CW01507311

CONTENTS

JOTTINGS IN SOLITARY

CLASSICS OF IRISH HISTORY
General Editor: Tom Garvin

Other titles in this series:

JOTTINGS IN SOLITARY

Michael Davitt

edited by
Carla King

UNIVERSITY COLLEGE DUBLIN PRESS
PREAS CHOLÁISTE OLLSCOILE BHAILE ÁTHA CLIATH

First published 2003 by University College Dublin Press
Newman House, 86 St Stephen's Green
Dublin 2, Ireland
www.ucdpress.ie

Introduction and notes © Carla King 2003

ISBN 1 900621 91 6
ISSN 1383–6883

Cataloguing in Publication data
available from the British Library

Typeset in Ireland in Baskerville by
Elaine Shiels, Bantry, Co. Cork
Printed on acid-free paper
in Ireland by ColourBooks, Dublin

ACKNOWLEDGEMENTS

I should like to thank the Board of Trinity College, Dublin for permission to publish MS 9639, 'Jottings in Solitary'; to quote from MSS 9320 and 9534; and to reproduce the photograph of Davitt in MS 9649/11A on the cover of this book.

Mr R. Eldridge, Assistant Governor of Portland Young Offenders Institution and Mr David Legg, historian of Portland Prison, assisted in supplying the photograph of the Prison which appears on the front cover of the book.

My thanks also to the St Patrick's College Research Committee for providing funding for a research trip to the Public Records Office and the British Library Newspaper Library in London. The staff of Trinity Manuscripts Library, St Patrick's College Library, the Public Records Office, the British Library Newspaper Library, the National Library of Ireland, Trinity College Library and University College Library have been most helpful

Thanks are also due to my colleagues in the History Department in St Patrick's College, especially to James Kelly for his invaluable assistance in reading and commenting on the introduction and footnotes. Others who helped in locating sources for references include Patrick M. Davitt, Mairead Dunlevy, Maria Luddy, Marian Lyons and John McColgan, for which I am very grateful.

Barbara Mennell has once again been a most patient and efficient editor. My son, Jonah, also deserves thanks for his unfailing good humour and for lending me his laptop.

NOTE ON THE TEXT

The manuscript of *Jottings in Solitary* was written by Michael Davitt in prison, without the assistance of dictionaries or many books of reference. It was never revised in this form for publication. I have endeavoured to retain as much as possible of the original text, including his spelling and punctuation, although for the sake of clarity and consistency some apostrophes and full stops have been added. Where names or terms were misspelled I have indicated this in the text. Davitt's underlining of words has been rendered in italics.

Carla King
Dublin
May 2003

INTRODUCTION

Carla King

On Thursday, 3 February 1881 Michael Davitt and two others from the committee of the Land League, Thomas Brennan and Matthew Harris, were crossing O'Connell Bridge from the Land League offices on their way to lunch, when Davitt was approached by two detective officers[1] and told that his presence was required in the Lower Castle Yard. He was taken first to Dublin Castle, where Chief Superintendent Williamson,[2] who had arrived from England that morning, was waiting for him and read him the warrant for his arrest. Then he was brought by the mailboat *Connaught*, from Dun Laoghaire to Holyhead, travelling first class but under heavy guard.[3] The government was extremely worried that there would be an attempt made to free him, so precautions were taken—two lines of police at Holyhead, a pilot engine preceded the train, and he was taken off at Willesden station, because it was feared that there would be demonstrations at Euston, and driven in a covered wagon to Bow Street Police Station. There he was formally identified, and after two nights at Millbank prison in London, he was sent on to Portland Prison in Dorset, where he was to remain for the next eighteen months.

This was the first move in a government crackdown on the leaders of the Land League. The Protection of Person and Property Bill had been introduced ten days earlier and the leaders were well aware that they might be arrested. [4] There seems to have been a feeling that 1881 would bring some kind of resolution to the conflict. Davitt's comment in his diary at the close of the year 1880 was: "Eventful year just dying out. 1879 Education; 1880 Organisation; 1881 Result?"[5] However, he did not appear to have expected his arrest before the Protection of Person and Property Act had passed into law,[6] and he had to write to his friend, Tom Brennan, five days after his arrest with instructions to put his affairs in order.[7] Indeed, there had been an assurance given by W. E. Forster, the Irish Chief Secretary, on 13 January that he had not broken the terms of his ticket of leave, which had released him in 1877.[8]

What had decided Forster and Gladstone, reluctantly, to re-imprison him was a build up of pressure behind the scenes.[9] The government's attempt to contain the deteriorating situation by imprisoning a handful of the leaders fell apart on 24 January, when the jury divided and failed to convict. The Land War was raging, but in addition to this the government had been made nervous by bomb threats. On 14 January there had been an attempt to blow up the Infantry Barracks in Salford, where arms were kept, injuring a passing woman and a child; the child later died. There were rumours of plots in Manchester and various precautions were taken wherever arms were stored. On 16 January, at a speech at Kilbrin in Cork, Davitt asserted that "the world will hold England responsible if the wolfdog of Irish-American vengeance bounds over the Atlantic at the very heart of the Power from which it is now held back by the influence of the Land League". He was not advocating violence, but what the administration heard was the vivid phrase "the wolfdog of Irish-American violence" and it drew its own conclusions. Forster decided on 31 January that Davitt should be re-imprisoned and the wheels of the judicial system were put into motion immediately.[10] Over the following months almost a thousand activists, including nearly all the leaders of the land movement, were imprisoned, among them Davitt's lunch companions of 3 February, Brennan and Harris.

Davitt's case was somewhat different from the other Land League leaders in that he had been released from a fifteen-year prison sentence in 1877 on a ticket of leave, having served

over seven years. It now seemed as if he might have to serve
out the second half of his term of imprisonment, which would
have kept him in jail until 1885.

When news of Davitt's arrest reached Westminster it pro-
voked whoops of delight from the Conservative benches and
howls of protest from the Nationalist side that resulted in
thirty-six of their number being ejected from the House in a
tumultuous scene.[11] The party then met in one of the
conference rooms of the parliament and, in a session that went
on for three hours, decided how to respond to the crisis. For
the third time that week the question came up as to whether
the Irish MPs should withdraw from Westminster "for consul-
tation with their constituents"—in effect a threat of abstention.
The situation was already extremely tense as the Irish party
had been vigorously obstructing the Protection of Person and
Property bill. The sitting of 25 January had lasted twenty-two
hours and on 31 January a sitting began which continued for
forty-one hours and was only brought to a halt on 2 February
by altering the rules of debate with the introduction of The
Closure. As F. S. L. Lyons has pointed out, the scenes in the
House were the outward manifestation of a tactical dispute
within the Party. On 17 January, Parnell had stated publicly
that the first arrest under the Protection of Person and
Property Act would be the signal for a general rent strike, in
which event the Home Rule MPs would return to Ireland to
co-ordinate the campaign. This policy of "concentration" had
been advocated by Andrew Kettle. Another line of action,
"dispersion", was proposed by Davitt, according to which
Parnell should go to America to collect funds, others should
stay in England and try to bring British public opinion round
to support the struggle, and Dillon, Davitt and other Land
League leaders should return to Ireland.[12] As it turned out,
neither plan was adopted. Davitt had not been arrested under
the Protection of Person and Property Act but his seizure was
deemed provocative none the less, and it could have provided
the signal for an escalation of events. Here, then, was Parnell's
equivalent of the decision that faced Daniel O'Connell at

Clontarf in October 1843.[13] In the event he and his followers decided to stay and fight the coercion bill in Parliament. Asked by a *Freeman's Journal* reporter on the day following Davitt's arrest, whether the party would return to the House, his reply was: "If we consulted our own feelings we should retire, but we must do our duty."[14] The Irish party was deeply worried, nevertheless, about the effect of Davitt's arrest, and was anxious that it not provoke a violent reaction in Ireland. To this end, it issued a manifesto calling on the Irish people at home and abroad "not to overstep by one inch the limits of constitutional and peaceable agitation".[15] At a special meeting of the Land League held in Dublin on Friday, 4 February, presided over by Dillon, who had replaced Davitt as Secretary of the League, resolutions were passed condemning the government's action. However, Thomas Brennan called for restraint on behalf of the League's supporters and a continuation of Davitt's policy of peaceful protest.[16]

The government was also worried about the effects of Davitt's arrest. Florence Arnold Forster reported in her diary on 3 February that the Lobby and corridors at Westminster were filled with police, who were also anxious to prevent a crowd gathering near the House.[17]

Strictly speaking, Davitt could have been returned to the hard labour conditions he had left in 1877, of which *The Nation* reminded its readers with extracts from his pamphlet prison life.[18] However, he was now a major political figure. Opposition to his imprisonment became linked to general protest against the coercion bill. On 13 February, ten days after his arrest, a protest march, attended by a large crowd variously estimated at between fifteen and fifty thousand people, moved from Trafalgar Square to a meeting in Hyde Park where the three resolutions approved stated: "That we condemn coercion for Ireland"; "That the arrest of Mr Davitt, is mean, cruel and unjust"; and "That we censure the conduct of the Speaker and the Government in suppressing freedom of debate".[19] Further public meetings were held throughout Ireland and Britain, and letters of protest sent from local

organisations of British Radical Liberals and even from the
Gympie branch of the Land League in Queensland, Australia.[20]
Newspaper responses were predictably divided, but coverage
of the arrest was considerable. Questions were asked in the
House about the grounds for Davitt's reimprisonment and the
conditions under which he was held; a petition signed by 104
MPs, delivered on 11 February urged that he be treated as a
first class misdemeanant.[21] Davitt himself sent a petition to the
Home Secretary, Sir William Harcourt, on 24 February vigorously protesting at his imprisonment and challenging its
legality on the grounds that his release in December 1877 had
in fact been an amnesty.[22]

Throughout his imprisonment, questions were raised
concerning his health and the conditions under which he was
held. These were in fact far more lenient than those he had
experienced in his first term, but they did not match the relaxed
conditions allowed to his associates in Kilmainham. For example,
although he was allowed more visits than normal, they were
still very strictly limited and most applicants were refused
permission.[23] He was clothed in prison dress, forbidden access
to newspapers and only a portion of his mail seems to have
reached him.[24] However, he was given a cell in the prison
infirmary, allowed to work in the garden, permitted a special
diet and kept apart from the other prisoners. His treatment
was not punitive; Harcourt's biographer claims that John
Bright described him as "the most humane Home Secretary
he ever encountered",[25] and he had the support of the Prime
Minister in favouring a relaxed policy towards Davitt. Despite
this, it took seven months and several efforts before he was
permitted writing paper on the advice of the prison doctor,[26]
and the prison governor was required to read everything he
wrote. The provision of paper and pen was practically unheard
of in the Victorian prison system and Sir Edmund Du Cane,
the chairman of the directors of convict prisons, objected to
the proposal and the precedent it might set.[27]

Davitt's prison manuscript, which he wrote on the paper
supplied to him by the prison authorities, consists of 358 pages

of heavy blue prison notepaper written mostly on both sides
in black ink. It is now kept in three files in the Manuscripts
Department of the Trinity College Library, Dublin. Most of
the pages are well preserved, although one is badly damaged
and several have crumbled at the edges. Davitt was issued 20
sheets every two weeks and he generally dated his writings,
the governor, George Clifton, initialling them after he had
read them. In places the writing is continuous on the front
and back of the pages but quite often Davitt wrote on a main
theme on the front of the sheets and interspersed this with
poetry, prayers, proverbs, observations or tables on the reverse.
Most of the writing is quite legible, although there are a few
places marked in this text where words were illegible, either
because of the writing or damage to the paper.

What was Davitt's purpose in writing all this? To begin
with, he loved to write; contemporaries remembered him
always with a pen in his hand. In part this was of necessity,
as he wrote for his living. But as a rather solitary person, at
times he carried on a dialogue with himself in his diaries, and
there are elements of a diary in the *Jottings*. In addition, he was
active by nature and probably found the enforced inactivity of
his prison life extremely irksome. His solitary state while in
prison did not have a punitive intention because he was allowed
visitors, but there must have been times of considerable lone-
liness. And as quite a poor man, Davitt may have harboured
thoughts of turning his enforced solitude to good use by
writing a work he could sell. Significantly, he published a
book, *Leaves from a Prison Diary* in 1885, which purported to be
lectures delivered to a pet blackbird while in Portland, although
that publication and the *Jottings* only overlap to some extent
(see below).

In part *Jottings* and the first volume of *Leaves from a Prison
Diary* belong to a series of prison memoirs that appeared in
the late nineteenth century. John Mitchel, whose writings
had exerted a profound influence on the younger Davitt, first
published his *Jail Journal* in 1854. Two decades later, Jeremiah
O'Donovan Rossa brought out his *Prison Life* (1874), an account

of his dreadful mistreatment in Pentonville, Portland, Millbank and Chatham prisons.[28] Davitt had already published an exposé of the conditions in Dartmoor and other prisons.[29] But *Jottings in Solitary* is not a prison memoir as such, although there are elements of this in it. It is more a collection of writings and reflections that deal with a whole range of issues. Much of it could have been written by someone who had never been inside a prison, let alone written from inside one.

In some ways *Jottings* is a surprising manuscript. Having been arrested at the height of the Land League campaign, one might expect that this issue would have been uppermost in Davitt's thoughts. In fact, he began to address it only in "Random Thoughts on the Irish Land War" on 11 January 1882, nearly a year after his imprisonment. It may be that he had found it too painful a subject to dwell upon, as he must have worried about how the movement he had built was faring as a consequence of the incarceration of its leadership (a little news of which had been conveyed to him). In any event, his matter was much broader.

Jottings in Solitary begins with a failed attempt at an auto-biography, but Davitt offers us only a fragment of his earliest memories. There were to be other such efforts although he never in fact succeeded in writing his own life story.[30] It is possible that as such a public figure, he wanted to preserve a part of his life as private, or simply that his own life story interested him less than analysis of the world around him. What he does give us, though, are some vivid early memories of his family's Famine eviction, their resort to a workhouse, where they encountered its penal regulations, and the decision to leave again, on his mother's refusal to be parted from her four-year-old son. This is followed by his description of a journey on a horse and cart to Dublin and emigration to Haslingden, where the family had to leave the house where they were staying because the young Michael contracted measles and the woman of the house did not want her own children to be exposed to infection. These recollections, burned into his early consciousness, provide an explanation for some of his later implacable hostility to the institution of land-lordism. Moreover, his admission that his father would never later mention that the family had sought assistance in Swinford workhouse following their eviction provides a valuable insight into the veil of humiliated silence that surrounded Famine memory among many of its survivors.

From describing the Irish communities in Britain, Davitt moves to a discussion of early empires, the dispersion of peoples and the spread of religions. He begins by questioning why the British Empire was so unsuccessful in impressing either its civilisation or its religion on its subject peoples. His answer is that its influence was limited by its blatant pursuit of its own self-interest, which he illustrates by reference to the plunder of India by the East India Company. He is likewise critical of Britain's "domestic civilization", which he finds condemned by the increasing levels of pauperism and crime amid the wealth created by industrialisation. He singles out the inadequacy of its educational provision for the poor, and he quotes Joseph Kay's assertion that if the land system were not improved "it would be wiser to get rid of every school in the country", because educating the poor under such an inequitable system would only make them more aware of its injustice and serve to exacerbate social discontent. Standing in the way of the achievement of any real equality is the British class system that perpetuates poverty and gives a monopoly of political and administrative power to the aristocracy. Here we have Davitt looking wider than at Ireland alone, criticising the British Empire and the British class system. This placing of the Irish situation within the broader context of the British Empire was in line with the nationalism of Davis and Mitchel and it was to characterise Davitt's nationalism throughout his life.[31]

Davitt next turns his attention to British foreign policy, where he questions the Empire's self image as a friend of oppressed peoples, before examining the failure of British policy to anglicise Ireland. He points to the inability of British administrations over centuries either to separate the Irish people from the Catholic faith or to overcome Irish opposition to the landlord system. The only success of its policies has been in rooting out the Irish language, which he attributes more to the efforts of the Catholic Church between 1798 and the Famine than to the British administration.

Davitt's next topic is "Secret Societies, ancient and modern". He begins with the observation that: "Up to the date on the head of this sheet [4 October 1881] I have undergone eight years, five months and five days' imprisonment as a convict, for a supposed connection with a Secret Society. If this penalty does not constitute me a reliable authority upon the subject at the head of this paper, it at least will supply one reason why I am interested in the enquiry it suggests . . .". He continues:

> My object is not to popularise, nor yet to pass sentence upon Secret Societies. I am aware that in many instances they have become as intolerable a tyranny as the greatest despot against which their mysterious *power* was ever directed; but I am also aware—and they must be blindly prejudiced indeed who have read history and will not admit—that the cause of popular liberty in almost every European country owes some measure of its success to the workings of those now generally condemned occult agencies.

He clearly intended in this section to move from a general examination of the history of secret societies in Europe to a critique of "the failure of Fenianism". Thus he begins with a discussion of secret societies in general, tracing their origins to a reaction against oppression. Addressing the subject of assassination, which he describes as "the foulest crime which it is in the power of man to commit," he offers a modest defence by noting that the commonest targets of assassinations are informers and that only a small proportion of the "scores of informers" who emerged in the state trials between 1865 and 1874 were assassinated. Returning to his main theme, Davitt embarks on an examination of Freemasonry, and the Illuminati[32] and later to a discussion of the Philadelphic Society[33] and its successor the Olympic Society the Tugenbund[34] and the Carbonari in Italy. He never did get to the subject on which he was most

qualified to write—the Fenians— perhaps owing to old habits
of secrecy. But it suggests that Davitt was reassessing his old
adherence to Fenianism, probably as part of the process of
discarding it.[35]

A theme to which Davitt returned repeatedly was his *critique*
of British government in Ireland. In this section of *Jottings* his
concern was not so much with historical wrongs as with the
operation of British rule in his own day. He offered a detailed
refutation of the argument that Ireland had the same laws and
was governed in the same way as England. On several pages
he carefully compared and tabulated the discrepancies in
electoral representation between English and Irish
constituencies. He criticised class rule in Britain as well as
Ireland, drawing here on Kay, Spencer and Henry George to
illustrate "the enormous wrong which land monopoly has
wrought and still inflicts upon the industrial population of
G[rea]t Britain and Ireland". His conclusion is that "the
Nationalisation of the land, the only logical, just, final, and
satisfactory settlement of the agrarian question of the present
day must necessarily follow the education of the masses and
meet the imperative wants of increasing population in these
countries".

Moving on to a discussion of the constitution as it pertained
to Ireland, Davitt denied the claim that the Irish were
naturally unruly by pointing out that in countries to which
they emigrated they were generally law-abiding and peaceable
citizens. Nor was unrest in Ireland attributable to alien
domination in itself. It was, he claimed, the result of misrule
by Dublin Castle, which he described as "the primary, if not
the greatest factor in the discontent of our people, and a
Depot of centralised despotism without a parallel in the
government of any other civilised country". This is his point
of departure for a detailed *critique* of British government in
Ireland, using the device of imagining the roles reversed, with
the Irish being the dominant power in England.[36]

Central to Irish grievances against British rule was the
maintenance of the Irish landlords and their supporters as a

"garrison" in control of Irish administration, and it is his contention that as long as it remained, any effort to win the Irish to obedience to British rule would be "as ineffectual as would all endeavours to close and heal a wound in the human body while the barbed shaft would remain embedded in the sensitive flesh". Addressing his arguments to "the serious and practical consideration of English statesmanship" (a reflection of his aspiration to build bridges between the Irish cause and a sympathetic section of British public opinion) he poses the question whether the maintenance of this "Garrison rule" and its inevitable accompaniment of unrest, distress and "morbid political excitement" was really in Britain's best interest.

Davitt, who was largely self-educated, saw educational provision as an indispensable precondition for a more equal society. "The people of any country," he declared, "will never really be the sovereign power of such country until 'the ignorant masses' thereof become 'educated' masses." While recognising the advances that had been achieved he criticised the "miserably inadequate salaries" of Irish national school teachers, pointing out the large discrepancies in the pay rates of teachers in Ireland and their equivalents in England and Scotland, which led to the conclusion that "the education of the youth of Gt. Britain was entitled to more consideration at the Imperial Treasury and a higher degree of proficiency in its teachers than that of the youth of Ireland".

One place that had offered the young Davitt the opportunity to further his education had been the Mechanics' Institute in Haslingden. He favoured the extension of this kind of facility to Ireland as a means of improving the circumstances of poorer farmers and agricultural labourers. He advocated the setting up of a network of what he called People's Institutes, based on the three hundred or so baronial districts of Ireland, which should be built as far as possible with local volunteer labour and paid for by a combination of a local tax of two pence per head of the population, voluntary subscription and funding from the Land League. Evening classes would provide instruction in improved methods of

agriculture and better household management for farmers.
Like so many of his contemporaries from all political back-
grounds, Davitt was appalled by the dirt and demoralisation
in which so many farming families lived, and urged the
promotion of improvements such as the removal of dunghills
from the doorways of houses, the construction of outhouses for
animals to remove them from the living area, and the provision of windows and chimneys in cabins. It is quite striking
how Davitt's belief in the need to ensure more comfortable
homes, educational facilities and agricultural advice coincided
with the policies later fostered by leaders of the co-operative
movement, such as Horace Plunkett and George Russell,
although party politics ensured they remained firmly apart.[37]

Davitt envisaged the leadership in a campaign to educate
the people being undertaken by the Land League, and he
criticised the neglect of this topic by Irish politicians heretofore. Here we see an example of the point made by Philip Bull
that the Land League and its successors, the Plan of Campaign
and United Irish League, went far beyond simple land
agitation to provide some of the functions of a proto-state.[38]
Emmet Larkin, in his studies of the Catholic Church in
Ireland and its relationship with the nationalist movement, has
also put forward the hypothesis that a "*de facto* Irish State"
existed in the consciousness of the Irish population.[39] The
Land League and the United Irish League distributed relief
to those suffering economic distress; normally the function of
the government. League courts were established as people's
tribunals to arbitrate in disputes, the Ladies' Land League
undertook the teaching of Irish history to the young in its
youth branches; and here Davitt was advocating the foundation
of evening schools, not by the state or local government, as in
Britain, but by the Land League. In a somewhat similar vein,
it was Davitt in particular who had pressed for the Land
League/Home Rule movement to seek to have its own
candidates elected to the Poor Law Boards to take control of
these bodies from the landlords. He had urged in December
1880 that the Land League should contest elections to the

boards the following March. He was in prison by that time, but the elections were contested and nationalist representation considerably increased.[40] He seems to have been keen to seize the opportunity for a peaceful expansion of a nationalist proto-state by the Land League. Of course, much of this vision was to be rendered unworkable by the abandonment of the Land League and Ladies' Land League shortly after his release, but a few elements of it were to reappear in the Plan of Campaign and the United Irish League. His People's Institutes were to remain a dead letter.

As a journalist and an acute observer of his own society, Davitt urged the need for a new study of human society and its functioning. He proceeded to sketch out his own ideas about how it could be done, dividing society's interests and activities under the headings of order and progress. His discourse at this point is more abstract than is usual in his writings.

On 23 November Davitt began writing the section he called "Traits of Criminal Life and Character". In his second long term of imprisonment, Davitt was generally isolated from the other prisoners, and so this is largely based on his observations during his first prison term, when he was serving a sentence of hard labour.

In the 1870s and 1880s, the treatment of prisoners permitted unprecedented levels of ferocity, which historians of the prison suggest mirrored society's deep fears about social unrest and crime. Davitt was outraged by the harshness of the system which, he believed, systematically removed all human dignity. As with other contemporary prison memoirs, there was a concern to show the barbarity of the treatment of prisoners. But Davitt went further, to look at the prisoners themselves and ask what it was that made people into criminals. He also analysed the different types of crime, explaining how various types of confidence trick and swindle were carried out. His approach here is often humorous and anecdotal, demon-strating the sense of the ludicrous that he claimed sustained him through hardship. But there is an underlying concern with the question of how criminality could be reduced in society and how prisons might be transformed into institutions of rehabilitation rather than punishment.

This section of the *Jottings* was to form Volume 1 of his published version, *Leaves from a Prison Diary*. It aroused considerable interest when it was published in 1885.[41] A modern authority on prison policy, Martin J. Wiener, has suggested that the book sounded a new note in prison policy, challenging the moral rationale of the prison and led the way for subsequent reformers.[42]

We are given another glimpse of Davitt's appreciation of the absurd in his account of his own arrest, written in mock-heroic style. It begins: "While crossing O'Connell Bridge Dublin in company with Tom Brennan and Matt Harris of Ballinasloe with no other intent against the peace of Society than what might be found in a resolution to subdue (temporarily) an appetite at a place of luncheon, I was met by an 'old acquaintance' who politely invited me to come and have a few words with a gentleman owning apartments in the Lower Castle Yard". There follows an account of his journey to London and identification to ascertain "that I was *really* myself and not somebody else," and his incarceration in Portland. It ends with the signature M. D. and W.822 (his prison number).

Davitt's excursion into parody is followed by a close analysis of Irish parliamentary representation, based on a combination of the lists in *Thom's Directory* and his detailed knowledge of both the representatives and their constituencies. This examination was undertaken in the light of an attempt by Parnell to introduce clearer definitions of membership of the Irish parliamentary party. On 27 December 1880, in a meeting in City Hall Dublin, it was resolved "that all home rule members should henceforward sit in opposition".[43] This presented the whiggish members with a clear alternative and on 16 January, just prior to Davitt's imprisonment, a revolt led by William Shaw, MP for Cork County, had taken place, as a result of which twelve members formally seceded from the party. [44] Davitt's aim in his table of constituencies and their representatives seems to be to ascertain which candidates should be replaced and where attention should be directed to strengthen the party's representation. It shows up the weaknesses in the Irish party and some of the difficulties faced by the party's leader, which Parnell vividly articulated to Andrew Kettle in 1885: "Does Davitt not know that I have to work with the tools that come to my hand? I have no choice. The men I would like to have won't come, so I have to use the men who will."[45] For obvious reasons, this section could never have been published in Davitt's lifetime but it does demonstrate his detailed knowledge of Irish politics. By chance, on 22 February, shortly after he wrote this, he was elected to Westminster to represent Meath, although he knew nothing of it until his release in May 1882, his visitors having been forbidden to discuss politics with him. His candidacy was rendered null by the fact that he was an undischarged felon,[46] and his election was in effect a protest vote.[47]

From the subject of parliamentary representation Davitt turns to what he calls "Random Thoughts on the Irish Land War", which he commenced on 11 January 1882. This was begun in response to a visit by Frances Sullivan the previous day. The American wife of A.M. Sullivan, MP for Meath, and herself a member of the executive committee of the Ladies' Land League, Frances Sullivan had informed Davitt that Archbishop Croke had misrepresented him as expressing approval for the 1881 Land Act at their meeting the previous September. On hearing from the archbishop of the provision that arrears of rent would have to be paid before tenants could avail themselves of the act, Davitt had pointed out that this would automatically exclude some 300,000 small farmers unable to settle their arrears. He concluded that the Archbishop had misunderstood him.

This encouraged him to examine the land question. He began by asking on what possible grounds the continuation of the landlord system in Ireland could be defended, drawing for his critique on Joseph Kay's *Free Trade in Land*, published in 1878.[48] Davitt criticised British commentators for their ignorance of the realities of squalor and degradation suffered by the Irish tenants. He denounces landlordism in passionate terms, describing it as "a blasphemous interference with the providence of God", and asks: "What power has given to Society or to a fraction of Society the right to make man miserable for no other crime than that of having come into being in obedience to the law of Nature? From whence the authority to make his life a burden, to starve him within reach of plenty, hover over his existence as if to snatch from his dreary path every semblance of hope and dash from his lips every draught of pleasure—to herd him or cast him forth shelterless like an animal, hunt him from off the land from which and upon which Nature intended him to live, and finally send him to the prison a criminal or to the grave a pauper?"

He points to the opportunity now presented to settle the land question and laments the "*total* want of tact which the leaders of the movement exhibited in neglecting, overlooking or despising the second, if not the most powerful and important factor in any settlement of an Anglo-Irish difficulty—*English public opinion*." Here we see him expressing what was to become a central part of his policy in the 1880s and 1890s— the need to win the hearts and minds of the British public to support the Irish cause. He argues that in succeeding in portraying the Irish as lawless, the British press had been allowed to do the work of the landlords, and reinforced already existing anti-Irish prejudices. Continuing agrarian outrage only confirmed this image and was ultimately self-defeating. He particularly condemns the mutilation of animals, claiming that the operation of the Whiteboy Acts only served to encourage the practice because the owners of the animals could claim compensation, and in some cases inflicted injuries on their own stock in order to do so.

After some short excursions into other topics, Davitt returned to the land question and in particular to the issue of land nationalisation. His publicly declared support for land nationalisation was to become a major issue and a cause of difference between him and other nationalist leaders following their release in May 1882. He had read Henry George's

Progress and Poverty prior to his imprisonment, and was so impressed he undertook that the Land League would promote it on its publication in Britain. Apparently he read it twice more in Portland, although he did not have access to George's pamphlet, *The Irish Land Question*, which was published while he was still in prison and was therefore not available to him.[49] In the *Jottings* Davitt proposed a solution to the land problem that would buy out the landlords, using a public loan. Here he diverged from George's policy of simply expropriating the landlords. While holding that "in strict justice they [the landlords] should not obtain their fares from Kingstown to Hollyhead",[50] he allowed that "as *conventional justice*" compensation would have to be paid. This would be done by the government taking out a loan of £140 million to pay off the landlords, which would be repaid at three per cent per annum by the Imperial Revenue then collected in Ireland by means of a land tax of ten per cent on all land values. Once the loan had been paid off, all civil and local government taxes could be abolished and the land tax would finance all government expenditure. Farmers would be secure, while only paying out the equivalent of one-half their present rents, whereas "all classes would be free from taxes, duties and rates, now imposed". He went on to investigate both the arguments in favour of land nationalisation and the issue of annual public expenditure in Ireland to work out how a system of land nationalisation might be put in place. Nor was land nationalisation the only model that Davitt was considering. He gave a lot of attention to Joseph Kay's *Free Trade in Land*, which, like J. S. Mill in *The Principles of Political Economy*,[51] advocated the replacement of landlordism by peasant proprietorship. It is entirely characteristic that this discussion is interrupted by a short examination of the religions of the Japanese.

In mid-February Davitt turned his attention to Irish history, to mark the centenary of the Dungannon Convention. He alleged that the Dublin parliament had only ever been a parliament of the Pale, elected from the Irish Protestant Ascendancy and, even then, with two thirds of its members returned for pocket boroughs. Nevertheless, the progress made by the country during the eighteen years of legislative independence gave it, he argued, a disproportionate importance. Lamenting that there had been no Irish Washington, he drew on Alfred Webb's *Compendium of Irish Biography* to examine the careers of Charlemont, Grattan and Flood.[52] He then went on to discuss "How Ireland was robbed of her Parliament", the background to the Act of Union.

There were some shorter items in the collection—drafts of letters,[53] brief biographical accounts of William Lloyd Garrison and the sculptor John Henry Foley, a list of ladies' precedence, and *Jottings* concludes with his entry on his birthday, 25 March, where he bemoans both the fact that he has reached the venerable age of thirty-six, and that he is recording it in prison. He was to spend just over a month more in prison but if there were more writings in that time, they have not survived.

In January 1882 Frances Sullivan, following a visit to Davitt in Portland, announced that he was working on a book. Henry George, who accompanied him to Scotland Yard on 11 May 1882 to collect his belongings a few days after his release, also referred to a manuscript of a book.[54] And yet the book that was eventually published in 1885, entitled *Leaves from a Prison Diary or Lectures to a "Solitary" Audience* was substantially different from *Jottings in Solitary*.

To begin with, *Leaves* is a far more coherent document. Published in two volumes, the first is based closely on the section 'Traits of Criminal Life and Character'. The second volume is substantially new material, although some of the same themes—education, poverty, crime prevention, state ownership of land, the iniquities of landlordism, inequalities between rich and poor, and the misgovernment of Ireland by "The Castle"—are familiar. More crucially, the content shows how much Davitt's thought had matured in the intervening three years, and there are chapters on "The organisation of labour", "State socialism," "State ownership of the railways" and "Political justice: how the Anglo-Irish problem could be solved". Taken as a whole, it is apparent that Davitt used

volume 2 of *Leaves* to outline a programme of social reform
that embraced land nationalisation and what he termed state
socialism. In effect, it provides an outline of his political and
social philosophy.

Apart from the development of Davitt's ideas, there were
other reasons for the differences between the two works. He
needed to sell the book, so he simplified the structure to two
broad themes: criminal life and comment on British and Irish
social and political structures. To this end, he took out all the
parts he presumably felt would be of less interest to the public.

One motif that Davitt introduced into *Leaves* was a pet bird
he kept while in Portland, which had been rescued from the
prison cat and given to him by the governor, George Clifton.
The chapters of *Leaves* are described as lectures delivered to
"Joe", his "pet blackbird", to whom he dedicated the book.
Pauric Travers has suggested that the original bird was in fact
a thrush, as Mrs Sullivan described, and that Davitt's description of it as a blackbird was a salute to Parnell (described
in popular song as the "blackbird of Avondale").[55]

An additional reason for the difference between the manuscript and the book is that the political context had changed
since 1882. For example, Davitt's vision of an expanded role
for the Land League was unworkable in a situation where the
organisation no longer existed and its successor, the Irish
National League, had become a tool of the parliamentarians.
By 1885 Davitt was now predicting the formation of a Labour
Party in Britain, although Gladstone's conversion to Home
Rule at the end of the year kept him loyal to the Liberals for
some time after the foundation of the Independent Labour
Party, in 1893.[56]

We can be reasonably certain that this was Davitt's first
lengthy piece of writing. It reflects his thinking at a time that
was to mark a significant turning point both in his own life and
for the movement he had begun. It demonstrates his wide
reading,[57] as well as his love of poetry and languages. The poems
are in a range of languages: French, German, Italian, Spanish
and Latin, and Davitt appears to have translated one poem by

St Francis Xavier from English into Latin and another by the German poet, Uhland, from German into Italian. *Jottings* also illustrates Davitt's developing interest in the wider world, one that was to increase over time, as well as an emerging *critique* of the British Empire and an understanding of the shared patterns of colonisation between Ireland and other countries that were to feature strongly in later years.

Davitt left prison a committed advocate of land nation-alisation. His decision to proclaim his position in public speeches a month after his release was to distance him, to some extent, from the rest of the Irish movement.[58] In his absence much had changed. The rent strike that Davitt had urged in January 1881 had been called the following October (too late in his view) and failed. Parnell had become convinced that the land war was unsustainable; he had decided not to revive the Land League and to focus his attention forthwith on constitutional politics based in Westminster.

Davitt was released on 6 May 1882, into a political context that had altered greatly from the one he had left eighteen months before. An exultant Parnell told him, in the train to London, that: "We are on the eve of something like Home Rule. Mr Gladstone has thrown over coercion and Mr Forster and the government will legislate further on the land question."[59] He did not tell him what Davitt was to discover to his shock several days later —that the price was to be the discontinuation of the movement he had founded. But by that time the Phoenix Park murders had taken place, and some of the political ground had already been lost.

The eighteen months of Davitt's imprisonment had also seen profound changes in British political life. The events in Ireland had effectively split the Radical wing of the Liberal Party, into a moderate wing, occupied by figures such as John Bright, John Morley and Joseph Chamberlain, not liking coercion but feeling that in the circumstances it was inescapable, and a more left-wing faction, represented by Joseph Cowen, Charles Bradlaugh and Henry Labouchère, who continued to oppose it. What happened in 1881 was a rallying of the furthest

left of the Radicals and socialists around the anti-coercion
movement. Socialism in Britain had been quiescent in the
1870s and although Marx and Engels had, in the 1860s and
1870s urged co-operation between the British working class
and the Irish, this did not take place until 1881. In late 1880
a weekly paper, *The Radical*, was established in London by a
working man, Francis William Soutter, and a publisher, Samuel
Bennett.[60] *The Radical*, throughout its short life (it folded in
July 1882), was consistently supportive of anti-coercion and of
the left of radicalism. In December 1880 Soutter had travelled
to Ireland to investigate the land war for himself, where he met
Davitt, Parnell, Egan and others. Soutter and Bennett tried
unsuccessfully to visit Davitt in prison in October 1881. When
United Ireland was raided and shut down,[61] Soutter and Bennett
brought out the next three issues and helped to distribute the
New York-based *Irish World* when the government tried to
curtail its sale.[62] Apart from Irish issues the *Radical* ran frequent articles on land nationalisation and women's suffrage.
Those in the forefront of the anti-coercion movement, trying
to bring together Radicals and Irish included T. P. O'Connor,
Soutter, Helen Taylor (John Stuart Mill's stepdaughter, who
took an active part in supporting the Ladies' Land League),
Joseph Cowen and another former Chartist, Charles Murray.
At the same time, it was suggested that a more defined organisation of what was termed "advanced Radicalism" should be
formed. Led by Cowen and H. M. Hyndman (translator of
Marx's *Das Kapital* into English), this became the Democratic
Federation, later the Social Democratic Federation, one of the
strands from which the British Labour Party was later to
emerge. So by the time Davitt was released from Portland,
signs of rapprochement between Irish and British radicals had
begun to emerge.

This edition of Davitt's *Jottings in Solitary* has been edited to
around one half of its original length in order to adhere to the
Classics of Irish History format. The material omitted includes
poetry, sayings, Davitt's account of Classical societies, his survey
of secret societies, his examination of Japanese religion, tables

of political representation, sketches of the lives of William Lloyd Garrison and John Henry Foley, a table of ladies' precedence, a note on John Ruskin's opinion of the Irish and the drafts of all but one of his letters. The longest section omitted is that on "Criminal Life and Character", which was closely reproduced in *Leaves from a Prison Diary*. The main criterion used in the selection was to include the longer, more coherent pieces that illustrate Davitt's working out of particular themes. The only lengthy sections left out are his discussion of secret societies, which is based on his reading rather than his experience or original thought, and his examination of "Criminal Life and Character". The omission of Davitt's choice of poetry is regrettable, but the other shorter writings were considered to be of less interest to the general reader than the more detailed expositions of his thought contained in the longer pieces. Davitt's later writings were to be more polished but what is here published for the first time provides us with glimpses of the early crystallization of his ideas and the impressive range of his intellectual curiosity.

JOTTINGS IN SOLITARY

Ná mol na cain tú féin
Neither praise nor dispraise thyself

Is fearr clú ná conac
Character is better than wealth

SYNOPSIS OF DATA FOR AN AUTOBIOGRAPHY

I have more than once been requested by friends who believe my life to have been more fruitful of events and adventures than it really has been, to write my biography. Having had something of greater moment to occupy my time during the three years and forty-six days between my release from Dartmoor Convict Prison to my re-arrest in Dublin on the 3rd of Feb. last than to sit down and write out a "history of myself", I have deferred the task until my old "friend" *misfortune* has placed more time at my disposal than I know how to usefully occupy.

I was born on the 25th of March 1846, in the parish of *Straide*—between Castlebar and Swinford—in the country of Mayo, Ireland, and am consequently in my thirty-sixth year at this time of writing. My father, Martin Davitt, though of the small farmer class, had received a tolerably good education for a working man in Ireland in *his* day—so near the time of the penal laws.[1] Besides a fair proficiency in the rudimentary branches of learning, he was well read in Ancient, Irish, and American history; and was the best *Sennacus*, or Irish storyteller I ever heard. To his narrative of the French Expedition to Killala under Gen. Humbert (in the time of his father)[2] the achievements of Patrick Sarsfield Earl of Lucan,[3] his repetitions of the prophecies of St. Columcille (in which he was a firm believer)[4] and to his vivid accounts of the horrors of the Great Famine of '47 and '48 in which himself and young family were sufferers, I owe whatever of patriotic feeling I may have for Ireland and *all* the hatred I feel for its chief curse— Landlordism.

My Mother, whose maiden name was Catherine Kielty, was born in the parish of Turlough—almost beneath its still perfect Round Tower—near Straide; and was also belonging to the same class as that of my father.[5] Being a Davitt, also, on her mother's side, *I* may consider myself of that ilk, "to the backbone," as the saying is. So far as pedigree or family history is concerned, I believe I may say with one of Napoleon's generals, *"Mon Ancêtre? C'est Moi!"*—Still the origin of the clan *Mac Dhivaidth*—the Irish pronunciation of the name—is neither obscure nor unnoticed in Irish history. Mac Dhivaidth (Son of David or, Davidson) denotes a descendant from Sir David O'Dogherty, Chief of Inishowen in the County of Donegal,[6] the ancestor of Sir Cahir of that name who, resenting an insult offered him by the English Governor of Londonderry Sir George Paulet (in 1608) "with the aid of his foster brother Hugh and Felim MacDavitt and their retainers, marched on Derry, when the town was taken, sacked, and burned, the governor Paulet falling amongst the first victims".[7] The rebellion of Sir Cahir and his subsequent defeat and death must have scattered part of the clan MacDavitt from their district of Inishowen and caused them to migrate down the western coast as far as Mayo—from some member of which part I am no doubt a descendent.

My mother though unable to read or write English—and for the greater part of her life not capable of speaking it near as well as her native tongue—was nevertheless a woman of great natural intelligence, being gifted with a remarkably accurate memory, great discernment of character and habits of unremitting industry. Her command of the Keltic tongue was perfect, and her delight in speaking it even after she had resided in England a score of years was such that all her children acquired whatever knowledge they possess of their native language from hearing her speak it while residing in that country—we all having left Ireland too young to remember much of our childhood there. She was very fond of enforcing a command or clinching an argument with one of our beautiful Irish proverbs—so rich in philosophic truth, sound morality and poetic sentiment—the frequent use of which by the people of the west of Ireland, I may add in their conversation, has had no little share in keeping alive the tongue in which Ossian sang and the Brehons wrote our ancient laws, until the present generation of Irishmen have been compelled to recognise their national tongue and make *some* little effort to effect its revival. Being a woman of vigorous imagination, earnest Christian feeling and strong human sympathies, the scenes of which she in common with my father had to witness during the progress of the great Famine left an impression of such deep horror on her mind that she could not through life get rid of the frightful picture which widespread suffering had imprinted upon her memory.

Being like my father thoroughly Irish in feeling and sentiment and having a healthy hatred of *Sassanach* rule, my Nationalist training was in consequence of the most orthodox character.

Of our home and condition previous to emigrating to England I know only what I have heard my parents relate in after years. At the time of my birth, just at the commencement of the famine, we were, as I often heard them remark, in "easy circumstances"—though the fact of my father being but a tenant-at-will was not calculated to make such circumstances very "easy". Three or four milch cows, a male donkey, pig and some sheep constituted I believe the stock of his small holding. When Public Relief works were started for the district between Castlebar and Straide he was appointed an overseer of roads. This position was taken from him in the midst of the famine and conferred upon a jealous neighbour. Thrown back upon the scanty means of his small holding, with entire failure of its produce and a family of six persons to support, it became a difficult matter to weather the storm of starvation which desolated Mayo in the years 1848-9.[8] Of positive hunger I do not think we had any experience; but undoubtedly "hard pinching" must have been the case when almost everything we possessed had to be disposed of to procure the mere necessaries of life—which *at that time* consisted of yellow or Indian meal, *sans* milk or other luxury whatever! In the summer of 1850 while my father was in England—whither he had gone for the first time to "earn the rent" as a Harvestman—our landlord came down with a demand for both rent and arrears. Some arrangement was made by which we were left in possession for another twelve months at the expiration of which time, failing I believe to wipe off all arrears, we were one morning thrown out on the roadside and our little house and home pulled down before our eyes by the reigning institution; the "Crowbar Brigade". I was then but four and a half years old yet I have a distinct remembrance (doubtless strengthened by the frequent narration of the event by my parents in after years) of that morning's scene: The remnant of our household furniture flung about the road, the roof of our house falling in and the thatch taking fire, my mother and father looking on with four young children—the youngest only two months old—adding their cries to the other pangs which must have agitated their souls at the sight of their burning homestead! Twenty-nine years after I took part in another scene of a different nature on the same spot—but upon which the home of my early childhood no longer stood. A grave near the valley of the far off Susquehannah [*sic*] was then the resting place of one parent, while another by the banks of the Schuylkill river was shortly to afford a refuge from trouble and wrong, to the other. I alone of those who witnessed the first was destined to play a part in the other scene, and experience something akin to exultation at the hope it inspired: Fifteen thousand people are assembled upon the small farm from which we were evicted. A platform is erected over *the very spot* upon which our humble homestead had stood, and while the air is resounding with shouts of "Down with Landlordism", "Death to Eviction", I, after an exile of close upon thirty years—

seven and a half of which were passed in prison—am there the representative of a Movement which, with God's blessing, may be destined for the overthrow of the home-destroying, robber-code of laws which has scattered thousands of families as it had banished mine, from the place of their birth. I recollect saying on the occasion:— "If I stand here today on the spot upon which I was born, but on the ruins of my levelled home, with memories of its once happy inmates crowding fast upon my mind, I may yet live to have the satisfaction of trampling in turn upon the ruins of Irish landlordism."[9] From what I learned from His Grace the Arch[bisho]p of Cashel when he honoured me with a visit in company with the Bishop of Ross last Wednesday (Sep. 7) *some portion of the iniquitous powers of landlordism are in ruins now.*[10]

The next step from eviction, generally speaking, is the Workhouse, fit offspring of its kindred institution landlordism; and like the majority of those who were driven from their homes in those black years, *we* did not altogether escape the degradation of having to enter such an establishment. Few people care about recording anything which should bear witness either to their "lowly origin," or their poverty in early life, especially if Fortune makes some amends in after life and they begin to "hang upon the precincts of society" where "empty pockets are the worst of crimes" and the Workhouse the only Hell that has terrors for those who make poverty an introduction to it, and a badge of shame; yet feel no shame in placing this stigma upon the many by grinding out of underpaid and unprotected labour what is necessary to minister to the tastes and luxuries of that same society. I know of nothing which I should be ashamed to acknowledge in connection with my life, save an action that would leave behind it a stain of moral obloquy upon my character, or a wrong inflicted upon the conscience, honour or just belongings of another. If Bethlehem had a workhouse among its institutions eighteen hundred and eighty one years ago it is probable that the Divine Nazarean would have been born there instead of in a stable; and as *He* was not ashamed to be poor why should one of His creatures be?

Swinford Workhouse was our destination after being evicted, and there we presented ourselves the same day, the family consisting of six persons: my father, mother, three sisters— aged respectively eight, three years, two months and I, being the second eldest, four and a half years old, at the time. Fortunately for our brief stay within such a place one of the regulations required that male children above three years of age should be kept apart from their mothers—for what reason or purpose I know not; but when this condition of enjoying workhouse hospitality was mentioned to my mother she snatched me to her breast, and declaring she would rather die by the roadside than submit to such an inhuman condition, left the establishment, inside the walls of which we had stayed *but one hour*. I never once remember my father alluding to this incident in the early life of our family, when recounting his experiences of the famine years, in after life, to those friends who had gathered round our new home in England; doubtless from that feeling of false shame which associates an entrance under *any* circumstance into the dreaded "poorhouse", with the degradation it inflicts upon the *pauper class* which its establish- ment in Gt. Britain and Ireland has created. My mother, however, never shirked the fact in *her* narrations of our family struggles, and I love truth and the memory of *her* action in my regard on that occasion too much, to conceal that fact of our having once reached the zero of adversity and crossing the portals of an Irish workhouse.

Emigration to England

From the foregoing brief sketch it will be seen that our experience of life in Ireland was such as might have reasonably reconciled us to leaving it for some other land where Fortune, should she prove ever so adverse, could scarcely place us much farther from her favours. Indeed until I had grown up towards man's estate and acquired that *amor patriae* which is the chief characteristic of Irishmen, I could never understand why my parents should be constantly lamenting their exile and longing to return again to a place which was associated with so much trial, suffering and wrong. In point of scenic beauty there was scarcely any comparison between the tame, uninteresting situation of Straide, and the rugged grandeur which surrounded the locality of our new home in one of the most picturesque, mountainous districts of Lancashire. But the mysterious attachment which can keep a Carraroe peasant on the side of a bleak and boulder-strewn slope of hills, or that reconciles a rational human being to a window-less cabin of mud in the midst of a boggy swamp, in preference to an exchange for probable better conditions of existence in a Stranger-land, cannot be accounted for by any comparison with those impulses or motives which prompt or direct the ordinary actions of men in the routine of social life. Well is it for the cause of human liberty that Nature has imprinted this strange love of country in such strong and enduring character upon the heart of mankind; for without its power and the sacrifices it is capable of exacting from men who experience its influence, there would be no check to the *supreme crime of Conquest* nor curb to the tyranny of unjust and arbitrary domination.

There chanced to be a family from the neighbourhood of Straide bound for England just at this time who were so well off in worldly affairs as to own a horse and cart and to be in a position which enabled them to take the same with them on their journey. An arrangement was entered into between the owner and my father whereby my mother, myself and sisters were to be "accommodated" with seats as far as Dublin in consideration of the future payment of a certain sum out of "the fortune" which we were to make in England. Among the few incidents of my early childhood in Ireland the one of riding in that particular cart is about the one I remember best. It was as innocent of springs as the watch which Brian O'Lynn "fashioned out square" from a turnip;[11] and as for the Animal which drew it, he manifested his patriotic displeasure at facing a journey to England by breaking the traces a half dozen times ere reaching Dublin and "bolting" towards pastures green, in preference to dragging a heavy load towards "pastures new".

He one day upset the whole of us in the middle of the high-
way and made such a run for "Ireland" as took his owner and
my father near the whole of that day to catch him again.
However we reached Dublin at last and on the 1st of November
1851[12] landed in Liverpool. After a few days stay with some
friends in that port we set out for our destination, the town of
Haslingden in N. E. Lancashire where we arrived in due time
after having "tramped" the whole distance from Liverpool.[13]
We "lodged" for a few weeks with the family of an acquaintance of my father[14] until our means prospered to the extent
of renting a house of our own—my father having at once
commenced work as a day labourer. At this period of my life
those troubles and misfortunes which somehow or other have
adhered to me to this hour, and which have envoled [*sic*] my
family in whatever trials and troubles they have experienced
since leaving Ireland commenced. My being the unconscious
means of saving them from a residence in a workhouse has I
believe been the only real service it has been in my power to
render those who did so much for me through life—such has
been the unpropitious star which influenced *my* unlucky advent
into this world of unfortunates. As it was Fate and not
propensity however which rendered me thus unable to be of
much help to my parents in their uphill struggle through life,
I can therefore consciously adhere to the second part of my
proverb "Ná mol na cain tú féin". Our stay in the house of
the parties with whom we "lodged" on our first arrival in
Haslingden was cut short by my being seized with the measles,
as the wife of the owner of the house gave us notice to quit
immediately upon learning the nature of the malady with
which I was afflicted. I recollect that night more distinctly than
any other event of my early life—though at that time I was
three or four months short of five years old. My mother made
a fruitless appeal to the woman's maternal love to allow me
to remain in the house until morning, as the night was a
bitterly cold one, it being December. The women's husband,
who was a kind-hearted, hospitable Irishman, but a mere
cipher in the household government, warmly seconded my

mother's appeal, but all in vain; the woman doubtless actuated by the same motherly affection for *her* children in an object removing of serious danger from contagion with them, as that which fruitlessly pleaded to her on my behalf. I was carried in a sheet and placed beneath a wall for shelter. Some fifty yards from where we had been ejected, my poor brave mother crouching down by my side in an agony of grief and despair at the pitiable plight in which we were situated—without shelter from the keen December blast which seemed to moan in sympathy with us as it flew by that shivering and weeping group: and without any hope of saving me from the inevitable consequences of a prolonged exposure to the winter's cold. Fortunately there are hearts so full of human sympathy to be found after all in this selfish world, which even serious risk to those they love cannot steel against helpless human suffering in need of Samaritan assistance or Christian Charity; and to one of such is it owing that my hapless career in this World was not brought to a close that bitter night thirty-one long years ago. Often have I regretted since then while experiencing more of the evils of life that such was not my destiny, though I am sensible of the suspicion of moral cowardice which such a wish even in the darkest hour of pain and adversity, invites. Still, there are moments in the lives of some beings when the whole psychological fabric of our nature seems to give way before a combined weight of mental and physical endurance, for the alleviation of which there is no seeming remedy at hand. All the vaunted fortitude of the Stoic philosophers who denied that suffering was an evil in discourses delivered to obtain the applause of an Athenian or Roman public opinion, could be exploded in *one hour* in our age of "advanced civiliz-ation" if that hour was among the first of days, to be followed by weeks, and months, and years; the amount of mental suf-fering to be borne during such whole time would present itself for calculation to the soul within the first few moments of that very hour, and be shown every succeeding hour afterwards to be of a nature that could only be appreciated in variety and intensity by weary, silent, hopeless, actual endurance.

Mr James Bonner,[15] ever afterwards an esteemed friend, was the good Samaritan who came to our rescue on the occasion of our second "eviction", by generously offering us the shelter of his house; and to this timely act of pure unselfish benevolence is it probably due that I survived the trials of that December night. Fortunately my admittance among that gentleman's household was unattended with any evil to his family from the contagious disease with which I was attacked, and in a few weeks time we were once again, though in exile, the occupants of a house which nobody else could call their own, and comparatively speaking quite happy in once again experiencing the felicity of an independence—somewhat limited no doubt—but which contrasted so favourably with our experience since driven from our first home.[16]

The strong prejudice which *existed* at this time among the English working and lower classes against the Irish, especially in the Northern counties of England, would scarcely be admitted by the comparatively *educated* tolerance of the present generation of Englishmen, so great was its virulence towards those which their own country's criminally negligent legislation at the outbreak of the Great Famine of '47 and '48 had compelled to leave Ireland.[17] Although this hostility had its origin in that mutual "absence of love"—to speak it mildly—which their near but (on one side, at least) decidedly unsatisfactory political relationship, engendered; it was intensified by the fear that this influx of hungry industry would glut the English labour market and cause a diminution in the rate of wages. The advanced doctrine of political economy which demonstrates the facts of increase of labour being an increase of wealth, and of labour and not capital being the creator of the fund from which wages are drawn, and that therefore this fund must *cetera paribus*, rise or fall with the state of the labour market, was scarcely admitted by English political economists thirty years ago, and could not, of course, mitigate the popular apprehension that the new-comers to all the manufacturing towns and villages of the North of England would reduce the price of labour to a starvation point.[18] Another cause of strong dislike to the Irish was their religion. Catholic places of worship began to spring up like magic and rear their symbols of the dreaded "Popish Faith" side by side with the numerous Protestant and Dissenting rivals which could brook any intrusion but that of Rome. Tracts and pamphlets full of dreadful prognostics of what was about to happen to the people and the faith of "St Harry the Eighth" if priests were to be tolerated in every town, were circulated among the masses, and of course effectively fanned the *double* flame of labour prejudice and religious fanaticism.*

A necessary consequence of this double-edged hostility against the Irish, was, their establishing themselves in small colonies in all the cities and towns where they intended settling down, for purposes of self-defence—hence the "Irish quarters" that are yet to be found in every large centre of population in Gt. Britain from London to Dundee. Riots attended with serious and often fatal results, were of frequent occurrence from 1850 to the break out of hostilities with Russia, when English popular feeling was turned against "Nicholas the Bear" to the considerable relief of the hitherto detested "Irish Patt".[19] To those who know of what metal the Irishrie of the North of England are tempered it will be needless to say that they did not tamely submit to the ill usage of which they were the frequent recipients. Of no portion of the scattered *Clan na Gael* wherever found throughout the world can, *Nemo me impune lacessit* [20] be more appropriately said than of the Irishmen who are to be found in the great manufacturing and industrial centres from Birmingham to Berwick-on-Tweed, and so thoroughly have the natives of these districts become satisfied on *this* point that little or no molestation has been given to our countrymen in such localities on account of either labour, race or religion during the past fifteen years. To the influence

---

* Mem.—Refer to "History of our Own Times" by Justin McCarthy M.P., to see if *he* refers to these troubles in the North of England from 1858 to 1860. [This is Davitt's note to himself. The book did not refer to the sectarian troubles of those years, although it mentioned tensions in the post-Famine period. Ed.]

of these small colonies in the midst of a hostile population—
of the same race as that which had treated their fatherland as
they were being treated—and the frequent encounters with
their English assailants, is to be attributed that intense
Nationalist feeling and indomitable pluck with distinguish the
N. of England Irish; as has been abundantly illustrated in the
daring, if unfortunate enterprises of the Chester Raid[21] and
rescue of Kelly and Deasy in Manchester in the year 1867.[22]

[here Davitt writes about conquest and the dispersion
of races and religions in the Classical world]

ENGLISH CIVILIZATION

(*continued*)

The contradictory character of English Civilization may be one of the causes why its acceptance by the races subjected to British rule has not followed their subjection, as in the instances given of the conquests of Rome, Mahommed, Spain and Portugal; but the chief cause in my opinion is to be found in the characteristic disregard of every consideration involved in an act of conquest by England save those which fall under the head of *British Interests*. Every one who reads the dispatches or speeches of the English Secretary for Foreign Affairs knows what is meant by "British Interests". They are not as a Stranger to English politics would imagine, the mere conservation of English political prestige, or safeguard of national honour. Nothing of the sort. The honour and prestige of England were concerned in the attack which Austria and Prussia made upon Denmark (in 1865?)[23] a friendly power, which she was bound both by treaty and the *public promise* of Lord John Russell to defend; but—as "British Interests" were not in any way jeopardised in the war, the Austrian Emperor and Prussian King were allowed to help themselves to as much of Danish territory as they at that time required. The honour of England was concerned in the fortunes of her Crimean and Chinese-wars ally in the Franco-Prussian War; but not her "British Interests"—therefore Prussia was permitted to cripple France (though not beyond rapid recovery as we see) by a partition of her territory and the imposition of the largest war levy ever demanded from a defeated antagonist by a triumphant power.[24]

But when certain Christian races of Eastern Europe long subject to the tyranny of Turkish rule and the rapacity of its provincial governors or pashas, rise in revolt and obtain for their righteous cause the sympathy of *all* Europe and the practical help of *one* of its Powers, mark the conduct of England.

From her high Evangelising pretensions and her national—but hypocritical—boast, that "the Bible is the secret of England's greatness," it would be supposed that if a Christian people in any part of the world stood in need of assistance in a just and praiseworthy effort against Infidel tyranny, the sword of "the Defender of the Faith," and "the Champion of Human Liberty" would leap from its scabbard in their support. The exact contrary, as is well known, was the course taken by England in the recent Bulgarian war.[25] "British Interests" lay in the direction of aiding rather than opposing Ottoman despotism in Europe, hence Bulgarian massacres of Christian women and children by Bashi-Basouks[26] are made light of if not palliated in the British Senate, and the press and ruling classes of England succeed in exciting the masses against the very power which had come to the aid of the Danubian Christian principalities!—For was not Turkey indebted to English Bankers? Could England allow her millions of Mahommadan [*sic*] subjects in India to believe that *she* would permit "a dog of a Christian" power like Russia to drive their co-religionists from Europe? Would not "British Interests" suffer in the East if an increase of Russian prestige was allowed on the Bosphorus? "Therefore let the Christian subjects of the Sultan be butchered or kept in continued tyrannous subjection rather than Russia shall be allowed to effect their emancipation or hurt the Turk. "Our interests" demand the continuance of Turkish rule in south-eastern Europe, so on with our fleet to Bisika Bay,[27] call out the Reserves, infuse a war spirit into the people and chaunt forth the New National Anthem:

> "We do not want to fight
> But by Jingo if we do"—[28]

What, then, are those "British Interests" which dictate the foreign policy of England, and render her Civilization so incommunicable to her subject races, by their being made the primal object of her rule, and the end and aim of every act of her administration? I have already described them negatively and shall now attempt to define their real nature from the character which they have given to English government in India and Ireland:—

It is unnecessary to travel over the history of British conquest and rule in India in order to form a just opinion of the infamous manner in which a company of unscrupulous Monopolists armed with the power of England, effected the one; or how a succession of rapacious and unprincipled Governors conducted the other. Some English writers who loved truth and hated injustice—even when perpetrated in the name of England and on behalf of "British Interests"—have left on the imperishable record of history the frightful story of India's subjection, "at which the world grew pale", though Histories from Heroditus [*sic*]²⁹ down to John [*sic*] Anthony Froude³⁰ have each had to narrate the crimes, plunders, perjuries and iniquities in general of those scourges of humanity, conquerors. A company of English traders obtain permission to establish a factory where Calcutta now stands, and in return for this privilege or rather *hospitality*, commence to plot and ultimately carries out the subversion of the power—the government of the country—which had done nothing but what should have earned the gratitude and loyalty of the intruders. Here at the very outset of the contact between the civilization of England and that of the east—between Christianity (as represented by Englishmen) and the faiths of Bramha and Mahommed,—duplicity, treachery, and ingratitude are made to appear the chief features of the former to the people who belonged to the latter—who in after years have doubtless, read but have most assuredly not been converted by, the millions of cheap bibles sent them by Exeter Hall³¹—British Interests are advanced—that is more goods are sold and *more* money sent to England—by these acts of the

Company; but who shall say that the interests of religion, justice, honour or public morals (which are supposed to be traits of our modern civilization), are advanced also?

The plea which the majority of English writers have set up in extenuation or rather justification of the Company's acts as well as of the subsequent rapacity and sanguinary proceedings of Governor-Generals, is in every way worthy of the countrymen of Warren Hastings,[32] Clive[33] and Judge Impey.[34]

"Successful crime *alone* is justified"

says some poet;[35] but only when the successful criminals are English and the crime the plunder of some race or country in the furtherance of British Interests. "The people of India were ruled by so many petty despots, who, under the nominal supremacy of a weak Prince, committed all sorts of injustices against the peace and well being of their groaning subjects; therefore the Company succeeded in substituting the 'blessings' of English government—to be followed by the Bible and 'our civilization'!"

True, the Company's Servants accumulated immense wealth, and shareholders in England received large dividends, but this was only to be expected from a country so rich as India and open only to the sale of English manufactures. "Governors and officials returned home after ten years experience of Calcutta etc. with fortunes of from fifty to three or four hundred thousand pounds; but, as they could have 'secured' (that is robbed, cheated or received as bribes) more than they brought away, there was something to be said in their behalf after all." If such be the accounts which English apologists give of the *best* of their countrymen's proceedings in India, what in the name of God must *the reality of those acts* have appeared to the people who suffered by them—and what their opinion of the "New Civilization" and religion of those who perpetrated them? If it be granted—as apologists for conquest do, but which Justice and Morality, and it is to be hoped *Religion*, do not—that right, honour and fair dealing must necessarily be suspended in such transactions as the subjugation of India, ought not the dictates of a higher principle than a passion for the wealth of the conquered and a sounder policy than a total disregard of *their everything*, but their money, commence at once to signalise the rule of the Conquerors? If in addition to the "inestimable privilege" of British government the other concomitant blessings of its religion and civilization are intended as some recompense to the newly acquired subjects for the loss of their political independence.

Unquestionably if "British Interests" had not alone prompted the acquisition and characterised the subsequent administration of the new British territory, the fate of its inhabitants would not have been left for as many years in the hands of the rapacious East India Company. Never had a conquering power such an opportunity of substituting a Christian and modern civilization for that of a barbarous and declining one, and of firmly planting the religion of the Gospel in the heart of Asia, than had England when she added India to her Empire. But the genius of her civilization is not to propagate itself but rather to infuse its views into those with which it is brought into contact, alike with the injury of its own higher attributes, and the races which are brought within reach of its demoralising influences. Whether a government be national or be that which a conquering power substitutes for it when overthrown, it is as essential for its own stability as for the good of the people which it is to govern that it be not grounded upon motives which are hateful to its subjects; but if of the latter it is of final importance that some compensating advantage for the overthrow of native rule should be plainly discernable in the acts and policy of those who are substituting another in its place. It matters not whether this compensating advantage be of a religious, social or political character, providing of course that the people believe themselves benefited thereby and are made to recognise the good intent of the government which confers it. It is in both these aspects where England has signally failed, alike to obtain the willing submission of her subject races and as a propagandist of her own civilization. The petty despotism and rapacity of the native rulers of India at the period of the East India Company's advent there, was such that any power which would lighten the burden of taxation or robbery rather of the Ryot or industrial population would be a welcome substitute for that which it had constantly to fear as an unscrupulous, plundering enemy. Yet so far beyond the Nabobs and Rajahs did the Company go in the rule of robbery (and so far of course as a necessary consequence did the Civilization and religion it represented go beyond the worst features of those of the people of India) that, to use the expressive language of Macaulay,[36] "the population soon discovered that the finger of the Governor General (Warren Hastings) was thicker than the thigh of Suraj Dowlah"![37] When to this disparaging comparison with Native rule is added the subsequent outrages of the English upon the Caste of the Brahmins in the judicial murder of Numcomar [sic] by Hastings and his tool Impey,[38] the mercenary action of the Gov. General in the Rohilla War[39] etc, and the violation of the sanctity of the Harem in the *robbery* of the Begums,[40] we see how fatal the rule of British Interests have been in India both to the people thereof, as well as to English Civilization, Christianity and good government.

I have alluded to the "conflicting elements" of English Civilization at the commencement of my remarks thereon, as probably one of the causes why it fails to leave a durable impress upon any but the Anglo-Saxon race; forming in this respect an unfavourable contrast with the civilizations of preceding conquering nations and in many others with those of contemporary peoples. I shall now, ere commenting upon its career of failure in Ireland, endeavour to point out this inconsistency. If the proud assertions of most English writers are to be credited their country is at once the most civilized, the most free from interference with individual liberty and the best friend to Human Freedom, of all the Nations of the Earth. Let us see whether this is mere boast or real fact. First, what are the tests of a people's *domestic* civilization? I shall advance *four.* 1st Such a state of social independence or enjoyment by a people of the fruits of their own industry as shall approximate nearest to an equality in the distribution of the wealth which their united industry has accumulated to the minimising of poverty and its attendant evils among them.

2nd The extent of the conformity of the individual and Society to the precepts of a professed religion, and to the canon of moral law, "do unto others as you would wish to be done by," as shown by the amount of crime and state of public morals.

3rd The development of the intellectual faculties of the people as manifest in their industrial arts and sciences, medicine, literature, systems of public education and organisation of labour.

4th Such a form of Government as best represents the interests and feelings of the entire people having a voice in its creation, as shown in the prevalence of moral order under its rule, impartial administration of the laws, and feeling of general security against class influence and disturbers of individual rights and privileges.

Before applying the foregoing tests to English domestic civilization it will not be amiss to glance at the manner in which its comparative value to the individual and society is generally but fallaciously estimated by English writers.

A comparison with the social condition of England previous to the invention of labour saving machinery and the locomotive, and before the discovery of the magical properties of steam and electricity, together with the increase of wealth which has followed in their wake, is the usual way in which the "progressive civilization" of the present day is lauded at the expense of that by which it was preceded. This mode of comparison however forms no just criterion because no one advances the proposition that pre-electric telegraph, steam and railway times were "any better than they ought to be": Nor is it denied that modern invention and the improvements in industrial arts which the application of science and chemistry have effected,

have not added to that productive power which supplies
English "Society" with its luxuries and its monied classes with
their wealth. But if civilization be what Guizot defines it, "The
improvement of the individual and society," and if by individual
and society the *whole* population of England and its "super-
organic invironment [*sic*]" be understood,[41] then does England's
domestic civilization stand condemned at the present hour by
an amount of pauperism, crime (and necessity for Emmigration
[*sic*]) among her population, unknown by any previous epoch
of her history, and greater than what is to be found among
any other contemporary civilized people. English civilization
fails in England, then, not in the production of wealth nor in
the permanent improvement of *some* of its classes, but in an
equitable and rational apportionment of its progressive results
among *all* its classes, so as to show in the social condition of
the masses the essentials of "healthy, happy human existence,"
and evidence of the enjoyment of those fruits of the industrial,
creative and contriving capacities of Englishmen by which
their civilization and what they have gained therefrom could
be recognised.

Side by side then with the undoubted increase of material
prosperity in England during the past fifty years is the no less
evident fact of a corresponding increase of pauperism and all
its concomitant evils. Is increase of poverty an inseparable or an
accidental accompaniment of England's advanced civilization?
In either case its presence to the enormous extent of *a million
of paupers* in addition to the amount of hardship and pinching
want among the well known "poor quarters" of English cities
and large towns, points out a *pernicious something* in that civilization which is responsible for it amidst so much wealth, and
indicates a danger to Society of the no distant future with
which neither education nor statesmanship attempts to grapple
at present. Writers intent upon blazoning forth the "glories"
of Great Britain and the super-excellence of its civilization,
keep this dark picture of shame and human suffering in the
background; either unwilling to exhibit its forbidding features
to the gaze of other nations or afraid to approach the everyday

widening gulf which the civilization of their country has placed between the Dives and Lazarus[42] of English Society. But to return from this anticipation of their consequence to the four tests by which a rational comparison may be made of a people's domestic civilization:—I have already in part shown that test no. 1 discovers an increase of poverty in England equal to if it does not surpass its increase of wealth; and the most superficial knowledge of the present social condition of the people of France, Switzerland, Belgium, Italy, Holland, Norway and Sweden, Denmark, the German Empire and Spain will be sufficient to prove how far superior that condition is; how much better are the houses, clothing and food of the industrial classes: how much less general is pauperism among their populations than in that of England; because owing to the prevalence of peasant proprietary in all those countries and the consequent division of their land into small properties, their wealth is more equally divided among their inhabitants to the bettering of the conditions of human happiness under which they live.[43] In all the foregoing countries, increase of material prosperity since the time of the French Revolution by which continental "landlordism" was overthrown has been general, and the diminution of pauperism and mendicancy equally apparent; while in England during the same period, the reverse is the case, saving the increase of wealth which has gone to the upper and middle classes, leaving *more than twenty per cent* of its people but one step above actual destitution. Test no. 2 will also by comparing the church-going population of England and the number of persons in its Convict Establishments and country prisons with those of any continental country, show results condemnatory of the religious and moral elements of English Civilization. If France and Germany exhibit more of *professed* infidelity in their large cities, their rural populations will more than balance this defect in a comparison with the irreligious tendencies of the English masses.

The state of public morals in England is probably no worse than that of most civilized countries, save that there is unquestionably more drunkenness and crime among the lower orders than among the same class of any other contemporary people. According to a late Bishop of Oxford over *80,000* prostitutes existed in London alone.[44] When the number of these unfortunates in such cities as Liverpool, Manchester, etc., is added to the foregoing estimate of what is to be found in London, what an amount of immorality does it point out in the people of this country. The proceedings in the Divorce Courts and the every-day scandal of "society" indicate anything but a high moral standard in the fashionable or "upper ten" portion of the English people. Finally on this subject of a people's public morals there is probably no country in the world where there is less confidence shown in the honesty of the public than in England. "Beware of pickpockets" seems to be the one grand caution which English civilization has taught all Englishmen who have anything to lose in their own country. "Thus conscience doth make cowards" etc.[45]

Test no 3 applied to the *whole* of England's population must place its intellectual development lower than that of the populations of Switzerland, Saxony, France, Norway and Sweden or Belgium; although England's middle, professional and upper classes can rank in literary merit, critical acumen and inventive genius with the best intellects of the world of learning. England's knowledge like her wealth has not been well distributed by her civilization. This defect however is now being remedied through the operation of the Compulsory Education Act—which by the way is somewhat of a misnomer as the act is not *compulsory* throughout England.[46]

The spread of intelligence among the masses in those continental countries in which *the land* has likewise been distributed into small holdings and become the property of the people, has rendered their agricultural populations, conservative and contented:— whereas the following is the effect which in the opinion of the author of *Free Trade in Land*,[47] the more general diffusion of knowledge will have upon the poor and lower-industrial portion of the English people: "The more intelligence spreads among the poor of our country the more will all this (social discontent) increase, unless we alter the laws which tend to prevent the peasants from acquiring property. The classes who are deprived of the natural means of bettering their social condition will rise more and more fiercely against the obstacles which beset them, the more clearly they perceive those obstacles."[48]

"If it be necessary or expedient that the present land system should be continued, *it would be wiser to get rid of every school in the country.* To give the people intelligence and yet to tie their hands, is more dangerous than to give fire to a madman. At present our peasants are deficient in intelligence and therefore they are quiet," (page 286 et seq.). Not very flattering this to the civilization which in the estimation of most English writers takes the lead of all those belonging to the nineteenth century.

The final test of the four by which I am comparing England's domestic civilization with those of other nations, is that of Government. The English is undoubtedly the best form of constitutional monarchy in the world—but certainly not the best form of government. However, as for anything observable to the contrary the English people are satisfied with and contented under its rule at present—though probably not one in twenty of its subjects are permitted to have a voice in the election of members of parliament. The House of Commons though Democratic in its privileges and functions is unquestionably an aristocratic assembly. Probably not two per cent of its members belong to the industrial ranks of the English people. Here again *wealth* absorbs everything—the political privileges as well as almost all the other benefits of English civilization—leaving the masses out in the cold—to become dangerous to *Monopoly* by and by.

Much can be said both for and against the administration of justice in England, just as it is compared with that of other countries. English Judges do not meddle in politics nor interfere in any way in the government of the country. In Ireland unfortunately they do both. English judges would be both disgraced and compelled to vacate their positions by public opinion if they were suspected of being the tools of either the court or prime minister; while the hungry favour-hunting

occupants of the Irish Bench think themselves disgraced in no
way by doing the dirty work of Dublin Castle whenever
required to prostitute the seat of Justice to party or vindictive
purposes. Partiality to offenders against the law who belong
to the "Upper Ten" is a well known "weakness" of English
Judges whilst their habitual severity against offenders among
the lower orders, show conclusively that English Civilization
has not yet reached that stage of progress in which *all* are
equal before the law. Class influence is probably more
powerful in England than in any other civilized country: and
though it cannot now interfere arbitrarily with the personal
liberty of any Englishman, the aristocracy has however a
monopoly of the Magistracy, Higher Commands in the Army
and Navy, Diplomatic Service, Royal Household, Ecclesiastical
preference etc., etc.

And now to test the Englishman's boast of his country's
being not only a friend, but the *best* among all others to the
cause of Human Liberty; this chivalrous championship of
Freedom being of course the outcome of England's "advanced
Civilization". I have already pointed out in the brief outline of
England's *external* civilization as shown in her conquest of India
and subsequent policy in reference to the dismemberment of
Denmark and her support of Turkey in the Bulgarian war, etc.,
how "British Interests" are made the *primum mobile* alike of her
conquests, rule of the conquered, and relations towards other
powers and peoples. I have yet to learn in my study of history
who that people is and where the Nation that owe everything
of the liberty they may possess to a disinterested act on the
part of England. True the majority of Englishmen are the professed friends of at least all *civilized* peoples seeking independence
from despotic home or oppressive foreign government—*the
Irish excepted*—and English public opinion generally speaking
when divorced from the traditional or "British Interests policy"
of the upper classes and government, is an unsparing critic of
arbitrary power and a generous sympathiser with struggling
Liberty all the world over—excepting Ireland. In fact this
abstract sympathy with and theoretic advocacy of freedom to

all oppressed Nationalities of the English people, joined to the generally passive and frequently active—hostility of its government towards the same, when British Interests are directly or indirectly involved, forms one of the prevailing inconsistencies of the English nation, and one of those conflicting elements of its civilization to which I have heretofore referred. "Dieu et mon droit",[49] sounds pious and well as the national legend of a people; but if acts and not professions should dictate a superscription to the Royal Arms of England, the present would be changed to "Meliore proboque, deteriore sequor"[50]—

"I know the Right and I approve it too,

Condemn the wrong and yet the wrong pursue".[51]

Although England had taught France and the world how to deal with "a Right Divine" King who persisted in governing wrong, she succeeded in combining all the kings of Europe in a league against the French people for their treating Louis Capet[52] as the English themselves had treated Charles Stewart [*sic*].[53] If that mighty Revolution from which *all* modern liberty and true progress has sprung was not strangled in its infancy in the interests of Continental despotism, it was not the fault of the genius of Pitt, the eloquence of Burke or the power wealth and valour of England. The history of the War of American Independence is another instance where the might of England is once again in the lists against human Liberty— and fortunately for the oppressed of all nations who want a refuge from tyranny and wrong, she came out of the contest defeated, baffled, humiliated. Nor was her sympathy with the Confederates in the great American Civil War more successful on the side of Slavery and Secession against Freedom and the Union of the U.S.A.

In conjunction with France—when that country was governed by the miserable "Man of December,"[54] England aided in the (fortunately unsuccessful) effort to subvert the liberty of Mexico in order to give an European Adventurer an "Empire" contiguous to the United States Republic.[55] She next declares war against the Afgans [*sic*], drives Shere Ali from his throne and deluges the country with the blood of her own soldiers as well as that of her antagonists—merely to extend the "Scientific Frontier" of her Indian Empire.[56] Next follows her espousal of the cause of the Turk and Eastern despotism in Europe against the Christian people of the Danubian principalities who were striving for freedom from a hated vassalage. Singular mode of furthering the cause of "Human Liberty" this, Madame Britannia and Messieurs the (self-styled) friends of oppressed peoples? English Civilization and the all-directing ubiquitous "British Interests" must explain the enigma. Her last and most "brilliant" exploit in the way of civilization and "help" to liberty is her war against the Zulus and Boers of South Africa; in which shameless and unprovoked aggression England however receives from the "barbarous," naked, Assagai-armed followers of Cetchwayo[57] (defending their country) the greatest blow alike to her prestige as a conquering nation and the vaunted courage of her soldiers, which any country has experienced in modern days at the hands of an enemy. One hundred years hence there will probably Englishmen be found who will wonder why English Civilization and the Bible will have failed with the people of South Africa!

In briefly sketching the failure of English Civilization in Ireland I shall travel over as little of the rugged path of history as possible. In my opinion the best, clearest and most convincing resumé of historical fact, devoid alike of passion or prejudice while palpitating with angry truth and fervid national feeling ever penned on the dark record of English rule in Ireland, is that comprised within the narrow limits of seventy pages and one chapter (the fourth) of Gavan Duffy's *Young Ireland Party*.[58] If every intelligent Englishman capable of reading could only be persuaded to devote *two hours* to the scanning of that wonderful "Birds Eye View of Irish History," and one hour more to a serious and unprejudiced reflection upon the facts there brought before his mind, I don't think I would ever be imprisoned again, at least with the approval of English public opinion.

If England's Civilization could be adopted by or imposed upon any of the races which have fallen under English rule, that race should have been the Keltic or Irish. Identical in origin with the ancient inhabitants of Gt. Britain; of the same religion as that of its people until the epoch of the Reformation; situated within a few hours sail of its coasts and more distant from the means of intercourse with any other nation, the fact of the Irish people remaining until the present day as distinct in individuality, feelings, national habits and national aspirations from their English rulers as if they inhabited an Island in the centre of the Atlantic, forms one of the most singular phenomenas [*sic*] of ethnological or political history on record, and in my humble opinion one of the most convincing proofs of the non-transmissibility of English civilization to any other race.

An explanation of this non-acceptance by the Irish people of English Civilization is not to be found in my opinion either in the vitality of that which obtained in Ireland previous to 1172[59] surviving in opposition to that of the invaders, nor yet in any inherent antagonism of Keltic blood to the composite race of the Anglo-Saxon,—as probably most of our countrymen flatter themselves into believing—but from the seemingly inseparable relationship of English conquest to all that sordid selfish lust of power, sleuth-hound unerring pursuit of object, and remorseless disregard of every humane feeling towards a defeated but unbending victim, or fear of moral responsibility in carrying out a pitiless policy of extermination towards him if he yield not a willing submission, which distinguished the followers of Mahommed in their career of conquest from Arabia to Samarcand [*sic*]. "Our rule and your unmurmuring obedience thereto, or your Extermination," has been the language implied in the acts and policy of England since her standard was first planted on Irish Soil—and it is only within the present century that this method of transplanting English "Civilization" across the Irish Channel has been changed or modified from the impossibility of converting us thereto or effecting the other alternative. Had England been guided by a sounder policy than the distribution of the land of Ireland (at that time National property—the patrimony of the people) among the Adventurers who flocked over from England in pursuit of fortune; and allowed wiser principles of government or statesmanship than the trampling upon the national feelings, habits and institutions of the Keltic inhabitants, to influence her Irish Administration, the sequel would be far different and much more profitable to the well-being of the British Empire, than what has resulted from the blind and persistent adhesion to the policy of "British Interests". Had Hugh O'Neill[60] and "Dauntless Red Hugh" O'Donnell[61]—the only two Irish Chieftains equal in warlike genius and diplomacy to the representatives of England in Ireland since the invasion, and capable of acting together and combining the strength of the country against the foe—had they been as they requested confirmed in their titles and belongings by the English Monarch in good faith, and favours conferred upon them such as sound policy would dictate, instead of the deceitful, treacherous conduct which ultimately drove them into rebellion and thence to exile and death; and had the national land code been likewise left intact and the people allowed to remain the owners, instead of the creation of the plantation scheme—from which Irish Landlordism is derived—and permitted also the same enjoyment of their religious creed, there is every probability that Ireland would be today in reality and not in name, "an integral part of the British Empire," and my countrymen as submissive to English rule as those of their kilted and Cambrian race north of the Tweed and west of the Severn. I say in "all probability," as almost every page of our history records instances of Irish leaders (from 1172 to 1798) demanding justice from English monarchs against their rapacious and sanguinary instruments in Ireland; and justifying rebellion against the rule of the same by their violation of previous treaties or agreements between either the Irish and the English King or the former and the (English) Parliament of the *Pale*.

Still under even a just and tolerant English—*foreign*—sway in Ireland such as I have pointed out (and such as England may yet be educated into adopting—when it may perhaps be on the verge of being too late), "in all probability" likewise there would from time to time arise Tones,[62] Fitzgeralds[63] and

Emmets,[64] who would indignantly spurn alien domination at any price, and claim for their fatherland at the risk of their liberties or lives the proud privilege of the Nationhood without which a country is like an individual bereft of his good name, "poor with all else beside".

It is essential for the successful planting of one civilization over that of another, or for the submissive acceptation [*sic*] of the rule of the conqueror by the subjugated for that which it is overthrown, that one or both should be grounded upon motives that are of paramount influence with the people who are to be won from their own. The two most powerful motives which determine the religious, social and political character of the Irish people have always been and are still, an enthusiastic fidelity to their National Faith and passionate attachment to the soil of Ireland, forming the two most prominent features of Irish civilization for over a thousand years—yet it has been England's one grand object blindly, unscrupulously, and vindictively pursued to detach them from the one and deprive them of all claim or title to the other. Three hundred years of a religious persecution equalled in atrocious fanaticism only by that which Christiandom [*sic*] waged against the Jews, succeeds only in rooting the Catholic Church more firmly on Irish soil today than among any other nation in the world. Penal laws[65] have to give place to Emancipation.[66] Tythes [*sic*][67] to the endowment of Maynooth,[68] until finally in 1869 the Disestablishment of the Church of the Conquerors leaves victory and religious freedom and equality to the Irish people.[69]

The "land war" has been equally long, equally unjust, sanguinary and impolitic on the part of England as the one she contemporaneously waged on the people's faith:—while the resistance offered to the Feudal System from its first introduction into Ireland to the present hour, has been equally determined, unceasing and heroic as that which has won liberty of conscientious belief from the same power by the same people. Will the struggle for "Free Land" be equally successful as that for "Free Altars"? *Tempus omnia revelat*;[70] and time *not too remote* will also unquestionably show the end of blood-stained Irish Landlordism as sure as there is a God of Justice who metes out to guilty systems of human oppression as to individual transgression of Divine Justice the period allotted to their career of wrong and the penalty of their crimes and misdeeds—*Latifundia perdidere Italiam*[71] was the mournful declaration of Pliny[72] over the crumbling edifice of the Roman Empire. If English statesmen persist in disregarding the teachings of history, the warnings of writers and philosophers like Mill,[73] Sismondi,[74] Kay,[75] De Lavaleye [*sic*],[76] De Laverne,[77] etc., and the examples of every other civilized country in respect to the great social question of Land Reform, and blindly adhere to the feudal code of land laws which every other people but the English have abolished, some future English Pliny will yet write a similar epitaph to the above over the tottering ruins of his country's prestige and civilization. (End of remarks on England's Civilization.)

The only victory scored in Ireland by English Civilization has been the supplanting of the Keltic tongue by that of England. This is no inconsiderable triumph it must be admitted; and the fidelity of the Welsh to the language of Ossian under similar political relations with the Anglo-Saxon, and *nearer* to the intruding English, should put Irishmen to the blush. Not that the acquisition of English would be a danger, but that we allowed our own to *almost* perish through neglect, by using in preference that of our rulers. I am of opinion that this sacrifice of our national tongue—and consequent loss of the treasures of the past and national stimulants locked therein—must be attributed to the teaching of the Catholic Church in Ireland from '98 to the time of the Famine of '48. *Qui bona?*[78]

. . . [Oct 4, Secret Societies—Ancient and Modern] . . .

IRELAND'S SHARE OF THE BRITISH CONSTITUTION: AS SEEN IN ITS GOVERNMENT AND PARLIAMENTARY FRANCHISE

"You have the same government and laws as we have and yet you are discontented and say you are not justly governed. Admitting that great wrongs have been inflicted upon Ireland in the past, in what does its present government and the administration of its laws differ from what obtains with us in England? You Irish are *never* satisfied." There are few Irishmen that have taken a prominent part in Irish national politics during the past twenty years who have not some time or other been addressed in similar language to the foregoing by English politicians or critics. It is also the text of the Anglo-Irish political lessons by which the foreign press has been taught through English newspapers that Ireland is in the full enjoyment of that great desideratum of most civilized nations, "the British Constitution"; and that therefore Irishmen have no legitimate cause for agitation or real grievance of which to complain. Similar questions have been put to me by more than a hundred inquisitive "Interviewers" during two lecturing tours in the United States; shewing that the American like the press of France, Germany and Italy is educated into the belief that we have no case whatever against England in ref. the enjoyment of the same liberties and laws as Englishmen and Scotchmen.

The great majority of Englishmen honestly believe this to be true simply because few of their countrymen ever care to rightly inform themselves upon the subject of their country's rule of Ireland. What they suppose is or think ought to be the case, is the opinion they express or the judgement which they form upon the matter. Now the answer which every Englishman who has learned to sing "Britons never shall be slaves" would return to the questions contained in the first sentence of this paper, if England stood in the same political relationship towards say France or Germany, as Ireland occupies towards her, would of course have no weight whatever when coming from an Irishman to an English critic, nor would it, I fear, be much more successful if given to the query of a disinterested foreigner. "The conquest of Ireland is a *fait accompli*—it forms an integral part of the British Empire—it has ceased to rank among nations for a longer period than the existence of many of England's contemporaries; and therefore, all claims to independence on its behalf can only be discussed upon a basis of abstract right," is the reasoning which such claims would invariably encounter outside of Irish Nationalist opinion. Whether Irishmen agree or not with the justice or political morality of such reasoning they must be alive both to the necessity of recognising its effect upon neutral minds and to the wisdom of adducing more convincing facts than those implied above if the sympathies of such minds are to be won to the cause of Irish political effort, or the moral support of public opinion enlisted on the side of our people in their rational or social aspirations. Will a dispassionate inquiry into the nature of English rule in Ireland, as manifested in its govern-ment and share of the constitution, produce such facts? If it does our case against England will, *a fortiori*, be more complete, and our chances of external sympathy for the remedies we demand be likewise increased; if it does not, we are left to struggle with our rulers bereft of the sympathetic interest of nearly the rest of the civilized world. Let us see, then what a peep behind the scenes of England's rule of Ireland will disclose:—

For the purposes of this inquiry it will be necessary, first, to point out what are the objective advantages which the citizen of Gt. Britain derives from the "British Constitution" and second, to see whether or not those advantages are equally enjoyed by the inhabitants of Ireland under English rule. In seeking to comply with the first of these requirements I shall not deem it necessary to institute any comparison between the British Constitution and that of any other civilized nation, as this would be shifting the controversy into the domain of another and irrelevant subject, the relative merits of monarchical and republican forms of government and institutions. It is quite enough for the purpose to consider the British Constitution as disconnected in the political as Gt. Britain is in the geographical world: It is also unnecessary to discuss whether or not the political and social rights of Englishmen under the same are all that could be desired by progressive mankind. To ascertain the equal or unequal participation by Ireland in its advantages—such as they are—with England and Scotland, is the essential and only object of this paper.

Let us see what are the prominent features of the British Constitution as perceptible in the Government, attitude of the people, and administration of the laws, in England:—

The surest test of a people's contentment with and confidence in the government of their country is the general state of social order which prevails among them under the same. A glaring abuse of power or arbitrary interference with the liberties or belongings of a civilized people on the part of its government, will as surely provoke some discontent or disturbance in the social system of the body politic, as the presence of a disturbing agent in our physical structure will manifest itself in the form of bodily disease or ailment. The prevalence of social order, then, and a patriotic or healthy tone in the National press— the pulse of the commonwealth—are indicative of popular satisfaction with the manner in which the government of the country is conducted. When in addition to this the maintenance of social order is plainly the result of a mutual confidence between the governors and the governed—when the former has but to concern itself in the interests of *material* order, that is in the preservation of individual rights and privileges, and the application of legal powers against infringements thereof or public wrongdoers; and the latter by their willing submission to the ruling authority and loyalty to the constitution uphold *moral* order, it is evident that the people are governed by themselves for themselves and that they are in the enjoyment of such political rights and liberties as they for the time being think necessary or sufficient for their own wellbeing and good of their country. If at any time, however, an extension of such political privilege is demanded by an exempt section of the people (who, however, enjoy an equal share of personal liberty with the rest of the community) the agitation for the same will show itself only in a temporary excitation of public opinion requiring none of the power in the hands of the Executive needed in the administration of material order, to be diverted therefrom— thereby insuring the prevalence of social order during periodical political excitement among any particular class of the people.

Almost *all* these conditions of Social Order exist in England. *None* of them are found in Ireland. Wherefore? There is probably more personal liberty enjoyed in England than is to be found in any other country in the world except the United States. If an Englishman be a householder in a city or borough and pays his poor rate, he is in possession of the Franchise, no matter how humble his house may be or how small the rent he pays for it. Whether he be a merchant, mechanic, or costermonger he is as secure from disturbance or domiciliary visits from the agents of the law as long as he is guiltless of any breach thereof—as Queen Victoria. He in fact enjoys the privilege which is the boast of Englishmen—his house is his castle. If he desires the possession of a gun or other firearm, he is at liberty to have one over his mantelpiece. If he wishes to travel through the country for pleasure or profit, he may go from one end of England to the other without being questioned or interfered with by the police—so long as he abstains from trespassing on enclosures, interference with game, or what else the law defines to be the property of others. If he is dissatisfied with any particular law or statute of the realm, conduct of cabinet minister, home or foreign policy of government or amount of money paid to Her Majesty the Queen, he can express his sentiments thereon in almost whatever language he pleases either by means of the press, village inn, city club or public platform, without any fear of a prosecution for sedition or annoyance from the presence of a government shorthand writer at his elbow. If he goes to law with his neighbour he is confident that the same will be administered impartially. If he commits any serious breach of the same he knows that the jury which is to try him will be fairly empanelled and that the judge will act independent of Downing Street, or Scotland Yard. If he be a politician he will of course be subject to party opinions, and rejoice or despond when his favourite statesmen are in or out of office; but in or out as his party may be he feels that the *permanent* government of his country—that which never goes out—is always the same, tolerant, patriotic, watchful guardian of England's coast, honour, interests and the individual belongings of every Englishman. He may grumble at the taxes which he is called upon to pay, but he knows that the House of Commons—the voice of the people—is the keeper of the people's purse, and that the Chancellor of the Exchequer will only ask for what the public service imperatively requires from the Nation for the management of its affairs. English judges are compelled by force of modern custom and public opinion to take no part whatever openly or privately in politics, and to keep the Seat of Justice as free from official dictation or court influences as if their power was derived directly from the people. They take no part whatever in the government of the country. The Magistracy throughout England is more or less of a representative character from being the creation of and kept under surveillance (more or less) by both political parties. Taken as a class in the possession of power they are neither obnoxious to nor distrusted by, the people—the preservers of public order are a *local* not a centralised force in England, never interfere in the political gatherings or ordinary concerns of the people, and are not allowed to carry arms, even when called upon to quell a riot. Scotland Yard has probably no more to do with the management of the police affairs of Buckinghamshire, Westmoreland or other county, city or town of England, outside of London, than in that of Paris or New York. The military force of the country is known to be distributed for defensive and not *offensive* purposes among its various depots and barracks.

Finally if the English citizen be a lover of monarchical or democratic institutions he will find his principles more or less represented in the constitution of his country. If the Court and Aristocracy no longer hold the national purse or appoint the Judges they have a monopoly of the higher commands in the army, diplomatic service—and of the House of Lords. The House of Commons is at once the National Assembly, overseer of public affairs, and paymaster-general for every department of English government. Its members may nearly all belong to the upper, monies and legal classes, but its functions are probably as democratic and its powers as great as that of any assembly of any republic in the world. As the vigilant guardian of public liberty its traditions can speak of one despotic king sent to the scaffold and another deprived of his throne. If an Englishman be molested or insulted in any part of the universe, he is almost certain that the House of Commons will hear of it and take action in his behalf. It is the preserver of the people's privileges at home and the powerful and watchful guardian of their interests abroad. Upon public questions of popular moment it can invariably be counted upon to side with the people against both crown and aristocracy—and in the creation of this most English of all English institutions one Englishman in every nine of the population has a voice.

Such appears to me to be the most prominent features of the British Constitution as seen in the government and administration of Law in England; and the liberties and privileges of citizenship pointed out in this brief sketch are what among others not specified, the citizen of Gt. Britain enjoys under the rule of such constitution.

Although it is no concern of this paper that the British Constitution is defective in some points of vital importance to

the wellbeing of the masses of Gt. Britain, it will be no harm
to make specific mention of the two most important, ere
proceeding to a review of Irish Government and the political
privileges allowed to Irishmen by the same. The principal
defect is the monopoly of land by a small class to the exclusion
of the nation from the possession of the same; and the severest
censure which can in my opinion be passed upon this great
wrong against the natural rights of Englishmen, is contained
in the two facts relating to this monopoly which Mr Froude,
the champion of the English land system, has frankly pointed
out. "The House of Lords owns more than *a third of the whole
area of Gt. Britain;* while *two thirds of it* belong to great peers and
commoners; whose estates are *continually devouring the small estates*
adjoining them." Two short commentaries bearing on these
pregnant facts by two well-known Englishmen will comprise
more censure on this defect of the British Constitution than
two pages of criticism. Lord Derby—one of the large English
landowners—has admitted that, "the class of peasant proprietors formerly to be found in the rural districts was tending
to disappear,"[79] and Mr Kay, the author of the widely-read
work on *Free Trade in Land* declares, "These (the foregoing)
statements are only too sadly true." "There is no doubt,"
continues this well-informed writer, "that England once possessed a large class of independent, well-to-do, self-supporting
yeomen proprietors. Old writers treat it as one of the boasts
of Old England that she had so many small freehold Yeomen.
Where are they now? By our system of Land Laws we have
been cutting away the base of our social pyramid, while nearly
all other civilized countries have been pursuing an exactly
opposite policy." (*Free Trade in Land*, p. 18). If this gradual
effacement of the most conservative class of any country, keeps
pace with the growing education of the landless people of
England, while pauperism advances among the masses in
proportion to the accumulation of landed wealth in the hands
of the ten thousand peers and commoners who own the two-
thirds of England and Wales, the "devouring" system will
some day commence at the other end of the social scale; and

if Macaulay's "Goths and Vandals" of overcrowded cities and towns of England swoop out upon the quarry, some other defective branch of the Constitution will probably go along with that of landlordism.[80] It only requires education to show the farmers, mechanics and labourers of this country the truth of what advanced political economy is now teaching; that to permit any one section of a nation to have a monopoly of its land is equivalent to the creation by law of a small wealthy and a great pauper class; that to allow the soil of a country to become the absolute property of a moiety of its people, is a surrender of natural and national right not for a compensating advantage, but for an evident wrong and a positive evil to society. That land is a natural agent—existing independent of either human law or landlord power; one of the primal, indispensable necessaries which God has supplied for the use of mankind; and that land is of no value in the economy of existence or of government without the application of labour, are self-evident propositions, the oft repetition of which by land reformers tends to excite the ridicule of interested critics, which the popular mind of Gt. Britain and Ireland is nevertheless eagerly beginning to grasp to the certain overthrow, sooner or later, of the system of land laws which gainsays them. Every individual who earns his bread in or near a city or town in Gt. Britain, no matter what his occupation may be has contributed and is daily contributing to the value of the land both in, and in the neighbourhood of, such city or town, whether he is aware of the fact or not. Hence the price of land is say one hundred guineas per square foot in parts of London—decreasing in value in proportion to the distances from the centre of busiest population, until some out of the way district is reached where rent for land, as good as that upon which the Bank of England now stands, may be no more than one pound an acre. Who or what has lent this surprising value to this land in and near large centres of industrial population? Have the landlords? Not a fraction more than has that old friend of comparison, the man in the Moon. The increment of its worth results from the daily wants of the

Community at large and its enormous revenues, rents, and charges are the taxes which landlord legislation in the past, has succeeded in placing upon the growing necessities of the society of the present and future in the interest of its own particular class. This national agency in the augmentation of landlord wealth has raised the rent of land in England to such a surprising figure that it is today 120 times the amount in money as it was 500 years ago according to Prof. Thorold Rogers,[81] and 14 times as great if measured in cereal produce; while the increased value of building land has been advanced even more enormously. According to such a reliable authority as the present Postmaster General the capitalised rental value of the land of England has reached the almost incomprehensible figure of £4,500,000,000!—a sum which if capable of being loaned out, would, at the rate of 3 per cent, *pay off both principal and interest of the National Debt in five years!* Yet this fabulous wealth has been created by the people of this country non-agricultural as well as agricultural in the application of their industrial, contriving and creative capacities in the progressive march of modern civilization, *independent of any exertion on the part of the privileged class which now claims it as its own*; while the same agencies in its production are called upon to pay 26 millions a year interest on the national debt, along with the other public charges of the country, out of the direct returns of their own labour. This triumph of Monopoly over the natural rights of Englishmen together with the pauperism, misery and crime which the unequal distribution of the wealth which is created by the application of human exertion and skill to productive natural agents, is alike the one grand defect of English civilization and the principal flaw in the British Constitution. The landlord commoners of the Long Parliament who abolished the military tenures of the feudal system knew very well what they were about. To send a despotic King to a scaffold was in its way no doubt a grand act in vindication of popular liberty, and a lesson in the application of which the people of France have since shown themselves willing learners; but the revenues or "knights service" and fees which landholders were hitherto compelled to contribute for the service of the state as an indispensable condition to the recognition of their territorial rights and privileges, were dexterously saddled upon the people in the name and on behalf of the spirit of liberty! True, the King could no longer turn an army against the nation if the representation of the nation resolved upon taking that powerful weapon into its own hands: but the King, despotic, false and treacherous however he may have been, made the national property—*the land*—support both the army and himself to the saving of the cost of the same to the people at large. And had the members of the Long Parliament not had an eye to the getting rid of the condition which made the landlords little more than stewards of the nation's property, they could have changed the form of the feudal dues so as to meet the requirements of the new arrangement, and thus obviate the necessity of the immense taxation and enormous national debt which have resulted from their "patriotic" acts.

Few English minds have yet grasped the full extent of the enormous wrong which land monopoly has wrought and still inflicts upon the industrial population of Gt. Britain and Ireland. They have seen the marvellous growth of their country's wealth and commercial prosperity from decade to decade without caring to give more than a passing notice to the equally rapid advance of those social evils which keep pace with, if they do not actually germinate within the development of modern progress. They have been taught by the literature which has hitherto influenced both opinion and thought upon the subject of tenures and property in land to explain away the pauperism, poverty, starvation, misery and crime among the lower classes, not by any references to their being shut out from their natural means of subsistence, but upon the Malthusian hypothesis that nature refuses to provide for dense populations, and therefore "The weakest must go to the wall" in the struggle of human existence. This inhuman and cowardly doctrine has in later times cropped up under a new name as the "survival of the fittest" and is doubtless accepted by the landocracy and those accomplices in the plunder of national wealth "the conservators of ancient barbarisms" as an indisputable dogma in the laws of political economy; but the *masses* themselves are commencing to think and reason upon this question of whether Nature's God has erred or not in bidding man to increase and multiply, and if any of those sudden popular upheavals of our time should bring the question of the "survival of the fittest" into the domain of practical politics, why the masses will not fail to recollect that *they* and not the *few* have the best claim to, and the most arms to secure, the provision which Nature has made for their natural wants and necessities.

One English writer who is far ahead of the Malthusian school has already exclaimed "had we to deal with the parties who originally robbed the human race of its heritage we might make short work of the matter:"[82] and Henry George of San Francisco[83] in his powerfully reasoned work, *Progress and Poverty*[84] follows up this declaration of Herbert Spencer[85] in the following trenchant style: "Why not make short work of the matter anyhow? For this robbery is not like the robbery of a horse or a sum of money that ceases with the act. It is a fresh and continuous robbery which goes on every day and every hour. It is not from the produce of the past that rent is drawn, it is from the produce of the present. It is a toll levied upon labour constantly and continuously. Every blow of the hammer, every stroke of the pick, every thrust of the shuttle, every throb of the steam engine, pay it tribute. It levies upon the earnings of the men who, deep under ground risk their lives, and of those who over white surges hang to reeling masts; it claims the just reward of the capitalist and the fruits of the inventor's patent effort; it takes little children from play and from school and compels them to work before their bones are hard or their muscles are firm; it robs the shivering of warmth; the hungry of food; the sick of medicine; the anxious of peace. It debases, and embrutes; and embitters. It crowds families of eight and ten into a single squalid room, it herds like swine agricultural boys and girls; it fills the gin palace and groggery with those who have no comfort in their homes; it makes lads who might be useful men candidates for prisons and penitentiaries; it fills brothels with girls who might have known the pure joy of motherhood; it sends greed and all evil passions prowling through society; as a hard winter drives the wolves to the abodes of men; it darkens faith in the human soul, and across the reflection of a just and merciful Creator draws the veil of a hard, and blind, and cruel fate. It is not merely a robbery in the past; it is a robbery in the present— a robbery that deprives of their birthright the infants that are now coming into the world! Why should we hesitate about making short work of such a system? Because I was robbed yesterday, and the day before, and the day before that, is it any reason that I should suffer myself to be robbed today and tomorrow? Any reason that I should conclude that the robber has required a vested interest to rob me? Consider what rent is. It does not rise spontaneously from the land; it is due to nothing that the landowners have done. It represents a value created by the whole community. Let the landholders have, if you please, all that the possession of the land would give them in the absence of the rest of the community. But rent, the creation of the whole community, necessarily belongs to the whole community."[86]

These ideas despite the cries of "Socialism" etc. with which they are met are taking root in the popular mind of Gt. Britain and Ireland, and they already menace the very existence of the only relic of feudalism extant in modern civilization—the English Land laws. The nationalization of the land, the only logical, just, final, and satisfactory settlement of the agrarian question of the present day must necessarily follow the education of the masses and to meet the imperative wants of increasing population in these countries.

Workhouses, prisons or emigration will not meet the growing evils of the existing social arrangement: Neither will a joint-ownership of the soil between landlord and tenant, or fixity of tenure—fair rents—arbitration courts or parliamentary commissions, solve the great problem which land monopoly will henceforth keep to the forefront of political questions, and with which statesmanship must grapple if society is to be defended from those popular movements which increasing want brooded over by the daily increasing intelligence of millions of human beings must create against those responsible for the injustice which drives rational men to reek relief in radical remedies. But how remove the existing system? What is to be done with the landlords? Property is a sacred object in the eyes of the constitution and to lay violent hands upon the recognised rights of any class is to disregard those principles upon which both society and government have their foundation. Desperate evils are successfully met by the application of desperate remedies. To base an argument for the continuance of landlordism upon the difficulty of abolishing it is equivalent to an admission that there is no other ground upon which to defend its existence. Nor can any other be advanced except the old alarmist cry of "revolution," "destruction of the constitution" etc. which those interested in social and political abuses have raised against every reform which has been carried in England during the last fifty years.

The irresistible advance which the cause of societary progress is daily making to the overthrow of the those wornout political and social maxims which have kept the mass of mankind as the slaves of monopoly, compels conservative ideas to follow in the wake of those of modern civilization and accept more or less of the to them, repugnant principles of reform, or be otherwise thrown out of the contest for political ascendancy. The "land for the people" will consequently soon find a permanent lodgement as the domain of English public opinion, and engage the thoughts of the social philosopher as well as the consideration of practical statesmanship like every other radical reform has done since public opinion became the ruling power of these countries; while the forty or fifty thousand individuals who are chiefly concerned in the maintenance of the existing system will learn to accustom themselves to the inevitable tendency towards the abolition of landlordism, and make the best bargain they can for the transfer of their territorial revenues to the service of the state and the needs of the people. The application of the rent which accrues from the land of England to the support of the state would simply abolish *all taxation direct and indirect* and leave to the breadwinners of Society the whole fruits of their skill and industry; while the removal of those restrictions which tie up the land in large estates and prevent the full development of all its resources, would soon check those social evils which now cluster in so foul an accumulation under the sway of the British Constitution.

The next defect in this great institution is the limited extent of the Franchise. There are over four millions of Householders in England according to the census returns for 1871, and of those, who beyond doubt constitute the backbone of the country, little more than *one fourth* are entrusted with the privilege of voting for members of the House of Commons. Why Household Suffrage should be granted to the rate payers of cities and boroughs and withheld from rate payers immediately outside the same and throughout the country is a political puzzle to strangers and an admitted injustice among all Englishmen who have confidence in the patriotism of their countrymen. The opposition which is offered to the assimilation of the County to the Borough franchise is as singular as it is impolitic and unjust. The counties are generally reckoned the stronghold of Conservatism and the boroughs that of Liberalism: Yet the Tories passed the reform bill of 1867 which gave household suffrage to ratepayers in boroughs, while they offer a solid front of opposition to Mr Trevelyan in his efforts to have the same privilege extended to the counties.[87] The arguments generally put forward by the opponents of further reform on this great national question are of the stereotyped alarmist complexion, "endanger the Constitution," "Advance of Republican ideas" etc., while it is as patent as history can make it that every extension of popular right which has been granted by Parliament during the past fifty years has strengthened the foundation upon which the constitution rests—the loyalty of the people. Where would the constitution be amid the political storms and social convulsions that have hurled Kings from their thrones and wrought such changes in Europe during the last half-century, if the genius of Reform had not guided the destinies of England during that period, and averted all danger by obtaining timely concessions of just measures for the public which clamoured for them? The safeguard of the Constitution is not to be found in an army or a specially privileged class or social influence of a landed aristocracy; but in the abolition of all those laws and systems which belong to a non-progressive past and which thrust their unjust and exploded notions of government and political privilege into the face of altered times and circumstances to the irritation and discontent of modern thought and opinion. When the abolition of feudal land laws and the extension of the franchise to every rational and intelligent Englishman are added to such enactments as the Repeal of the Corn Laws, Reform Bills, Municipal Corporations Act, Free Trade measures, Navigation laws etc., then but not till then will the British Constitution represent the genius of liberal minds and free institutions, and stand upon a firm and invulnerable base.

IRELAND'S SHARE OF THE BRITISH CONSTITUTION: AS SEEN IN ITS GOVERNMENT AND PARLIAMENTARY FRANCHISE

(continued)

I will now pass on to a review of the Government of Ireland, attitude of the people towards same political status of the Irish citizen, state of the Franchise etc., in order to comply with the second requirement of this inquiry—"Whether the advantages— such as they are—of the B[ritish] Constitution are enjoyed by Irishmen equally with the citizens of Gt. Britain".

Almost every traveller who has visited the United States is familiar with the story which is told at the expense of New York politicians and a newly arrived Irish Emigrant: Two eloquent canvassers for the Republican and Democratic "Tickets" (it being election time) introduce both themselves and the political virtues of their separate party-principles to the newly arrived stranger the moment he lands in Castle Garden. He is hailed as a citizen of the Gt. Republic without having to await the legal conditions for naturalisation—on the understanding of course that he votes straight for either of the parties' candi- dates. Failing however to either fully understand the new political privilege with which he is invested or comprehend the exact meaning of their respective party platforms, the story makes him ask the importunate party agents, "Have you a *Government* in this country?" "Why certainly, Sir. The most powerful, free and enlightened." "Well then," interrupts the

Irishman, "I don't understand the Democrats or Republicans but I will vote *"aginst" th' government anyhow.*" Whatever truth or fiction there may be in the foregoing story, it however illustrates the ideas of "the Government" which nineteen out of every twenty Irishmen leaving Ireland entertain towards the power that has been before their eyes since childhood—and which they associate with the cause of their exile—the power that represents the *British Constitution* in that country. To seek for a satisfactory explanation of this strong and bitter antipathy which three fourths of *the people* of Ireland entertain towards its ruling authority, either in a national insubordinate trait in Irish character which renders the Irishman discontented and trouble-some under all societary restraints; or in a quenchless hatred of that power which has deprived his country of its nationhood and made himself the subject of another people, would, in my opinion, be overlooking a plain and palpable cause for the gratification of English prejudice on the one hand, and the patriotic feelings of Irish nationalism, on the other. Those Englishmen who are in the habit of flinging the insult of "unruly Irish" at our people seldom take the trouble of noting their peaceable and orderly behaviour when resident *anywhere* but under the English—Anglo-Irish government of Ireland; or from the contrast between this discontent under the sway of "Dublin Castle" and their contented, prospering and law-abiding dispositions in Canada, Australia and New Zealand, etc., etc., draw a correct and logical inference from indisputable facts. The British flag floats over Quebec and Montreal, Melbourne and Sydney, Auckland and New Plymouth as well as over Dublin, and yet Irishmen are as amenable to the powers that be in those cities as the citizens of any other nationality. This being matter of well-known evidence even under conditions of British rule out of Ireland, there is no need of citing testimony from countries where English supremacy is not recognised in defence of Irish citizenship from the prejudiced aspersions of certain English critics.

The next theory, that of national irreconcilability to alien domination, while having more solid ground to rest upon will not however explain the problem of our country's disquiet, unless we claim for ourselves greater hatred of political subjection and a stronger love of independence than can be recognised in any other race or people of the civilized world. It is as true as it is creditable to Irishmen that they have, as Auguste Thierry[88] has declared, made a longer and more perseveringly unceasing struggle to overthrow the rule of their conquerors than has any other European nationality; but whether this be the result of unique patriotic virtue on the part of our people, or a consequence of the blind, vindictive ruling capacity of Englishmen in Ireland, is not determined by the just and handsome compliment of the French historian. If we have maintained an insubordinate attitude towards the power which has supplanted our country's liberty, longer than any other subjected people have done, may it not be because that power and its representatives have always maintained against our country, its religion, social system and natural and political rights of its inhabitants an unjust, unwise, impolitic, and equally lengthened, persecution. No other portion of the human race has yet withstood for so prolonged a period the superiority of numerical strength in a dominant power if united with a just and tolerant rule of their country's interests. The patriotic and desperate stand which an invaded people generally makes against a more powerful invader, followed by examples of personal sacrifice and virtuous effort in the cause of nationality are or rather have invariably been the steps by which extinct nations can be traced in history from political individuality to an amalgamation, social and political, with the race that has subdued them. The Scotch and Welsh are of the same Celtic stock as the Irish. Their histories and traditions are replete with battles stubbornly fought, deeds of heroic virtue performed and examples of self sacrifice and patriotic devotion innumerable against English conquest and usurpation—the same as are found in the records of Anglo-Irish strife. Yet Scotland and Wales are today as satisfied with and contented under the sway of their conquerors as if Caledonian claymore had never been crimsoned in English blood—or Welsh Bard had never evoked the patriotic vengeance of the sons of Cambria with such strains as

> God's wrath upon the Saxon!
> May he never know the pride
> Of dying on the battle-field
> With justice on his side—

Flattering however as it might be to our national vanity to suppose that our forefathers had scorned the like submission which defeat had won from the hands of Wallace and Llewellyn,[89] and that Ireland had sacrificed the peace and prosperity which Scotland and Wales now enjoy, for a desperate and continuous effort to regain the lost privilege of guiding her own political destinies, we must look to less exalted causes for a solution of the problem of her discontent, and seek for an explanation of the "Irish difficulty" in a policy of government which if pursued towards Scotland and Wales in the same manner as history traces its career in Ireland , would have made the Scotch and Welsh of today as troublesome to English rule as ourselves.

My purpose during this inquiry is not however to rely upon historic data for an explanation of the continued disjointed relationship of the two countries; but to endeavour to point out in the administration of Ireland's political and social affairs of the *present day*—after so many grievous wrongs have had to be redressed—evidence of the same fatal policy which has characterised English rule since it was first thrust upon our country.

If "an intelligent Foreigner" were asked "what was the form of Irish Government" he would probably either answer "the same as that of England" or confess his ignorance upon the question. An Englishman who had neither resided in Ireland nor troubled himself in acquiring any correct information upon the subject would of course reply "it has the same constitution as England, with a viceroy to represent the Queen." While an Irishman's answer would simply be "Dublin Castle". The singularity of the last definition of Irish government consists in its being absolutely true, while 999 out of every one thousand Englishmen are as absolutely ignorant of what "The Castle" means in the rule of Ireland; of its constitution—*modus operandi*, and unlimited powers, as if it were situated at the mouth of the Yang-tse Kiang river and was identified with the rule of the Celestial Empire, instead of standing on the banks of the Liffey the representative of the British Constitution.

I will endeavour in this brief sketch to remove this ignorance by presenting a picture of the absolutism and anti-Irish character of this singular institution, which will prove it to be at once the primary, if not the greatest factor in the discontent of our people, and a Depot of centralised despotism without a parallel in the government of any other civilized country. In order that Englishmen may better understand the workings of this Headquarters of Irish government; and head cause of Ireland's discontent, I will endeavour to describe what a similar administrative machine would be in England, if the relative positions of both countries were reversed and the mode of conducting respective civil and military affairs exchanged: the Home Office would be the English "Castle". The Queen and Viceroy would of course change residency and Buckingham Palace would become the Vice Regal Lodge of England. The Home Secretary would become the head of the government of England; but as he would be an Irishman and a member for an Irish constituency, he would be almost entirely ignorant of English affairs and have to depend upon the Under Secretary and ordinary staff of the Home Office for all information relative to all public matters which would concern the internal peace and welfare of England, particulars of occurrences,[90] characters of officials in all public departments, and general knowledge of the country and people, their customs and peculiarities, all necessary to be understood in the work of superintending the rule of the same.

As the Chief Secretary for England would be absent in Dublin during the session of Parliament, in that city, he would have to rely exclusively upon the permanent staff of his department for the answering of the numerous questions with which he would be plied by English members concerning the whole internal administration of England in his absence:—

such as evictions, suppression of public meetings, misapplication of public funds, state prosecutions, etc., etc. and other incentives to social disorder which would result from the un-English and unconstitutional bureaucratic or "Dublin Castle" government of England.

Actually during the absence of the C[hief] Sec[retary] and virtually at *all* times, the conduct of public affairs and rule of England would be in the hands of a "Select Ring" which would be composed as follows from the salaried heads of various departments:

President of the "Ring"

The Under Secretary of State for the time being—who would be an Englishman, ardently devoted to the cause of Ireland; and representing the important interest of his—salary.

Vice President: Alarmist general, and *de facto* Governor of England,

The Inspector General of English Constabulary
(who would be an Irish Col. Henderson)[91]
(with Deputy Inspector and Head of
Detective Department as aids and advisers)
Privy Councillors of "the Ring":
The Commander in Chief of the force in England
(who would be an Irishman)
The Lord Chief Justice
And all the Judges who "go circuit" in England
(-who would be true and tried servants of the Home Office or English "Castle" having served a faithful apprenticeship of several years as Westminster—Home Office – Hacks.)
The Law Adviser to the Home Office;
with two Ex Officio members who should represent and edit two daily papers in London, the sole object of which journals should be to offer daily insult to the national feelings of the

English people and hold them up to the contempt of Ireland and the world as at one and the same time, the best governed and most ungrateful people on the face of the earth and that by "people of England" should be known the Irish garrison which ruled them. Their duties should also embrace the task of selecting from the Alarmist Department of the Inspector General of Constabulary the accounts of all such occurrences throughout the country as are to be manufactured into "horrible outrages", "midnight drillings", "attempted assassinations," and evidences of an "intended resurrection" for the establishment of an English Republic. In order that external public opinion—especially that of Ireland—should be kept thoroughly and officially informed of all these bloodthirsty and revolutionary doings of the English masses, members of the staffs of those two journals should be the representatives in London of the leading Irish, Scotch and American papers, through which all news relative to the "State of the country" would be transmitted from England. Finally the gist of the leading articles in the journals of these Ex. Officio members of the "Select Ring" would be that there would be no peace in England, adequate protection of life and property or real prosperity and progress until Irish statesmen should have the courage to govern England by means of a continuous suspension of the Habeas Corpus, abolition of trial by jury, and the application of Martial Law to all "Disturbed Districts". These papers would be known as the official organs of the Irish Government of England (as well as being the mouthpiece of the Select Ring) and their proprietors be in the knowledge of how the Secret Service money granted in the Estimates for Irish Government is—in part at least—applied.[92]

The "Select Ring" thus particularised would consist of about Thirteen Members, drawing an aggregate salary from the taxes of the English people of over £50,000 not counting extras, and having the entire disposition of the revenue of the country in their hands: the management of all public offices: disposal of some 3,000 government posts: the legal drilling of all Resident Magistrates in Home Office or "Castle" tactics:

the creation of all county Justices, Lord Lieutenants and Deputy Lieutenants of counties, selection of High Sheriffs from the lists returned to the Lord Lieutenant for such offices; indirect control of Grand Jury proceedings throughout England; and grand preliminary Secret Star Chamber Tribunal for the reconsideration of political offences, and the arrest of those suspected of same.[93]

Two very important functions of the Ring would be the English political education or State Training of the two Irishmen who would for the time being hold the office of Lord Lieutenant and Chief (or Home) Secretary. These Officials upon visiting England (probably for the first time) after their appointment by the Irish prime minister, would be taken in hands by the Ring or some chosen members thereof, and inoculated with the alarmist doctrines and rule-by-state-of siege principles which have obtained in the council-chambers of the Home Office (or "Castle") since the Irish first landed in England and selected that ill-omened installation from which and by which to govern the English people. The Irish Nobleman who would be the nominal head of the English Government would be instructed that the dignity of "Her Majesty's Lord Lieutenant-General and Governor General of England", would be best consulted by attending exclusively, both himself and lady, to the holding of petty levées or Brummagem courts; some public building in London (which would correspond to the establishment on Cork Hill, Dublin) that would stand protected by a military barracks on one side, and surrounded by various police offices and detective departments on all the others would be selected for this purpose, as proof that the headquarters of government and fashionable assembly were poetically situated in the hearts of the London people and resting for foundation upon the sympathies of the country. The parties who would be honoured with invitations to the Home Office Assemblies would be named by the Ring, and these would consist of the Irish, Scotch, and English Officers whose regiments might be quartered in London; such few Anglo-Irish M.P.s as might have obtained their seats in

Parliament by the influence of the Ring and who should be distinguished for their defence of the same in the House from the attacks of the English popular members; while the remainder of the favoured would be made up of judges, government officials, bankers, county squires, landlords, London aldermen and such fortunate Grocers, Butchers, Drapers, Pawn-brokers, Hotel-Keepers, and office seeking Lawyers and Barristers as might have "caught the eye" of the Ring in the transaction of their various callings or through some special circumstance which might have made them peculiarly obnoxious to the mass of London citizens. When the "Nobility and Gentry" of England would condescend to appear at one of these Brummagem courts, the fashionable consort of an East-End Tradesman who might have also received a card of invitation would have to occupy the *Eighty second place* in the "roll of ladies' precedence" as established by the authority of (an English) Sir Bernard Burke,[94] and from thence contemplate with feminine pride and generosity of sex the exalted position of her eighty-first-degree-more-favoured-sister in the possession of Vice-regal notice. All public men who held rank in the estimation of the English people such as Joseph Cowen,[95] Sir Charles Dilke,[96] Mr Labouchere,[97] Mr Chamberlain,[98] Sir Wilfred Lawson,[99] Mr Howard,[100] John Bright[101] etc., etc., would be rigorously excluded from all Home Office gatherings or Viceregal Lodge festivities by the all powerful influence of the Ring.[102] If the Lord Mayor of London should chance to be a popular favourite or in any way have distinguished himself in the people's cause the Ring would succeed in making the Irish Lord Lieutenant select some public occasion upon which to offer the chief magistrate of the city a polite insult in the form of a refusal to dine with himself and the City Fathers.

The remaining duties of the Irish Viceroy of England would mainly consist in delivering an Annual Speech upon an exclusively viceregal subject: the growing prosperity of England, particularly since his party came into power and himself into the country. It would be his duty to show by a formidable array of figures—prepared by his Secretary and the best statistician of the Ring—that notwithstanding bad harvests, increase of pauperism, depression of trade and continued political agitation by misguided men, the prosperity of England was advancing in a most satisfactory manner. By the amount of deposits (which the landlords' agents and civil service employees would be placing) in the banks it would follow that the average savings of the population of England was on the increase. True, thousands of English farm labourers and artizans might be leaving the country; but then the number of cows and horses were multiplying, while pigs were being reared much more efficiently and economically than twenty years ago. Finally all that England would want in borrowed-viceregal opinion would be rest from public agitation, rigorous application of law, and the continuance of his party in office. If after these onerous duties the Irish representative of Royalty in England aspired to make himself exceedingly popular with the citizens of London he would condescend to visit a ragged school once a year and express his admiration of the management of the same—in a public letter written by his Secretary at the dictation of some member of the Ring. On the anniversary of England's patron saint he might chose to appear with a rose in his coat, while an Irish military band would be playing "Rule Britannia"; and from the top of a wall somewhere between the Home Office and Scotland Yard show himself and his generosity to the two or three hundred people whom the music would attract, by scattering fifteen shillings or a pound in small silver among the urchins and corner boys who would cheer his name. If during the rest of the year he had an eye to the augmenting of his salary of £20,000 per annum, he might follow the example of a recent L. Lieutenant of Ireland by grazing the cows of the viceregal establishment in St James' Park and selling the surplus milk to the guardians of the London Workhouses.[103]

The training of the Home (or Chief) Secretary by the Ring would offer more difficulty than what would have to be surmounted in the governing-education of the Viceroy. He might be a man imbued with liberal principles and come to the

performance of the duties of his office with a mind pre-
possessed against the suggestions and promptings of the paid
English Underlings who had guided the policy of his predeces-
sors in the Home Officeship, which made him so unpopular
with the English people. The wrongs which the stupid
legislation of the past had inflicted upon the inhabitants of the
country might have made an impression upon his unofficial
sympathies and prompted him to make every honest effort to
remove any just or crying grievance which he might discover
in operation to the injury of the popular interests.[104] If in
addition to all their dangerous proclivities he should turn out
to be a man of independent character, firmness of will, and
honesty of purpose, the obstacles which would be thrown in
the way of the continued absolute rule of the Ring would be
of a most formidable nature. The genius of the Ring would
however be equal to such critical emergency. The occasional
experience of such more or less perversely disposed Chief
Secretaries would suggest the employment of "Castle" tactics
for winning the newcomer over to the hereditary policy which
generations of absolutism had handed down to the present
guardians thereof, the Ring, aforesaid. There is scarcely any
feeling of the many which pain the mind or wrench the
sympathies of a public man so keenly disappointing as that
which results from a suspicion, or seeming discovery, that those
in whose welfare he is labouring or upon whose behalf he has
sacrificed political friendships, days of thought and nights of
repose, are the ungrateful, perverse, and unworthy people
their enemies have always declared them to be. He may have
maintained a hundred times in Senate or on platform that
such traits of character were foreign to the observed natural
dispositions of such people; and that if their conduct did occasionally form an unfavourable contrast with that of another
race or class, it could be both logically and charitably accounted
for by recollecting the numerous deteriorating moral and
national agencies which unjust government, ignorance, poverty
and political servitude have always engendered in a conquered
people. But let the belief that he was in error once approach

his mind—that the class which dominated such people, socially and politically, and which had derided his generous efforts on their behalf, were in the right after all, and he becomes disheartened and discouraged in the pursuit of their welfare, as well as a prey to doubts which accidental circumstance may confirm and throw him into the ranks of the powerful adversaries of his former clients. He feels like the man who has succoured a seeming helpless cripple in the belief that those in whose service he had been maimed had done him grievous wrong and injustice in turning him out upon the public thoroughfare to beg—and discovers afterwards that the police have arrested the object of his charity both as an impostor and on a charge of larceny. Human sympathy like human law in such a case would not be proof against appearances. Circumstantial evidence has often deprived the really destitute and deserving of that charity which should have spurned its suggestions, as it has frequently robbed the innocent of their liberty or good name through the non-recognition by a corrupt society of the real, divine attributes of justice. In the higher walk of political effort—that course of public labour which disinterestedly seeks the accomplishment of the greatest good of the greatest number (and which is alike above the ends of the mercenary office seeker and the aims of the unscrupulously ambitious) the motives which set human action and sympathy in motion for the good of mankind are of the same nature and susceptible tendencies as those which cause to be undertaken without consideration of reward the task of a Howard[105] or the work of a St. Vincent de Paul.[106] They want the stimulant to activity which the presence of existing wrong or suffering awakes in the generous soul and an inducement to perseverance in an appreciation by those who have been wronged or rescued, that labour in their behalf has not been barren of results. The heroism or sublime pursuit of noble aims, however, which carries the philanthropist through the repulses of natures hardened by crime, or bears up the apostle of the poor amidst the vices which poverty begets in its victims is wanting in the field of political strife and very rarely lends its supernatural aid to the encouragement of the social or political reformer who encounters both the sneers and opposition of the upholders of political or social abuses, and the apparent apathy, ingratitude or opposition of those who suffer therefrom. Pursuit of public ends upon ideas of abstract moral duty may be the motor factor in the labour of disinterested public men; but the power or influence which alone is capable of keeping their labours in the groove of continuous effort is the appreciation, more or less by that particular section of the community, of the intentions, talents and influences which are exerted on their behalf, and the cessation or absence of which often takes from the advocacy of a popular cause or support of a privileged class the loyalty and energies which would otherwise be continued in their service. Party discipline and the ordinary ambition of educated minds will of course direct the actions and fix the political sympathies of public men, to a considerable extent; but in my opinion the final course which their inclinations and endeavours will take in the pursuit of the public good will depend in no inconsiderable degree upon the recognition and appreciation of the *higher motive* which enlists the heart and soul of a generous man in the service of his class or species. To ignore the existence or offer an affront to such motive and recognise only the baser springs of individual effort is often the determining cause which drives a public man to the abandonment of his first and disinterested course of action into the adoption of views and policies which have earned for so many prominent politicians of the present day the epithets of renegades and political blacklegs.

These influences which in a more or less degree guide the class of public men, who are above the consideration of salary in the performance of any particular public function, are thoroughly understood by the mercenary class of officials who are seldom heard of by the public until they become berthed in some important government situation. Salary and the possession of influence for the advancement of self and friends, are everything to them while motives of self-denial or sacrifice for the common weal are the very principles which threaten with opposition the exercise of such influence or the permanency of their stipends, and are dreaded when recognised in chiefs of departments as a dangerously infectious disease would be by the father of a family of young children. Reformers are to them what policemen are to card sharpers—the only enemies who menace the continuance and profits of their "little game"; and if the members of the "Select Ring" which now rule Ireland (and in the suppositious circumstance which I am assuming would have the government of England in their hands) could put their wishes into the form of law, political or Social Reformers would be treated as was the custom in the dominions of a Tyrant of Southern or Grecian Italy who encouraged the reform of abuses in the state on the condition that, any citizen who should propose any scheme thereon should be brought with a halter around his neck before the community in meeting assembled, and if the proposals were not acceptable to the whole of the same their author was to be strung up on the spot as a warning to future innovators. The advent of a Home (or Chief) Secretary to power who should by his previous utterances or acts exhibit any evidence of those traits of virtuous motives or independent bearing in his public career which I have pointed out, would call forth all the contriving faculties and inventive genius of the Ring in order to meet the impending danger to their exclusive direction and management of the ruling power of the country and the application of the public revenue. In this and in the support of the traditional policy of the "Castle", the Ring would have both the countenance and active aid not only of the other government officials throughout the country but of the entire landed aristocracy, its agents, lawyers, and dependents; and this from a very obvious and intelligible reason: All the land of England (to continue the comparison with the state of Ireland) would be in the hands of a few thousand Irish and Anglo-Irish peers and Commoners who would hold the same in virtue of the deeds performed by their ancestors in the Conquest of England. This right by force of conquest together

with the entire neglect of those reciprocal duties which the
feudal system of land law exacted from landlords towards their
tenants in return for rent; the heartless and tyrannical acts
perpetrated in evictions, capricious and unjust; and the draining
away of the resources of the country by the system of absenteeism, would make the landocracy hated and dreaded by the
mass of the people. In a word they would hold the land of
England by the force of the military and police of Ireland
alone. In order to do this the more effectually all the
administrative powers of the country would have to be in their
hands or in those of their tools; consequently the incoming
Chief Secretary would find Irish rule or rather the interests of
this class, thus "secured" upon his taking office; the direct
government of England would be centralised in the Home
Office (or Castle) and be in the hands of the Ring as I have
already described. The conservation of mercenary motives in
these officials would correspond with the situation of the
landed interest and make the continued rule of the one a
necessary condition to the upholding of the abuses of the
other. The law of reciprocal dependence would make the rule
of the Ring the perfection of government in the eyes of the
landocracy, while the continuance in full swing of the rights,
privileges and monopolies of the latter in the matters of landlord exactions, levying of county rates, and functions of county
magistracy would be guaranteed to them by the influence of
the Ring. The Chairmen of Quarter Sessions and County
Court Judges before whom cases of eviction for non-payment
of rent or other offence against landlordism would be tried
would be all the nominees of the landlords or of the Ring.
The High Sheriffs of Counties would be all landlords and the
sub Sheriffs either middlemen (small landlords) or land agents.
The Lord Lieutenant of each county would be a peer and a
landlord, and the twenty or thirty Deputy Lieutenants for
same would be all landlords also. Of the three or four
thousand county justices who would be entitled to administer
justice at petty sessions throughout England 98 per cent would
be landlords' agents and retired military and naval officers—

the remaining 2 per cent would represent the rest of the English people. The Resident or Stipendiary Magistrate would be recruited from retired military and naval officers, 4 Inspectors and Sub-Inspectors of Constabulary, and from former legal hangers-on of the Ring, while near two-thirds of their number would be Irish. The Grand Juries of Counties would be entirely in landlord hands as the people have no voice in their election. (This system of county government is unknown in England under the present mode of governing that country.) They would have the levying of taxes for county purposes in their hands—and the appointment of cess collectors, surveyors etc. and the entire disposal of the funds thus collected. If a murder should be committed or property be injured in any parish, barony or union of a county, the Grand Jury would be empowered upon application by friends of the murdered person or owner of injured property to levy a special tax upon the people of the locality of any such occurrence, for compensation to the claimants—though the offender might belong to another county, country or continent. The *elected* members of the various Boards of Guardians for the management of the country's poor rate would be of a mixed representative character—part belonging to the landlord class and part to the people, but as the system of Ex-Officio membership of such boards provides for an owner of property or landlord member for *each elected member*, the landlord interest and influence would prevail in this important department of county government, as in all others.

This, then would be the position of central and provincial authority on the advent of the new Home Secretary to power. The higher branches of the country's government would be under the complete control of the Select Ring, while the subordinate county part of same would be in the hands of the landlords and their nominees. Not a single individual would he find in the performance of any government duty or holding any position of public trust that would have been placed in such position on account of his being the representative of the industry, feelings, or wants of the people of England. All without an exception would have reached their posts through landlord patronage or influence of the Ring.

He would thus find the country divided in a distinct and unmistakable manner into two clearly marked divisions—one, comprising nine-tenths of the population which would be paying nine-tenths of the taxes and producing all the wealth of the country while having no representation whatever in the higher branches of the public service of England or voice in the disposal of its revenues; and the other composed of the remaining tenth of community and having both the government and fat of the land as its exclusive privilege and belonging. This arrangement would necessarily separate the inhabitants of England into antagonistic classes, the national or people's party and the Ascendancy Party. The former by their representations would naturally aim at a control more or less of the resources of the country, extension of political rights and a curtailment of the governmental monopolies of the latter; while these in their turn would strain every nerve to keep down popular power and innovation in order to retain the continued rule of England, management of its revenues, and the preservation of their favourite systems and laws, intact. To effect this the more securely, they would virtually constitute themselves an Irish Garrison for the preservation of their privileges and interests and represent to the Irish Government that the continued maintenance of its rule over the English people would depend upon the support which should be given to its proved loyal Garrison in the work of upholding imperial supremacy. Any concession to the people of England by the Imperial or Irish Parliament would be strenuously opposed by the representatives of the Ring in that Assembly by the whole Garrison and by every individual of the Ring itself, as an encouragement to the disloyal tendencies of the English masses, a sapping of the foundations of Society upon which law and order rest, and a menace to the constitution. Every and all popular agitations and movements in England for the redress of admitted political or social abuses would be denounced to the Irish Government, first by the two newspaper organs of the

Ring and next by all the garrison, as "seditious proceedings", "attempts to supplant the authority of Government"; "veiled rebellion", and "insurrection against Society": while "additional powers" with which "to strengthen the hands of the Executive" (i.e. the Select Ring) would be loudly and imperiously demanded in a chorus all along the line of the garrison.

The leaders of such popular movements would be all declared to be enemies to law and order, emissaries of an organisation established by Englishmen in America for the overthrow of Irish Government, or at best they would be represented as misguided men imbued with dangerous republican or Communist ideas.

To endeavour to convince an incoming Home (or Chief) Secretary that something like the foregoing was the real interpretation of the state of England, would be the tactics employed by the Ring, for the double purpose of prejudicing his mind against a turbulent and disloyal people irreconcilably opposed to Irish rule, and to win him over from ideas of reform to the continuance of the old policy of "Castle" government. The very look and atmosphere of the Home Office or "Castle" would speak of treasonable conspiracies and anticipated insurrections. The absence of crime in the assize calendars would be given as proof that the lower orders were engaging again in illegal associations against the state. Reports confirmatory of this would crowd in from every Stipendiary Magistrate and County Inspector of Constabulary in such parts of England as were formerly more or less associated with abortive attempts at rebellion. Judges going circuit would make it the theme of their addresses to the Grand Juries and lament that criminals continued to elude the administration of the law—(not of course owing to any inefficiency in the Constabulary in the matter of preventing or detecting crime)— but through the sympathy which the body of the English rural population would feel towards the perpetrators thereof, and cause them to refuse volunteering information which the constabulary could not obtain. The Grand Juries—from being in the hands of the landlords, and Ring—would pass resolutions in the same strain. County Magistrates—all landlords—would convene meetings and demand an increase of military or constabulary for "the better protection of life and property" in their respective localities—and thus would the rule of physical force continue, the Ring retain its supremacy and monopoly of influence and the new Chief Secretary be satisfied that the English were unfitted for and undeserving of those extended electoral and other political privileges which the Irish and Scotch enjoyed from their superior love of law and order and attachment to the Irish Constitution.

That the foregoing is no fancy or overdrawn sketch of Dublin Castle and its mode of "ruling" Ireland, requires very little showing beyond the simple statement of facts (which can be gathered from a study of the official Directory containing the particulars of the Government of Ireland, names and salaries of heads of public departments) etc.,[107]—and an observation of the manner in which the affairs of the country are centralised and managed in that unpopular and unsightly establishment. If such a system of government fell by any chance to the lot of the English people (as in the circumstance which I have just been considering) there is not an Englishman breathing who feels for the honour of his country and hates the mercenary instruments of injustice, who would not strive (metaphorically speaking) to kick such a den of arrogant and unscrupulous underlings into the Thames. There never *can* be anything like peace or regard for the administration of Law in Ireland, while the sensitive people of that country see their fatherland in the clutches of such a gang and themselves and their rights as civilized men maligned, insulted and trampled upon by those who flaunt the stigmas of official, race, class, and religious ascendancy before their face in almost every transaction of Irish government. "Same Constitution as the English and Scotch" indeed! We have about as much of the "British Constitution" in Ireland today as the people of Liverpool would have of the efficiency and trustworthiness of the present police system of England, if all the force required for the preservation of the peace and protection of property in that city were recruited from the gamblers, blacklegs and pick-pockets of London, Dublin and Glasgow. In the law proceedings and administration of justice in England, the judge is expected to be—and always is—either a neutral power between the accused and the State which prosecutes, or to incline more or less towards the side of the former; but whoever witnesses or hears of anything of the kind in Ireland? There is not a dozen men in that country outside of the landlords and officials who would not count upon having the judge as an assisting public prosecutor to the Crown side if arraigned for any offence against the law or state. The two latest instances of this shameless custom belonging to "Castle" rule, happened in connection with the recent State Trial of "Parnell and others *vs* the Queen".[108] A few weeks previous to the commencement of the trial, two of the Traversers brought an action for an attachment (or [illegible] to certain statements calculated to prejudice their cases when tried) against one of the organs of Dublin Castle, the *Dublin Evening Mail*.[109] The case against the proprietor of this paper was argued by Mr Macdonagh Q.C.[110] on behalf of Messrs Parnell and Egan, the two Traversers who demanded the attachment, and was heard by the Lord Chief Justice May[111] and Mr Justice O'Brien.[112] The conduct of the Chief Justice on the occasion was of so violently partisan a nature that the *whole press* of Gt. Britain and Ireland—the two organs of Dublin Castle excepted—virtually cried "shame" upon the intemperate harangue against the Traversers who were not yet on their trial, which came from the head of English law in Ireland, and the Chief Justice was in consequence compelled by force of public opinion to withdraw from any part in the subsequent state prosecution. No such conduct would ever be heard of in England; yet this man is still Lord Chief Justice of Ireland and drawing £5,000 a year from the revenue of the country. The next instance of a Castle Judge acting as assistant to the Irish Attorney General was on the occasion of the State Trial just referred to. Mr Justice Fitzgerald—third judge of the Irish Queen's Bench—was the presiding judge in consequence of the forced withdrawal of the Chief Justice; and the whole of the Traversers without an exception accepted him as an advocate for the Crown—or rather for the landlords—with a seat on the Bench.[113] Nor did the sequel belie their expectation. In his interruptions of the Traversers' counsel, in his every remark during the proceedings and his whole demeanour and conduct, a looker-on could not possibly recognize a single instance or occurrence which would lead to an opinion of his impartiality. His summing-up (from after some preliminary remarks as an introduction to same) was simply an elaborate and envenomed accusation of the Land League, and a supplementary speech to the attorney general's against the Traversers. Not a single word did he utter on the side or in behalf of the latter; and after the Jury had returned and one of this number declared that ten were for an acquittal and but two for a conviction, he actually became white with rage, turned upon the spokesman and rated him for mentioning the numbers; and then gave orders to the High Sheriff to bring in sufficient police to clear the court if any further manifestation of sympathy for the Traversers should be shown by the audience. Such however is the frequency of turning the Bench of Ireland into the position of an assistant Crown Prosecutor that exhibitions like those of Justices May and Fitzgerald excite no surprise among the Irish people. They accept such administration of the "Castle law" as one of the many evils belonging to that institution; and their undisguised contempt for and antipathy towards such parodies upon *English* law, and such prostitution of the seat of Justice, is but a necessary and inevitable result of the whole system of Irish Government as at present constituted. What would the English people say or do if *all* their judges in virtue of the office took an active part in the extra-legal rule of England and shamelessly acted the part of Ministers' tools upon the Bench? Would there not be a national outcry against a return to the custom of the days of Jeffrys[114] and Scroggs?[115] Yet such a disgraceful custom obtains in Ireland under the all-penetrating eye of the press, and under the (supposed) sway of the British Constitution without a single comment thereon from any organ of English public opinion. A further examination of the Castle system will show that every other branch of the law in Ireland is made to subserve either the ends of its Ring or the interests of the landocracy of the country:— The 75 Stipendiary or Resident Magistrates of Ireland (excepting perhaps those of Dublin) are all ex-land agents, ex-constabulary officers, retired military and naval officials or former legal dependents of the Castle—all believed by the people to be what their general conduct proves them—tools of Dublin Castle. Near two thirds of their number are English and Scotch, while there are not half a dozen Roman Catholics among the 75. The Justices of the Peace or County Magistracy of Ireland number over 3,700; ninety-eight per cent of whom belong to the landlord and land agent classes, *leaving two per cent to represent the remaining five millions of the population*! The religious population of Ireland, according to the census of 1871, gives over 4,000,000 to the Roman Catholics and a little above 1,000,000 to *all* the other sects combined; yet the proportion of Catholic J.P.s to Protestant is probably not more than 3 per cent of the 3,700 or more Irish magistrates created by Dublin Castle. Here we have the most obnoxious class in Ireland (the landlord-agent) having ninety-eight out of every one hundred justices of the peace belonging to its interest; while religious ascendancy is still upheld by Dublin Castle in maintaining the ratio between the Protestant and Catholic Magistracy, of one of the former to every 290 of their co-religionists while the Catholics have one to every 35,000 of their number! The county court judges and chairmen of Quarter Sessions before whom all land disputes and cases of ejectment must be heard are with scarce an exception recruited from the class of office seeking Irish lawyers who have pro-pitiated the Castle or won the patronage of the landlords by either toadyism or by anti-national records or expressions.

The constitution of the next branch of the Castle govern-ment—the Royal Irish Constabulary—is in entire keeping with the other departments which I have been describing; while the force itself forms the most singular of all the strange features in the political life of Ireland; and as an agent in the work of preserving the peace of society is the most unique body of "police" to be found in any part of the civilized world. Why a body of men who are dressed, drilled, accoutred, armed and quartered like soldiers, should be named "a Constabulary," and a "police force," is one of those puzzles which meet an inquirer at every step of a comparison between the administration of government and law in England and Ireland. In England, "Bobby" is a popular institution. It very rarely happens that he "runs in" the wrong man, nor can habitual disturbers of the peace or enemies to other people's property hold his vigilance, intelligence or pluck in defiance or contempt. Yet he is never seen with a rifle on his shoulders, or met with a "buckshot" pouch at his side. He would probably feel as awkward if thus equipped as his fellow countrymen would look astonished and indignant at such an un-English picture as an *armed* guardian of the peace. His truncheon is at once the symbol of his authority and the weapon with which the law permits him to defend himself if molested in the discharge of his duty; and no other does he desire nor is permitted to carry. Even when called upon to quell a riot or to disperse disorderly street crowds in large cities the English police force can never arm with any other weapon. Rifles and side arms in the hands of an English police force! Why it would be a direct menace to the liberty of Englishmen and would cause the downfall of the strongest administration that should permit it for a single week. The results of opposite systems of unarmed police in England and armed soldiers attempted to be disguised under the name of "constabulary" in Ireland, is seen in the respective attitudes of both peoples towards their particular forces: An Englishman loves individual liberty and respects the law which recognises his title to that privilege; therefore he holds in equal respect the agents of the law who are never associated in his mind with the performance of any other duty but what is to his advantage as a member of society—the duty of defending the persons and property of the whole community from the enemies of society. The Irishman has an equal if not a more passionate attachment to freedom of movement, speech and action; with a corresponding enmity or antipathy towards whatever maintains a continued espionage upon the exercise of any or all of these prerogatives of personal liberty. He can have no feeling of respect therefore towards the Irish Constabulary simply because he knows that it is an imperial, *political* body in every essential point of its organisation, and that it is not either an Irish civil or English police force in a single particular; and that its extra-political duty is the formation of a special body-guard to Irish landlordism. In England and Scotland the expense of both County Constabulary and Borough police is defrayed between the ratepayers and the state; for the well-known reason that Englishmen object to have such an important factor in the rule of Society in the hands of (even their own) centralised authority. Hence the English police are under the control of and dependent upon the local governing powers throughout the country. In Ireland the case is reversed. Since 1846 the charge of supporting the Irish Constabulary is undertaken entirely by the Government for what purpose and policy is very well known; and the annual cost of this Imperial force averages over £1,000,000 sterling. While Scotland has but a police force of 3,662 and England and Wales only 13,342 (not counting the Metropolitan force of London) Ireland's standing army of "Police" numbers 11,019, exclusive of the 1,163 which constitute the Dublin City force. From the manner in which this large body of *select* armed men (probably the finest corps, physically speaking, in the world) is distributed over Ireland; from their presence (with arms) at every gathering of the people, public meetings, markets, fairs, athletic sports, races, and their constant attendance at every railway station in the country, the nature of the work for the performance of which they are in the pay of the Government (like the other regular forces) can be easily seen: they form the advanced guard and corps of observation of English Rule in Ireland. Added to the twenty-five or thirty thousand other troops which England maintains in the "Sister Island" they form *the physical force Government of Ireland* which constitutes *our* share—of the British Constitution.[116]

"But then you have the Franchise and a Representation in the House of Commons"? True; but let us see what Facts and Figures have to say on these heads as on that of the preceding part of this inquiry into Ireland's "Share" of the British Constitution:

The population of Ireland according to the census of 1871 is 5,412,377; and that of England and Wales (per same) 22,712,266. Ireland has 64 constituencies and returns 103 members of Parliament. England and Wales 296, and electing 493 members. The Irish franchise is distributed into 170,698 county electors; 57,290 city and borough, and 3,548 Dublin University; giving a total number of parliamentary voters to Ireland of 231,536. England and Wales have 903,658 for their counties; 1,584,877 for their cities and boroughs, and 13,141 for the Universities—total 2,501,676, or 2,270,140 more than Ireland, England and Wales with little over *four* times the population have more than *ten times* the number of voters allowed to Ireland: the province of Ulster with a population of 1,312,879 (exclusive of its cities and boroughs) has but 67,131 voters distributed over nine county constituencies or 15,966 less than the two boroughs of Birmingham and Nottingham, in England.

Belfast, Armagh, Carrickfergus, Coleraine, Downpatrick, Dungannon, Enniskillen, Lisburn, Londonderry and Newry, cities and boroughs of Ulster, with a united population of 261,946 have but 28,708 voters—or 6,327 less than those of Dudley and Wednesbury with united pop[ulation] of 199,058.

The two provinces of Leinster and Munster, comprising eighteen counties, have a population of 2,674,054 (exclusive of their cities and boroughs) and have but 86,184 electors,—or 6,218 less than Cheshire and Derbyshire with a pop. of 912,218.

Dublin, Athlone, Carlow, Drogheda, Dundalk, Kilkenny New Ross, Portarlington, and Wexford—cities and boroughs of Leinster, have a united pop. of 346,823, and but 17,125 electors—or 9,068 less than the borough of Hull, pop. 123,408.

Cork, Bandon, Clonmel, Dungannon, Ennis, Kinsale, Limerick, Mallow, Tralee, Waterford and Youghal, cities and boroughs of Munster, have a u[nited] p[opulation] of 237,744, and but 10,582 votes—or 12,752 less than the borough of Salford with p[opulation] of 124,861.

Eighteen Irish counties with twenty cities and boroughs (Dublin, Cork and Limerick among the number) having a total population of 3,258,621, have but 113,891 voters between them—or 11,289 less than Liverpool and Manchester with u.p. of 872,779.

Mayo, Galway, Sligo, Leitrim and Roscommon counties, with the borough of Galway (comprising the electoral province of Connaught) have a total pop. of 881,553, and only 18,258 voters,—or 1,718 less than the borough of Stoke-Upon-Trent, with a pop. of 130,985.

Dublin—the second city of Gt. Britain and Ireland—with a pop. of 267,717, has but 13,599 voters; or some thousands less than either Edinburgh, Aberdeen or Dundee in Scotland, or these following second and third rate boroughs of England and Wales: Bolton, Norwich, Portsmouth, Oldham, Sunderland, Dudley Leicester, Merthyr-Tydvil [*sic*], or Swansea.

Glasgow has 2,630 more voters than *all the cities and boroughs of Ireland combined*—including such largely populated cities as Dublin, Belfast, Cork and Limerick.

Yorkshire—exclusive of its boroughs large and small of Bradford, York City, Huddersfield, Halifax, Dewsbury, Middlesbro' Whitby, Thirsk, Scarbro', Richmond, Ripon, Pontefract, Northallaston and Knaresborough—has still over 20,000 more electors than all the thirty two counties of Ireland combined; while finally, Lancashire has 110,562 more than the whole of Ireland, counties, cities, boroughs and universities, together!

I think I have in the preceding pages successfully negatived the frequent assertion of Englishmen that Ireland has "the same government and laws as England"; and shown also that we have practically speaking no portion of the British Constitution in unfettered operation in the "Sister Kingdom". Government by physical force is contrary to the spirit and letter of that constitution so often lauded as the guarantee and guardian of personal liberty and the emancipation of any slave who touches the soil over which it extends its aegis as a protection against tyranny. Its aversion to despotic government is such that it places it within the power of the elected representatives of the English people to curtail or even to *abolish* the Army and Navy (by the provisions of the Mutiny Act) during any session of parliament, lest such powers might by any chance be turned, by the governing power, against the liberties of the people of England. No traces of any such anti-constitutional mode of ruling the people of Gt. Britain is to be seen in the government of this country, or Scotland, or Wales, or in Canada, or Australia: India and Ireland alone of the countries subject to England are virtually ruled outside of the British Constitution. The rights and liberties of the Irish people are in the hands of a corps of officials and an army of occupation. In the appointment of the one or control of the other they have no voice whatever, either directly or by their parliamentary representatives. Questions can be asked and criticism made of course in reference to both these agencies in the government of Ireland by Irish Members in the House of Commons; but anything like *opposition* to either can be successfully met by the combined representation of Gt. Britain (six times that of Ireland) or by the temporary suspension of the parliamentary rights of Irish members . . . i.e. the application of the *Gladstonian Gag*.[117]

I will now endeavour to meet and answer such arguments in defence of "the Castle" or existing mode of ruling the people of Ireland as would be advanced by a supporter of such a system of government.

The continual presence of a large proportion of the British Army and necessity for the maintenance of a special corps of military police, is needed in Ireland to uphold Imperial supremacy and to meet any attempt on the part of the Irish people to separate the two countries.

This argument is at once an admission that the people of Ireland are still inimical to English government after more than seven hundred years of a political connection and that the pretence to rule the country by the same constitution as England is ruled or upon any other principle than that of physical force is a delusion of a madman. The first of these admissions would be anything but flattering to the genius of English rule as it would amount to a condemnation thereof, while the other is an acquiescence in the position I have upheld in this inquiry, as to the nature of Ireland's "share" of the British Constitution. But admitting that England by virtue of her possession of Ireland is justified in asserting and upholding her authority there, have I not pointed out sufficient of inherent wrong, injustice and impolitic procedure *in her system of doing this*—or rather in the Dublin Castle mode of accomplishing these ends of Imperial sway—to account for if not to justify the hostility of the Irish people towards the power of which such system is the outcome and representative? If there really be in the Castle system of government enough of intrinsic hostility towards the civil and political rights of any people that might be subjected thereto—as much as would cause the English, for instance, if thrust upon *them*, to kick it after the absolutism of the Stuart dynasty—there is in the facts which establish this hostility towards the people of Ireland an explanation of their continued discontent sufficient to palliate the same as well as to encourage them in a desire for Home Rule or Separation—without reckoning the influences of National desire or feelings as factors in such aspiration.

If, then, we can afford to eliminate the national wish of our people for a government of their own from the causes which keep their country in periodical political ferment and themselves in an inferior social and political status to the English or any other civilized nation, our case against the power which deprives us of the right to rule ourselves and which persists in ruling us contrary to the principles of its own Constitution, is conclusive; and the necessity and justification of keeping the cause of Ireland before the civilized world must be obvious to every rational and unprejudiced mind.

The ground upon which the possession by the landlords and their nominees of the whole internal administration of Ireland is sought to be defended, is, that they constitute "the British garrison" which holds the country for England, and that they must necessarily have the use of such powers as will enable them to watch over the interests of the Imperial government. This same "garrison argument" is also advanced to justify the support which Irish landlordism receives from England against the desire of Ireland for its abolition; in fact an English Radical M.P. made use of this not very convincing and equally unconstitutional mode of reasoning in a discussion upon the Irish Land Question with me in Dublin in the beginning of this year.[118] If this candid acknowledgement of how Ireland actually *is* governed and wherefore, would only be admitted by those who make a pretence of ruling us otherwise, there would at least be that amount of honesty in the system of government, and an end to all controversy as to our share of the British Constitution—though the Irish difficulty would of course remain the same.

This garrison rule may appear very satisfactory to Englishmen—but we Irish must be excused if we fail to see either an advantage or a convenience to *us* in such an arrangement—especially after the experience we have had of it since we were robbed of our own parliament and what little of the Constitution we enjoyed under the same.

In fact in this "Garrison" is centred the whole "Irish Question". So long as Ireland is thus held and ruled so long will there be discontent and disturbance. Attempts to win our people to a willing obedience to English rule and to an abandonment of all efforts towards a Repeal of the Union or an abolition of landlordism by the continuance of such a system as that which is the joint result of Castle policy and landlord monopoly, will be as ineffectual as would all endeavours to close and heal a wound in the human body while the barbed shaft would remain embedded in the sensitive flesh. This Garrison is the first of Irish wrongs. It has always been the major grievance of which our people complained, and will continue to be the source from which every Irish movement, agitation or party will draw a justification for open or passive hostility towards the power which sustains it with mailed hand in the teeth of the Irish people. If the Castle system of government had been specially planned to be a constant irritation to the country, a check upon its material prosperity, and an insulting badge of conquest to a once independent nation, no more fitting instrument could have been devised for the successful accomplishment of such designs. Why should it be continued? Are the comparatively few landlords and mercenaries who constitute the Garrison, of more consequence to the British Empire, than the remaining five millions of the Irish people? Does any one imagine that the latter will ever tamely submit to see the government, resources and wealth of their country in the hands of those who have already worked them so much wrong, and caused Ireland so much misery and pauperism? Are attempts at insurrection, agitations and popular ferments to be increased *for ever* in Ireland in order to afford a pretext for rule by physical force?

These are questions well worth the serious and practical consideration of English statesmanship at the present hour. It cannot possibly be to the advantage of England to see the "Irish difficulty" of the past one hundred years continued in the future; no more than is it the desire of the leaders of the Irish people to see their country a prey to periodical distress, morbid political excitement, and occupying the position of a non-progressive member of the family of civilized nations. The suspension of the Habeas Corpus and imprisonment of a number of such leaders for seeking *some* redress of admitted wrongs may not always be as easy and safe of accomplishment as when resorted to against an open and constitutional movement. O'Connell's maxim that "England's difficulty is Ireland's opportunity" must be practicable of application *some* time or other amidst the future conflicts of European Powers, if the maintenance of "Garrison-Castle" rule will continue to encourage our people to watch for such a contingency and endeavour to profit thereby. If such a system of government were persisted in towards Canada for instance—if all the land were recognised by English law as the absolute property of a few Englishmen, and these few or their creatures again recognised as the monopolists of power and the ruling caste of the country despite the continued opposition and emphatic protests of the remainder of the whole community—is there a sensible Englishman alive who does not believe that the colony would have revolted and be by this time divided into States of the neighbouring Great Republic? British statesmanship has simply accomplished for the Canadians what is alike indispensable to the contentment of any civilized and enlightened community and the stability of any central authority over the same—it has moulded the constitution of such authority to the feelings of the people and the needs of Canada.[119] A government to be permanent or to obtain the willing submission of those subject thereto must be grounded upon motives which are all powerful with the people or which will at least harmonise with their social system, established customs, and ideas. It matters very little what the peculiar nature of such motives, customs or ideas may be, providing their recognition by and the conformity of the system of governing power thereto, is what such society requires and is satisfied with. To impose a republican form of government upon China, a despotism upon Switzerland, or a celibate system like that which obtained in the Papal States, upon Utah, would be simply a declaration of war against the institutions and principles of those countries and insuring a prevalence of discontent and incentive to rebellion among their inhabitants against the powers that should thus act blindly, stupidly or vindictively against the dictates of sound policy and principles of good government. Yet it is precisely in this respect where English rule has failed in Ireland and still blunders in the persistence of a policy and

support of a system which are indefensible upon any hypothesis except the planting of a British colony in Ireland by the
effacement of all its national landmarks, or the banishment
therefrom of the Celtic race which has resisted this design,
born of the days of Cromwell and yet to be traced in the latest
Imperial provision for the emigration of the (always) "surplus
population" of our country. Instead of attempting to adapt
their rule or manner of government in accordance with the
maxims of rational policy, similar to those mentioned above,
that is to make their possession of Ireland as little offensive to
the susceptibilities and as uninjurious to the interests and social
wellbeing of our people as would be consistent with the continued supremacy of their Executive Authority, English Statesmen,
impelled by some fatalism, blindness or vindictive spirit, have
pursued an almost exactly opposite course, as the sad record
of Ireland's history but too plainly declares. The ideas to which
the Irish people have been most warmly attached—to which
they have devotedly clung through centuries of trial and
persecution—are those comprised within a desire for the
possession of some remnant of their country's nationhood; an
enthusiastic devotion to their religion, and a clinging attachment to the soil of their Fatherland; in fact their passionate
loyalty to each and all of these principles, national, religious
and social, has always been, and is to the present day, the chief
characteristic of the people of Ireland. Yet it is against those
very principles which have ever formed the very life of our
country as it were, that the whole animus of England's policy
in Ireland has been levelled—that has engaged the plans of
her statesmen and enactments of her parliament for their
abasement or destruction from then to our own day, when *one*
of these principles has triumphed over all or nearly all the
elements which have been pitted against it during three
hundred years. It is unnecessary to call upon historic data to
prove the truth of this almost inexplicable policy of gratuitous
aggression in the rule of Ireland—it is plain and palpable to
any one who has ever read of English plotting against the
parliament of Ireland until the Act of Union was finally passed

by Pitt and Castlereagh; of the penal laws in force against the
Catholic religion in Ireland until fifty two years ago—and the
influence arrayed against it until 1869[120] (and *still* maintaining
the practical ascendancy of the faith of the minority)—and the
evil system of land laws which is yet upheld in its warfare
against the peace and prosperity of Ireland. Instead of endeavouring to conciliate the national feelings of our people by
continuing the native parliament of the country a system of
rule was substituted which virtually renders an Irishman a
stranger in his own birthland and arouses all the bitterness of
his nature against the power that has given the rule and the
destinies of his country into the hands of a janissary Ring of
anti-Irish mercenaries ever but too ready to sally forth from
Dublin Castle in an attack upon any national effort or sentiment
of the people. Of the war which England has waged against
the faith of the Irish down to the present generation there is
no need to make lengthened allusion here as its crimes against
the rights of conscience and the atrocities perpetrated upon
the people who defended the same, are too well known to
need repetition. It is only necessary to remark—for the purpose
of this inquiry—that the enactment and enforcing of penal
laws against the religion of a subject people is not a policy
either sanctioned by sound maxims of government or calculated
to win the affections or willing submission of such people to
the power which pursues it. If the Catholic faith has a free
scope of exercise and a firm footing in Ireland today, it is
simply in spite of every effort which "the depraved ingenuity"
of English statesmen and the might of England's Arm could
make to destroy it—and any Irishman and student of Irish
history is aware that this fact and not the religious tolerance
of Irish government, is the reason why.

It is the same story of perverse antagonism to Irish custom
and institutions in respect to England's treatment of the third
of those principles to which our people are peculiarly attached—
the land. She found a system of land laws in Ireland which
had existed for all ages and against the justice of which no
portion of the community could reasonably object. This

system recognised the soil of the country as the property of the people; or as the county was at that time divided into kingdoms and principalities and again into Septs or Clans, the inhabitants of any such divisions had their portion of land as their own property, while each community or congregation of owners had a certain amount of land in common for purpose of pasturage. No such code as "landlordism" was known in Ireland until England, for her own purposes, introduced that fatal system into the country and confiscated the property of the people thereby insuring the ruin of its social peace and prosperity. By aiding ten or fifteen thousand adventurers and soldiers and encouraging Irish traitors in the plunder of the land, England has rendered the present inheritors of such ill-gotten property a very wealthy and therefore a very loyal class: but at the expense of making thereby almost the remainder of the Irish people the poorest of any in Europe, as well as the most disaffected to her rule of any of her subject-nations.

I have now passed in review the various points in which the present mode of ruling Ireland differs from the rule of Gt. Britain, and shown what the real nature of Ireland's "share" of the British Constitution is: I have analysed the "Dublin Castle" system and proved it to be both antagonistic to the spirit of such Constitution and virtually a Bureaucratic Despotism, resting for support upon an army of soldiers and military police, accountable alike for that disregard in which the Irish people hold its laws and law officers, and for the antipathy which they manifest towards the Government of which the Castle is the Irish Deputy: I have also shown that the *whole* policy of governing Ireland—of which the Castle system is a part—has ever been and is still the reverse of what any power would pursue which would honestly desire to govern a subject-people as it ruled its own, and the conclusion which I am enabled to draw from the facts, and particulars which I here instanced, is the same as the assertion with which I commenced this inquiry, namely: that there is *in the manner* which England rules Ireland *today* sufficient of injustice towards and disregard of the political and social rights of our people, as will both logically explain and rationally justify their discontent, *independent of all influence from purely National sentiments or aspirations.* There is but one more point in the rule of Ireland upon which I shall deem it necessary to offer a remark in concluding, and that is, the worth or nature of the remedial legislation which parliament has effected for Ireland during the present generation. Englishmen have themselves named each portion of such legislation "an instalment of justice to Ireland," thereby impliedly admitting that *full* justice was still to be rendered to that ill-fated country. An "instalment of justice" to Ireland, judging from the worth of what has been thus named resembles the taking of a loaf of bread from a hungry man, giving him after much ado a slice thereof, and then removing the remainder still further from his reach. In addition to this not very generous mode of treating us to our own—or to what the British Constitution insures to the citizens of Gt. Britain— it has always been and is still the fate of English statesmanship never to know *how* to remedy any of the admitted wrongs, requiring such instalments in a politic or conciliatory manner. Our people must be driven, either to open attempts at rebellion, or our country put in a ferment of political agitation ere ministers or parliament will either recognise or admit that such wrongs or questions come within the domain of practical politics; and then before they can be partially or wholly redressed or the [illeg] "instalment of justice" given, the Habeas Corpus Act must be suspended and Dublin Castle propitiated with an equivalent "instalment" of political prisoners.

Thus the credit which might be gained from a proverbially grateful people by the removal in a politic and judicious manner of some restriction upon political privilege or the affording of some protection against Castle monopoly, is lost to England through the vindictive spirit in which her concessions are granted or by which they are invariably accompanied, to Ireland.

When English Statesmen will learn to do *full* justice to Ireland, then and not till then will our people be contented or satisfied. If *after* the accomplishment of this desideratum of our country *the National* question of "Dependence or Independence," should give trouble to the Empire, Englishmen could *then* say with some share of reason "You Irish are never satisfied"—but not till then.

What do I mean by "full justice" to Ireland?

The Disestablishment of the Dublin Castle Ring and the Repeal of the Act of Union.

THE EDUCATION OF THE IRISH CITIZEN

With a corps of 10,842 Teachers, male and female—7,522 Schools; over one million of pupils on the rolls of same; and an average daily attendance of over 400,000 pupils, the education of "Young Ireland" must be making rapid progress in comparison with the days of old Ireland, 50 years ago, before the National Schools commenced their career of usefulness among our people. In addition to these schools which are in almost exclusive connection with *the people* (or as we are more frequently termed, *the masses*) there are numbers of superior schools, academies, colleges etc. together with Trinity College and the latest "University Arrangement" for the higher intellectual training of the present and next generations of Irishmen.[121] Added to this there is now in operation the Intermediate Education Act, which promises to prove one of the best measures of its kind that we have yet received from Westminster.[122] We are, thus on the whole fairly in pursuit of learning in Ireland after the eclipse of its ancient fame in that art during the prevalence of the penal laws; and the stigma of "ignorant Irish" which those who were responsible for that ignorance were in the habit of casting in our teeth, will soon be heard of no more. Of the merits or demerits of particular *systems* of education in vogue in Ireland—either in the higher or lower establishments, I know nothing beyond what can be inferred of their comparative worth or defects from the general education of those of our people who have been taught or educated in Ireland. From the miserably inadequate salaries, however, which are paid to teachers under the National

Board—averaging but £40 a year for male and £33 for female teachers—it is simply impossible for that most useful of all classes of society, to receive the training which is requisite to form able and efficient Instructors in the science of mental cultivation, such as are now to be found in schools throughout America and in most Continental countries. Until Irish School Teachers are placed on a nearer footing to those of England and Scotland, in the matter of recompense for their labours, the primary education of Ireland's youth must be wanting in those essentials which carefully trained and fairly remunerated Instructors alone can supply. While admitting that food and other necessaries of life are somewhat cheaper in the country districts of Ireland than in those of England, and that the expenditure of Schoolmasters and Monitors will be proportionately less in consequence of the disparity of food prices in the two countries, it does not follow that the difference in the salaries of Irish and English Teachers should be as it stands at present. The average stipend taken upon a number of 12,452 certificated Primary School Teachers in England (for the year 1879) is £120.11.9, and £139.3.0 average upon 3,034 of the same in Scotland, while 5,817 of the former and 1,755 of the latter are provided with houses rent-free. In Ireland as already seen the average salary of its staff of 10,842 Teachers is *but £40 including school fees,* and only one third of that number is exempt from house rent. Schoolmistresses in England are paid at the rate of £72.3.2 (an average taken upon 16,196 such Teachers) and in Scotland £72.6.4 (average on 2,028; while 6,000 or more are provided with houses rent free in Gt. Britain. The average pay of Irish Schoolmistresses is £33, *or less than half what is received by their Sister Teachers in England and Scotland.* This is not as it should be, and cannot be justified upon any ground except one which would suppose that the education of the youth of Gt. Britain was entitled to more consideration at the Imperial Treasury and a higher degree of proficiency in its teachers than that of the youth of Ireland. In the parliamentary grants for educational purposes in the year 1879 the sum of £30,000 is advanced for "Evening Schools" under the

[A large part of the page is missing. Here Davitt refers to the fact that there was no mention of evening schools in government grants to Ireland. This he attributes to]

lack of will among our public men . . . owing to our own neglect of the same classes among our people. This I take to be a severe censure [of] the *public* of Ireland in the matter of feeling an [interest?] in the improvement of those classes [who?] [. . .] keep the wheels of Society in motion and upon whom all dependence must be placed for the procuring of essential necessaries of life. . . . Anyone who was conversant with the mental and moral condition of the working classes of the North of England some twenty five years ago (or previous to the initiation of the Mechanics Institutes or Evening Classes for Artizans and labourers) cannot possibly appreciate the benefits which the mechanic and artizan class in that part of England have derived from the labours of the late Sir James Kay-Shuttleworth[123] and his associates in behalf of the operative classes of their fellow countrymen. These Institutions, especially in Lancashire and Yorkshire, have been chiefly the means of forming the present intelligent industrial character, fame for mechanical invention, and application of chemical science to the improvement of the industrial arts which have earned for the skilled artisan of the North of England a world-wide reputation. What little stimulus to education which I have been fortunate [enough to gain by my?] own individual effort [was at?] one of those Mechanics [Institutes in?] Lancashire. A fee of 2/6 per . . . entitled me to the benefits . . . per week during the winter months; the use of a library of two or three . . . — out of which library by the way I first [learned?] of Ireland— and of a newsroom . . . the leading newspapers, reviews and periodicals of England, all the year round. Round this establishment might be seen every evening, after labour, men from the factories and workshops who like [me had?] an ambition to make self-help and leisure from toil supply to some extent . . . of an education beyond our worldly means to attain. "The Mechanics," as the place was familiarly termed, soon became the line which separated the sober industrious and intelligent working man of the locality from the rest of that class which (at that time) spent large portions of its earnings in public houses after each "pay day", and taxed the vigilance of the police in the exercise of "pitch and toss" and "pigeon flying" on Sundays. Although the number of Irish families in the neighbourhood was over two hundred, myself and a companion, I am sorry to say, were the only Irish members of "The Mechanics". I have since then met many of my former labour acquaintances and countrymen scattered over England, Scotland and the United States, and found them just as they were fifteen and twenty years previously, labouring men "hewers of wood and drawers of water" like the majority of our race; while my English associates of the Mechanics Institute Evening Classes have probably all become either skilled artizans, superintendents in workshops, or employers of labour on their own account.

These facts—the signal benefits derived from these labouring men's Institutes by those compelled to toil at manual labour during the day; and the influences for good which they have exercised over so large a portion of poor struggling toilers who are generally left by society a prey to all the demoralising agencies of ignorance and comparative poverty, have often forcibly reminded me, when travelling in Ireland, how much good could be effected among our rural and inland-town population by the extension of such evening labourers' institutes to our country. The industrial pursuit of our country people being almost exclusively agricultural leaves them little or no occupation for their idle season during the winter. Here, then, would an Evening Institute supply a means for intellectual improvement without interfering with the time required for the cultivation of the land or any other daily pursuit; while the good which would assuredly follow from an intelligent farming class acquiring new and practical ideas of agriculture from books and occasional lectures on the proven methods of cultivation, would soon more than repay the community for whatever little expense might be incurred in the erection and management of such Institutes. It has more than once struck me while engaged in the land agitation of the past two years, that the Land League could extend its sphere of usefulness to our agricultural classes by the practical encouragement of these Institutes among them; but Irish Movements as a rule are too selfishly [illegible] and too exclusively occupied with the particular idea or object which calls them into being, to attend to any collateral work which appears to lie outside the scope of their immediate programme. This may be defensible upon the theory which will always find favour with indolent and selfish beings, that too many irons in the fire is bad policy, but not with such as believe that the French proverb, *personne n'a fait tout ce qu'il pouvait*[124] is equally applicable to organisations having the command of volunteer talent, popular enthusiasm and ample funds. A national organisation like the Land League embracing a membership of over 200,000 of our agricultural population, and having almost the whole of the active intellects of *Celtic* Ireland as volunteers in its service, must effect something more than a change in the land system of Ireland if it is to earn from the next generation the credit of having permanently elevated its social status by the removal of all impediments to anything like material progress among our people. In the hoarding up, as it were, of powers and means for the accomplishment of some one object for the popular weal, which may fail after all in the full realization of *all* the benefits calculated or predicated to follow therefrom, there is often the same want of skilful enterprise and foresight as characterised the action of the individual mentioned in the Scriptures who hid his talent in the ground instead of using it so as to increase his wealth. Any organisation claiming to be National, should, to a certain extent, model its labours upon those of a Government and endeavour to discover in how many ways it can assist the people in the bettering of their social position or in supplying aid for such wants as appeal for attention and succour to all who can lend a helping hand. No one can travel through Ireland in an observing mood without noticing the natural intelligence of the country people and their quickness of understanding, and regretting—if at all subject to feelings of human sympathy—that such natural parts were not the groundwork upon which rested a practical education similar to that which the peasantry of Switzerland, Belgium, Saxony, the Rhine Provinces of Germany and France, are admitted by all travellers to possess; and which has worked such wonders in their improvement and happiness during the past fifty years. I am of course aware that the prime factor in the work of elevating the social condition of the farming classes of these countries has been the sweeping away of a similar system of Land Laws to that which is accountable for all the evils and adverse influences which prevent the same advance by our own people; and which keeps them in a state of existence where the cooperative demoralising agents Ignorance and Poverty hold them almost helpless in a condition of mental and physical deterioration. Still the question which an Irish Reformer—or an organisation of Reformers—should consider is, cannot something be done to minimise the misery of our poorer agricultural classes by endeavouring to remedy the negative evils of their condition, while the positive ones are appealing for redress against the agent that is responsible for both? The household economy of the poorer farming and labouring classes of Ireland is beyond doubt the very worst to be found among any other people. Traces of the same want of anything like systematic arrangement or careful provision in the management of the homestead may be found in parts of North Devonshire and in portions of Dorsetshire in England, as well as in some districts of the Scottish Highlands; but nothing akin to the utter want of order in and around an ordinary Irish cabin can be seen among the rural population of any other portion of Gt. Britain or be met with by the traveller in any other part of the civilized world. Again, the same extenuating explanation enkindles the indignation against the system which, as is well known, has kept our people imprisoned in squalor and dark smoky miserable habitations by the imposition of a tax in the form of an increase of rent upon any appearance of comfort or improvement in themselves or their dwellings. Of all the crimes which rack-renting landlordism has committed against Ireland, this one is the most maddening. It arrests the hand of the father of a family who would otherwise seek to secure his children's home from the winter's cold and make the improvement of his little world the constant care of his leisure hours; while the thousand and one duties which the fond mother of a family would always seek to fulfil round the seat of her domestic empire, are held in check by the fear that their performance may but invite a demand from the landlord for what is needed to provide her offspring with food.[125] Hence the tumble-down rickety and horrible looking dens which are to be seen surrounded with a noisome vapour in summer, arising from the seething dunghill by which they are invariably flanked, as well as the filthy puddle which laves their walls in winter. No wonder that the peasantry of the west and poorer parts of Ireland should exhibit traces of physical deterioration which threatens the reputation for strength and configuration of the Celtic race with lasting traces of defect. That the victims of Irish landlordism are not all become the horrid unshapen beings which Mr Punch loves to depict us all as really being, is to be attributed to some preservative element in the soil or climate of Ireland.[126] This monster-evil of a monster system is however in the course of being arrested in its work of destruction as the Land League agitation has given a death blow to rack-renting and threatens likewise to stay the hand of capricious eviction in the future. It is time then for the social reformer to turn his attention towards the eradication of those customs and habits of slovenliness which add to the misery and unhealthiness of farmers' and labourers' dwellings, now that the agency which encouraged their existence is checked in its hitherto unbridled career. It will be very difficult, no doubt to infuse sufficient confidence into our worst-housed peasantry to venture an investment of some of their scanty earnings in the improvement of their homesteads until the law shall recognise them as the absolute property of the builder, or occupier who may have acquired the ownership thereof;

but if public opinion be once interested in this House Improvement Movement, it will see also to the protection of the capital which may be expended in such work, from the vulture claws of landlordism.

Nothing will encourage the class which stand most in need of this reform, to commence the same, as the concentrating of the public opinion of a district upon some centre which will be identified with this and other projects for the benefit of the people of such district. For this purpose among others which I shall specify, I would propose the erection of a "People's Institute" in such of the 300 or more Baronial Districts of Ireland as require most aid in the work of improving the condition of their people and have the same to be recognised as the property of the people of each Barony. The situation of these buildings to be determined by such favourable circumstances as might arise in connection with same—such as the gift of a site, proximity to largest town or parish in Barony, etc., but their central position for the district to be still a first consideration. It would be necessary to awake sufficient enthusiasm among the young men of each Barony as would enable the project to have as much volunteer labour in the work of erection as would reduce the cost thereof to as small a sum as possible. The gifts of stone, etc. from owners of quarries, or permission to procure such where no quarries are being worked, would be an object for the consideration of those who should take the initiative in the enterprise. With the gratuitous help which could be obtained in building, and the other assistance that could reasonably be counted upon in such a nonsectarian and non-political undertaking, I would put the average cost of building each Institute at £100. Assuming that half of the 322 Baronies into which Ireland is divided would both need and undertake the erection of an institute each, this would require a sum of £16,100 to cover the building part of the undertaking.

I would propose to raise this sum by the solicitation of *two pence* per head of a contribution from each of the inhabitants of such Baronies, which (counting upon *half* the population of Ireland as concerned in the work) would produce about

£21,000. Reckoning upon £10,000 from sympathising external sources, and £5,000 more from the funds of the Land League, this would represent a total working capital of say £35,000, which, after defraying the expense of building, would leave near £20,000 for the supplying of books, furniture and the other modest necessities of the Institutes. To maintain the Institutes from year to year in light, turf, repairs etc., and cost of care, would devolve upon the Baronial Committee of Management, and would cost but a mere trifle that could be covered by either small subscriptions from members, entertainments, athletic sports etc., etc. The teaching of evening classes could be made an honorary labour of love and would be certain to enlist the assistance of those in each Barony as would be qualified to aid their less fortunate brethren in the rudimentary branches of learning. A staff of permanent lecturers upon Agriculture, application of science to improved methods of cultivation, machinery, management of manures etc., etc. could be supported from a central fund which could be easily obtained when once the benefits of these Institutions could be demonstrated to the public at large. Grants from the Government or Board of National Education might also be obtained for the support of purely educational work in connection with the evening classes. When one of these Institutes became a recognised centre of good intent and practical usefulness in a locality, it would be very easy to organise such a plan of Homestead Reform as would meet both the wants of the district and run parallel with the feelings and desires of the people. If the keeping of animals in cabins along with the inmates was once proscribed as a lowering of the dignity of the individual and a cause of filth and vermin which must alike impair the health of male and beauty of female children, the construction of some sort of outhouse shelter for cows, asses, pigs and hens would soon become a work of pride among those who now share their dwellings with such animals. The next custom that could be attacked with equal success and benefit to the health of those who would abandon it, is the proximity of the dunghill to the cabin or farmhouse. For this slovenly habit and evidence of want of all refined taste in those who practice it, there is no excuse, and I have often wondered why priests and others who constantly visit such hovels and cabins and who must know how great a portion of the evils of poverty can be modified by the influence of cleanliness in the persons and surroundings of the labouring poor, have not endeavoured to effect some beneficial change in this respect. The usual situation of the dung heap is right in front of the doorway, and occupying space which could be utilised in the planting of cabbages or other vegetables, or in the formation of a flower-bed. As this accumulation of filth generally forms a stagnant pool and is usually the recreation ground of "the gintleman who pays the rint", it would both conduce to the health of the owners and the appearance of their homes, if both these nuisances were removed to some part of the holding or potato plot, where the manure could be preserved and the ground be improved by the percolation of the liquid portion of such manure through the same.

As these reforms in the customs of our poorer people would cost them nothing to effect but would on the contrary soon exhibit beneficial results, little or no opposition could be expected in the carrying of them out in any district: Yet what a desirable change it would prove from the prevalence of dirt and animal-like taste which at present characterize the Homestead life of a great proportion of our agricultural classes? The better lighting of cabins by the insertion therein of even one additional inlet besides the door for the admission of the sun's rays, together with the formation of some outlet akin to a chimney for the smoke which is invariably seen escaping through the doorway, would also be both easy and cheap of accomplishment when once the influence which a cheerfully lighted dwelling exercises upon the character and happiness of individuals would be demonstrated to those who have lived in such dark and smoky dens, any portion of their lives. The absolute necessity for some reform in the direction of better and healthier dwellings for the poorer portion of our people cannot be more convincingly shown than by the simple statement of the startling fact, that out of the 1,067,598 families which made up the population of Ireland in 1871, *no less than 227,379 were living in "houses" built entirely of mud and having only one room each!*[127] Over a million of human beings—male and female—herding together in mud cabins *with but one common sleeping compartment for both sexes!* Surely a system that is responsible for this demoralising condition among others well known, of more than a million of Christians, must have something of a devilish and inhuman character inherent in its nature. Englishmen either cannot or will not understand why we Irish hate landlordism so thoroughly and wage such incessant war against its continued existence over us; but if they only knew it as we do—had they but an experience equal to ours of how it treats those whom it compels to pay a tribute of fifteen millions a year, while dooming them to live like the beasts who share with them the roof of their one-roomed-hovels of mud, they would make short work of such infamous laws and of the political party that would endeavour to perpetuate them.

I am fully convinced that if some such scheme or movement as I have briefly sketched for the "improvement off the face of the earth" of the one-roomed mud cabins of our country, and the substitution of healthier abodes, and a system of cleaner surroundings, was once fairly started, that results would follow which would astonish all who now imagine that the miserable condition of life so peculiar to the lower order of our people is beyond the power of mere reformers to radically change. If the neat and comfortable farm and labourers' houses which a traveller sees almost everywhere on the continent are ever to be met with in Ireland, and to be allowed to work a beneficial change in the physique, habits and minds of two-thirds of our people, a reform in that direction must be set on foot sooner or later. Waiting for the abolition of landlordism won't do. I don't believe in the *waiting* policy no how—"act, act in the living present"—wherever humanity is suffering either from the injustice of evil laws or through the prevalence of habits or customs born of such laws for ages until they seem to be a defect in the character of those who

practice them. People long subject to the miseries of an impoverished existence, and strangers to the ordinary comforts of
civilized life, do not rise from rags and squalor spontaneously—
they must be helped and taught to do so by those who have
influence over them or who are identified with labour for
either their spiritual or social welfare. The work once commenced could not fail of support, nor of effecting objective
permanent good alike to the individual and society, and could
not possibly meet with opposition from *any* class whatever in
the country—which of itself would be as singular an event as
fortunate in a purely Irish movement.

No doubt my plan of operations would encounter opposition
from some quarters and give rise to doubts as to its practicability in many others; but if difference of opinions as to *how*
this absolutely essential reform of the homesteads of Ireland is
to be effected was the only drawback to the commencement
of the work, no obstacle would be placed in its way by any
predilection for my own method of how to accomplish a good
work for Ireland. My reason for advocating this reform along
with and through the means of the establishment of Peoples'
Institutes, is that such would in my humble opinion, prove the
best way for educating our labouring poor into the adoption
of such improved conditions of homestead life as would
withstand the continued adverse influence of their impoverished
social condition—should landlordism still be able to hold them
victims to the same.

Along with the inculcation of ideas in this direction and of
assistance in the putting of them into practice being identified
with a Baronial Institute, the teaching of how to till the land
better than at present, how to manage manures skilfully (like
continental farmers) and how to obtain the best possible return
for the outlay of labour and capital, expended in the cultivation
of the soil, would form an important branch of such establishments. That something in this direction is necessary for our
farming classes needs only to be mentioned in order to obtain
general concurrence. The best soil in Europe for most of the
cereals belonging to Europe is growing to be one of the

poorest to be found therein because it is the worst managed and most neglected of the soils of any other European country. In the palmy days of eviction and rackrent—now fading happily away—this ruinous treatment (or neglect of the soil) was easily accounted for. Men refused to expend their toil and scanty earnings upon the land from which they could count not upon any secure return. To till the soil so as to increase one's own store of food and worldly comfort is a work which very few would refuse to perform when confident that no other hand could snatch away the fruits thereof—but working and investing in order that *others* may enjoy the proceeds, is not, never was, and never will be conducive to increased exertion, or careful contrivancy on the part of a rational being.

In proportion then as those adverse influences to the comfort of the homes and security of the earnings of our agricultural classes are disappearing before the combined attacks of public opinion and repressive legislation, should be the efforts to bring those classes to conditions of life and practises of husbandry which would gradually but effectively efface the two great evils which at present afflict them—squalor and poverty. Let these reforms be effected through an educational medium and they will cling to the ideas with which they have been associated, and remain permanently lodged in the popular mind, and beget therein the sources of other necessary changes which time and material progress will demand in the social status and habits of our people.

A People's Institute for a whole Barony and to be erected at a cost of £100 may appear two very weak points in the plan which I have outlined for aiding the education of our rural industrial classes and of reforming their habits of homestead living. I would much rather see one in every village and have it as handsome and as well-built a structure as are the Mechanics' Institutes of England; but I know that the poverty of our people and country cannot afford any such undertaking at present, and hence the modest character of my proposals for a commencement.[128]

I believe that with the volunteer labour which could be obtained from the young men of any district where such a work would be set on foot for the good of its people, a suitable building could be erected at the estimated cost specified. For the participation of the male population of a Barony in the benefits of the evening classes, it would be only necessary to set apart certain nights in the week for certain districts and villages; while the homestead or house reform work could of course be carried on throughout the whole Barony when once the Institute should get into working order. Plans for altering and improving existing cabins, and for the construction of new and cheap dwellings would be provided by the central committee in Dublin, and if funds permitted, assistance be given towards effecting same. A local Inspection and Encouragement Committee in the work of house reform could be elected each year for the purpose of making the rounds of the Barony and seeing to the undertaking of the proposed changes in the dwellings, etc., where most needed. Prizes of useful articles could be offered annually for the best internal improvements effected in previous one-roomed cabins; also for external bettering and ornamentation of such and other dwellings belonging to the industrial classes; conversion of old dung-hill sites into vegetable plots or flower beds, etc. etc. By a slight encouragement of this kind, together with the spirit of emulation which the whole project would be sure to beget among an enthusiastic people like ours, standing so much in need of external suggestion and encouragement, the conditions of human misery under which more than a million of them are now living might soon be changed to others of comparative comfort; which the effect which such a reform in the Irish cabin and its surroundings would have upon the character and industrial habits of those who are now almost utter strangers to traits of systematic contrivance in the ordinary concerns of life, would be certain to manifest itself in a marked and speedy improvement in the whole rural economy of our country.[129]

I have been led into this digression through reflecting (some pages back) upon how much of permanent future good could

have been effected by the Land League independent of its
special mission for our farming and labouring classes by the
undertaking or initiation of a purely non-political work similar
to the at which I have just pointed out. I had fully intended
proposing such a movement to be set on foot after returning
from my last lecturing tour in America,[130] but the rapid march
of English public opinion towards the sanctioning of the
suspension of the Habeas Corpus Act occasioned other thoughts
and labours—until my arrest put a stop to all effort on my
part for some time to come.

Returning to the consideration of the Education of the Irish
Citizen (without special reference to any particular class of our
people), it is a matter of considerable moment to the future of
Ireland that the systems of education or courses of intellectual
training which obtain in our various schools and colleges should
approach in their efficiency to the level of what is to be found
in those countries with which our rising generation will be
brought into contact by commercial and other pursuits. If I
should form an opinion upon the merits of Irish education as
seen in the mental habits and reputation of our educated and
professional men, and in the business systems of our commercial classes, I should conclude that whatever success might
be obtained in their respective pursuits by those who belong
to the educated portion of our people, would be due to natural
parts and not to the influence of manner or methods by which
those natural parts were aided or supervised in the process of
development. Evidence of careless superintendence of studies,
want of system in the general acquisition of knowledge, and
of too much appearance of hurried endeavour to "learn and
be off" seems to me apparent in the present mediocrity of
nearly all the learned professions in Ireland, as compared with
the observed results of mental culture in England or Scotland,
Germany, France or America. There is not among the present
occupants of the Irish Bench a single individual who would
have risen to any such position in England through the efforts
of ability or acquired reputation in Westminster Hall.[131] We
are "favoured" at present with very industrious political and

very earnest party judges: but an *able* judge is not, by general admission, to be discovered in Ireland today. Any one who was present during the State Trial of Parnell and others *v.* the Queen, when the whole Bar might be seen in the Four Courts and its *elite* heard on both sides of the case, must have concluded that the legal profession was poorer in talent and weaker in eloquence than at any previous period of its career in Ireland. Not a single speech of the many uttered or laboured efforts made in the handling of law or witnesses could awake the ghost of a comparison with the illustrious names included within the periods which embrace the union of Irish forensic achievements—from the days of Curran[132] down to those of Isaac Butt.[133] The little evidence to be seen of any marked ability in philosophical research, historical writing or critical acumen; scientific discovery or mechanical invention; improvements in medicine or surgery, or trace of learning in theological works or religious discourses, exhibit a similar non-progressive state of the rational mind in all our learned professions.

My remarks however upon the Education of the Irish Citizen will be confined more to what is required for *the people*—or the mass of our population—rather than a criticism of that which the "better to do" portion thereof receive at Colleges or Universities. The people of any country will never really be the sovereign power of such country until "the ignorant masses" thereof become "educated" masses. When they discover what their *natural* rights are, through the means of their own reasoning faculties, their *political* rights will be soon conceded by those who have a monopoly of everything at present in consequence of the comparative ignorance of the greater portion of Society. The *quality* of this education thus, which the normal and other schools for the industrial classes of our people are now teaching, is of the greatest importance to the future welfare of Ireland.

What is the special education of the citizen?

That is to say in addition to the cultivation of a sound reasoning faculty, and the acquisition of a general insight into the world. What is the particular species of knowledge or information that qualifies for deciding the questions that are now beginning to be referred to the sovereign people? It must be a knowledge of human society, and must amount practically to a power of discriminating between the things that enable society to prosper and the things that obstruct its prosperity. But on this head "where is wisdom to be found?" What book embraces it, what teacher imparts it, in what school or college is it to be acquired? It cannot yet be said that modern education has compiled a compact body of complete information as to the workings of human society. Many works of high repute have been produced on particular departments of social welfare, such as the writings of political economy, or on the means of favouring the production of wealth or material abundance. But what this enquiry demands is not to make up a catalogue of books on social subjects, but to seek for or draw up such a sketch of the field that has to be explored as will give a plan for whatever information is valuable, and assist in discriminating among the masses of rubbish the particles of genuine worth.

The information relating to human society, the experience of past and existing communities, and the infinity of distracting opinions on this experience, lie recorded in books, which are either *histories*, having reference to what is past, and to the succession of events, or geographies, statistics, surveys, and pictures, giving an account of the situation and manner of existence of congregated human beings over the surface of the peopled earth at the present time. Thousands of volumes are taken up by one or other of these departments. It is evident, therefore, that to make the study of the human race and human society possible, not to say easy, we must be enabled to select out of this vast wilderness, such facts and opinions as may be of use to ourselves; we should require to possess a 'philosophy of history'; and of society, if by that is meant a collection of general ideas and general laws, that would afford both a *principle of arrangement* and a *standard of value* to historical and statistical information; something to guide us both in organising the materials we already possess, and in following our researches into the present and past conditions of nations and peoples.

In order to simplify the complex subject of human society, it is of advantage, in the first place, to distinguish its interests and activities into two fundamental classes: into those relating to *Order* and those relating to *Progress*. *By Order* I would mean to be understood, the stability, security and harmony of the collective arrangements and institutions of any society at any one time; the fulfilment of the great purposes for which men keep up society, so as to produce individual contentment and happiness, or at least a general acquiescence in, and compliance with, the regulations of the governing powers. *By Progress* is meant the change from one set of arrangements to others which call into exercise and gratify a higher and nobler order of human feelings and capacities, or diffuse more widely among the community the standard of elevation achieved for the few. The methods of maintaining Order, are totally different from the methods of promoting Progress; and although the two interests are, on the whole, not only compatible, but mutually indispensable, they often appear in temporary collision. All change unsettles for a time and may produce a certain amount of disorder, which, in the opinion of the parties interested, may be sacrificing more than the proposed improvement is worth. Order is of course the first thing to be attended to, otherwise there would be general shipwreck and destruction both of the present and the future, but so long as the human mind is capable of suggesting improvements, there should always be openings for admitting them into our practice—that is, our system of Social Order will not be Order unless it admit of Progress. In any enterprising community, the progressive classes, the men of originality or genius and their adherents arrayed against any existing system are capable of effecting its overthrow. Let us first illustrate the conditions of Order: In any complex machine the different parts must not only be good in themselves, but be well fitted to one another, and none must be wanting; the machine then goes on

well, and may be said to be *in good order*. In like manner the
life of a man may be said to be orderly when everything
contributing to health and happiness is regularly supplied, and
when at the same time, the wishes and desires extend no
further. On the other hand our lives are in disorder if we can
neither procure things suitable for us nor keep off things
deleterious. A person may require wine in a teetotal age; or
animal food and be a Brahmin,[134] or be supplied exclusively with
compositions of oatmeal. One man is liable to rheumatism
and has to wear a kilt: the special gift of nature to another
may be a delicate hand, and he is a barrowman; the greatest
pleasure of a man's life may be music, and his wife may break
his flute on his head.

There is no difficulty in extending the notion to Society
when we consider what are its characteristic operations. A
captain for instance carries a commission from his government
to take the command of his ship: the crew refuse to serve
under him. A tax is imposed, and John Hampden and others
resist the payment.[135] A service-book is sent from London to
constitute the worship of the Scotch people, and the country is
up in arms to resist it.[136] These are obvious instances of disorder;
and, moreover, they plainly point out an exact definition of
disorder,—disobedience to the supreme authorities. The one
thing essential to every society, great or small, is government.

As the institution of government is repeated in many shapes
throughout an extensive and complicated society, so is the
possibility to disobedience and disorder. There is not only the
supreme central unity of the civil government, or temporal
sovereignty, and its numerous deputies and subordinate
authorities, but also innumerable local and voluntary societies,
carrying on important affairs and demanding strict obedience.
We have, moreover, the spiritual government, which dictates
the more elevated duties of life, and administers consolation for
its irremediable ills. The great Family system involves agreement
which cannot be violated without very disastrous effects. The
organisation of labour demands control and obedience. The
process of education in schools creates the relation of teacher

and pupil, which must to a certain extent be a relation of rule and obedience. Wherever men meet together for any common object, they feel it indispensable to erect a temporary head or ruler and to submit themselves to his authority.

Such being the *appearances* that enable us to recognise Order or Disorder, it become necessary to inquire what are the conditions that produce the one or the other. Anything that throws light upon these must be of the first importance in the pursuit of knowledge as to what advances or retards the well-being of society. A few general principles may now be indicated to show into what shape the doctrines of Social Order have been put by thinking men:

1. It is essential that the government, whether political, moral or spiritual, should ground itself upon motives that are all powerful with the people. It matters little what the motives are or whether they owe their power or nature to circumstances, or express education. For example the Chinese government rests upon the paternal principle, which in the people is educated into an unusual degree of strength. The Emperor is the father of his subjects and opposition to him or to any of his sub-ordinates is filial [im]piety[137] and is regarded with horror. Having once established a system of education and a style of conduct by which the filial virtues are intensely cultivated, the Chinese government may be considered as very securely grounded upon its identity with parental sway; and disorder can never arise until the people acquire sufficient intellectual insight to perceive that the identity is false and sophisitical. Many governments have reposed on an assumed Divine Right, and have been secure so long as the people retained submission to the Divinity, and believed that the allegation of divine sanction was well-founded. But if either on the one hand, the divinities themselves are renounced in a fit of impiety, or, on the other hand, the relation between existing powers and the divinities is denied, there is nothing to prevent

revolution or disorder from happening. In a people whose character tends strongly to clanship, like the Scotch Highlanders, the head of a clan possesses a very secure tenure of authority. Among men differently constituted, as for instance, among the Teutonic nations, such a pretension could not sustain the arm of power. In the rudest stages of society, among savage tribes whose public life is war, hunting, and plunder, the most knowing is made the leader; and neither divinity nor hereditary claim could of itself maintain a dynasty. A government may often trust much to its having been long established. Custom or habit is very powerful in men; in certain mental constitutions that are not rare it is almost omnipotent; and rulers have in many cases presumed far upon this principle.

The surest of all foundations of government is the direct approbation of the people: obedience will then be spontaneous and certain. The government may be a very bad government—may do unwise, unjust, and ruinous things—but if none of these displease the people, it will be supported. Unless violent differences arise within the Community itself, or offence be given to powerful foreign nations, a people ruled by their own consent will enjoy internal stability. It by no means follows, however, that they shall enjoy the highest social prosperity.

The worst foundation of government is physical force, or a standing army, which, when used as the sole support of the supreme authority, requires to be made up of foreign mercenaries. Soldiers derived from the people themselves must share the popular feelings, and cannot, unless of a base and servile race, be turned against their own blood and kindred. A government may do much for its own permanence by controlling the public education, and suppressing every kind of knowledge that might lead the people to form opinions against itself. The Continental despotisms practised this policy. By a censorship of the press, and a check upon imported literature, they kept away from the people the examples and theories of free governments. If communication were less abundant, if the free countries were remote and insignificant, and if the spontaneous thoughts of men did not suggest inferences hostile to despotism, this species of policy might have been more hopeful than it has proved to be. Probably no government maintained itself yet upon the ground of its merits alone. It has almost always happened to pre-eminently good rulers not to be appreciated in their own time.

The French writers on politics are accustomed to distinguish between Material and Moral Order: meaning by the first the preservation of individual rights and privileges, and the full enforcement of the law against wrong-doers; and by the second, the *willing* submission of the people, and their full approbation of the constitution and doings of the government. Grumbling, discontent, and dissatisfaction, expressed or unexpressed, are opposed to Moral Order; actual outbreaks and open defiance threaten the maintenance of Material Order.

2. It may be laid down as a second fundamental principle of Social Order—that the extent of freedom permitted to individuals should be in proportion to their fitness, natural or acquired, to do of their own accord what is required of them in the interests and well-being of the whole community. In the education of the young we begin by controlling them in everything they do. As their intelligence and self-control are developed, they are allowed more and more latitude. They have leave to choose their own sports, and consult their own tastes when it is seen that they can keep themselves out of harm's way. When they have grown somewhat older, and show the possession of average discretion, they may wander from home for whole days, and carve out their own employments and recreations, and in a great measure regulate the routine of their existence. In short

they obtain more and more of liberty according as it is presumed that the self-directing force within them has been tuned to the rectitudes and proprieties of life. It has been assumed by many writers that the domestic slavery of the ancients was indispensable to the breaking in of savage humanity to habits of regular industrial occupation.

In those rude times if a man was allowed liberty of employment, he chose war, or hunting, or plunder, or something that was fiery, exciting, and brief. The promise of bed-and-board and pocket money, could not induce people to toil steadily from six to six at the dull drudgery of the plough, the loom or the oar; hence compulsion had to be resorted to. But the moment that self-interest became powerful enough to create propensities to labour, it was time that the compulsion should be withdrawn.

Freedom is a nobler state than slavery, and human beings ought not to be prevented from the exercise of their most elevated capacities. The modern workman can choose his own master and possess his own home (when not an Irishman) in opposition to slavery; he can choose his residence (when not ditto) in opposition to serfhood; he can choose his trade (if not living in Ireland where there is none) in opposition to guilds and restrictions; he can rise to be a master in opposition to the exclusiveness of ranks; (questionable under aristocratic and other monopolies in *these* countries) and we find that with all this freedom the work in done, and better done, and the workman's life rendered happier. While progress allows freer range of action, the conservative forces of society keep up and impose restraints: To preserve existing religious beliefs and observances, it has been common to punish and put down all dissent; to maintain the civil constitution, the liberty of free discussion on political questions has been generally denied, and public and popular agitations put under restraint. The keenest and most sensitive parts of human nature have been violently crossed by regulations issued in the name of good order.

Liberty of conscience—when people have consciences—is rightly considered the most indispensable of liberties—yet this has been both restrained and denied—presumably in the name of good order.

Liberty should not be confounded with popular power. Liberty has invariably been the result of the popular acquisition of power, but the two are not identical. Liberty of conscience and religious observance, liberty of thought, of speech, and of doing good to our fellows in our own way (except in Ireland), liberty of education, of choosing our occupation, liberty of using our gifts and talents to advantage, liberty of doing what we please with our own, liberty of trading, liberty of guiding our own movements—all these may be enjoyed without any vote in the appointment of government, and many of them may not be permissible under a popular form of government—as in Ireland.

The illustration now given of these two great principles may serve to point out one of the ways in which history and the experience of Nations may be useful to our political education—namely, by showing us how the foundations of government and the extent of freedom are related to the security or insecurity of societies; and in general, by teaching us that one object of our study ought to relate to the means made use of in any community for the maintenance of Social Order.

Progress:

We will now pass to the consideration of Progress, which means the passage from one state of existence to another, in which human nature has its desires and capacities elevated, and their gratification more perfectly secured. Amid the bustle of movement and change, it is desirable that we should be able to apply the scale or standard of real progress, and clearly discern whether we are going forward or backward; for it would be easy to assign many periods of retrograde activity in the history of the world.

Civilization is the sum total of all the progress achieved by human Society; and we may therefore conduct our exposition of progress under the title of the Elements and Tests of Civilization. Various definitions have been given to the term "Civilization". That given by Guizot[138]—namely "the improvement of the individual and of Society", is perhaps the best known; but it is not a complete or satisfactory one. Let us first indicate a few things essential to human existence and happiness that are *not* civilization. Civilization is *not* natural advantages, such as land, sea, mountains, climate, fertility, mineral wealth, variety of vegetable and animal species; it is *not* the goodness of our bodily or mental constitution; it is *not* mere good fortune favouring our exertions; it is *not* individual dexterity or skill in the shape of an incommunicable gift; it is not temporary fits of heroic virtue, devotion, courage or effort, even though a whole generation should be exalted thereby; it is *not* mere emotion, neither does it mean happiness in the common acceptation of that word any more than the greatness of an individual man means that he is happy. Happiness, if it be understood to signify satisfaction, serenity, contentment, arises from the proportioning of our desires to our means, and of our attempts to our abilities, and may be present or absent in every stage of human elevation and culture. The apostle Paul was miserable because his brethren the Jews would not partake of the benefits that he was sent to dispense;[139] Alexander was miserable because he had only one world to conquer;[140] "the Irish Ditcher", with seven squalid heirs, is miserable because his shilling a day is not enough to provide them with food; but no one would assert that the three situations are equal, or that it were irrational to prefer the one to the other. Lastly civilization is *not* Social Order.

Civilization is the permanent improvement that man has effected in his condition by his own intelligence and exertions. It is the artificial half of our existence. Nature has given us so much; whatever we have added by the use of our contriving and creative capacities is Civilization. Genius (or intellectual originality) and civilization define one another; but the definition will be best supported by the detail. The separate portions or streams of Civilization may be divided into eleven heads, and considered as follows:

1. *The Industrial Arts*: the methods of handling to advantage the material resources of the globe. The three divisions of this department of Civilization are the agricultural, commercial and manufacturing—or production, distribution and transformation. It is comparatively easy both to understand the course of progress in these arts, and to appreciate their degree of advancement at any one time.

The lowest state of humanity that we know of (in reference to the application of the industrial arts to the purposes of life) is the condition of the fruit-eaters, such as the Guanacas of the Orinoco, who derive their entire subsistence from the Sago palm.[141] They eat its fruit and bark, drink its sugary sap, and from its fibrous stalks derive cordage and weave hammocks, which they suspend from the branches of the trees like birds' nests—these operations constituting their entire industrial life, a life that could hardly bear comparison (in the exercise of contriving faculties) with the existence of ingenious and laborious beaver.

In advance of the root and fruit-eaters, are the fishers and hunters, who must possess *tools*, and therefore be included in the career of industrial improvement. If there were not many other virtues in man besides the skilful handling of material objects, Franklin's definition of him as a tool-using animal[142] would be unsurpassed in faithfulness; for his tools are what show his industrial intelligence, and the history of machinery is a vital portion of human history. Among the earliest benefactors of the race are the tool-devising, machine-inventing men—those who taught the formation of bows and arrows, of huts, cordage and mats, of cutting instruments and hammers; who commenced working in wood, stone and metal, in skins, teeth, bones, membranes and fibrous manufactures; who found out the properties of fire, and extracted the juices of plants; who discovered combinations of savoury food; who brought into use the mechanical powers, and hit upon the first application of wheel movement, who gave the earliest models of land and water-carriages; and revealed to astonished humanity the luxuries of bedsteads, chairs and tables. (The genius who first invented a Bed was named Murphy. Hence the corruption "Morpheus" given to the supposed "god" of sleep. If Murphy isn't a Saint, he ought to be.)

To pass from fishing and hunting wild animals to the keeping of permanent flocks in the Tartar fashion is accounted a great step, but to settle in a place and till the ground is a far greater. This involves not only the possession of additional tools (besides a considerable advancement in many of the other elements of civilization), but great knowledge of the properties of vegetables, due to the long and patient studies of superior men, and to many abortive attempts to plant, and sow, and impose upon the spontaneous operations of nature. Subterranean production or mining seems to have been always in advance of super-terranean agriculture.

In comparing one state of agriculture with another in regard to comparative advancement the conditions under which the soil is tilled must be considered, as well as the use of tools and machinery, soundness of methods of cultivation, acquisition of germs and seeds, and the increase of vegetable varieties. We may dismiss the first condition—that of rent for land—as the greatest drawback to improved agriculture in *modern* times; and if the individual who first invented or exacted rent without giving a full equivalent in return to the labour which alone can produce rent, was only known—his name would not be popular with the *Irish* people anyhow. Some kind of corn, the vine, the fig, and the olive seem almost to exhaust the agriculture of the Jewish patriarchs. The Egyptians must have been considerably in advance of their neighbours and one time captives, in this the first of arts. I have grown some peas this year which are the produce of a few found some three or four years ago in the hands of a mummy in an Egyptian catacomb—after lying there for upwards of three thousand years. The discoverer is a friend of Governor Clifton's—from whom I received a few of the offspring of the originals which were sown in Mrs Clifton's garden, where they grew after such an extraordinary lapse of time.

Nov 14th 1881

THE EDUCATION OF THE IRISH CITIZEN

(continued)

The Industrial art of *Commerce* is perhaps, of all the elements of civilization, that on which it would be most superfluous to enlarge at the present day. How it follows up and gives scope to agriculture—is improved by every improvement in the mechanism of carriage, roads, vehicles, and draught power—calls into existence a vast multitude of business arrangements and devices, money, credit, weights and measures, arithmetical calculations—demands freedom and security against violence—creates a numerous and energetic class of men—and expands with geographical discovery—is well known to all readers of the daily newspapers. In a word the steps by which commerce has improved, and the tests of its actual progress are sufficiently understood by the people of these countries.

It is in like manner, difficult to avoid having an intelligent conception of the nature of *manufacturing* improvement. We read daily of the creation of new manufactures, and of devices by which the fabrication of articles already in use, is quickened and their cost reduced.

Improvements in the handling of capital, such as the institutions of Banking and Joint Stock, affect all the Industrial Arts equally. New methods of book-keeping, and improved forms of transacting business, also work for the common good.

On the whole, it is evident that the law of the evolution or increase of Industrial Civilization, is the addition of device to device, and of one experimental suggestion to another, through the instrumentality of the superior intellects that have been engaged in the various operations. And of late years the sciences have had such a degree of advancement, as to become applicable to the arts, and by their assistance the progress has been immensely accelerated. Chemistry is come into play in agriculture; mathematics, astronomy, and various other sciences have improved commercial conveyancing; and mechanics, general physics and chemistry, have been concerned in creating large regions of manufacture.

The methods of fostering and furthering industrial improvement are therefore very obvious. Encourage individual ingenuity by good patent laws (a thing yet to be accomplished) diffuse accurate scientific knowledge, and carry on the general exploration of the world and its resources.

The state of this branch of Civilization in any place or time is likewise apparent by observing the character of the material necessaries, conveyances, enjoyments diffused among the people; how they are fed, clad, housed and carried from place to place; and whether the commonest of the people have come to enjoy comforts and refinements as well as the most opulent.

2. We shall take next in order the *Healing Arts* or the methods devised by human intelligence for restoring or maintaining the healthy action of our wonderful frame. Man's industry exerted on the rich and fertile earth brings forth a large array of material products, which he must learn to apply according to their various powers of acting upon his living system; and considering the abstruseness of the action that goes on between the bodily organs and the things that feed, sustain, and rectify them, we are not to wonder that the adjustment of the one to the other has been one of the most difficult problems which humanity has had to grapple with. And yet, how much of the sadness and pathos of human life has been connected with the hopeless irremediable disorders that have prematurely terminated the lives of the large majority of every generation since the very beginning of the race!

In forming a judgement as to the degree of advancement of any people it is exceedingly pertinent to inquire to what degree they have progressed in the operations of healing. There are three departments of the art under which inquiries may be separately made: First, *pharmacy*, or the knowledge of substances and influences that act medicinally or healthfully upon the human body. The more we search among natural products and acquire trading connections with the wide earth, and work out manufacturing operations, the greater will be the acquisition of such substances. It is, however, requisite to ascertain by observation and experiment the precise actions and power of each—a very complicated and laborious process, on which men have gone far astray, and indeed at this hour, it may be said that we have attained very little satisfaction on the subject. A second branch is *physic*, or the power of judging of organic derangement and applying from the pharmacy appropriate remedies. This demands an intimate knowledge of the human constitution, of its morbid changes and their symptoms. The third is *surgery*, which is concerned in local derangements, such as wounds, sores and injuries of particular parts of the system, of which the natural application is somewhat external. Here there is a large assortment of tools demanded, and great skill of eye and hand to use them upon such a precarious material as the human framework.

In the rude ages of the world, charms, incantations, pilgrimages, relics, and magic were the substitutes for the drugs of modern days. Compared with the past the medical skill of the present is very high; compared with the future, rather low. The highest gift of the physician is to economise to the uttermost the forces of the constitution, or to maintain the health under the greatest possible amount of expenditure of its powers. The prevention of disease is now expected at his hands, and not the cure alone.

3. Following out something like natural order we shall name the *Training Arts* as the third branch of the stream of Progress.

We have in this department a certain portion of the Agricultural Art; next Gardening, which, as distinguished from field-culture, is highly artificial, and has been very much improved by the application of human intelligence. The rearing of the lower animals is still more subject to human control. We regulate the breeding, food, motions and required habits of all our domesticated animals, and can thus produce types of character quite different from what Nature left to itself can do. Lastly, we have acquired a vast range of methods for guiding the Education of Human Beings. We have first a system of Physical training—or of securing a healthy, rigorous, and enduring bodily constitution. *Secondly*, the arts of Intellectual Training—in languages, sciences, habits of thinking, etc. *Thirdly*, Moral and Religious training to develop the affections, sentiments, habits of obedience and the like. *Fourthly* Technical Training—the teaching of special arts, or capacities and endowments for performing particular functions in human society. *Fifthly* Esthetic Training, or the polished arts and accomplishments.

The ancient world had made very high progress in every one of these departments; the raising of vegetables and animals seems to have been well understood; and the *methods* of educating human beings were probably little inferior to those of modern times. The Greeks and Romans could make an athlete, a soldier, an orator, a dialectician, a statesman, a man of virtue and piety according to the notions of the time, as well as, if not better than can be done in these our own days. Both ancient and modern times have produced individual teachers of extraordinary merit; but a system of teaching that shall be uniformly successful in the hands of average men is yet far distant. Recent years have seen much progress in the art of conducting primary schools (particularly in America) though it is to be feared that very little of this progress is to be found in connection with the Irish National (primary) schools owing chiefly to the scandalously low salaries paid to the teachers and monitors. In the colleges and Universities of these countries (Gt. B[ritain] and Ir[e]l[an]d) the curricula of study still points to a bygone age; while in the formation of superior minds there is no room for boast over the methods of the ancients. The Training Arts, like others spoken of, owe their improvement for the first three or four thousand years of the world to empiricism, or experiments of trial and error. When the sciences have been carried forward to a certain pitch, a new and far more rapid career commences. But the sciences of living beings—Vegetable and Animal Physiology, and Psychology are yet in a very youthful state.

4. The next head of Civilization is a very extensive and complex department—the *Arts of Social Intercourse*. Of these the foremost is *Language*, whose origin and laws of progress are still obscure, although great progress has lately been made in the study of them. There is also much misconception as to what are the merits or demerits of any given language. The prime requisites of a language for common purposes, are to have a name for every nameable thing, and not to use the same name for different things. But as the progress of observation and thought is constantly bringing forward new objects of consideration, it is essential, in order to satisfy these requisites, that a language should be flexible and fruitful, that is should readily yield, by a combining process, new terms to express the new things. Hence the praise bestowed upon Greek and German, and the unfavourable view sometimes taken of the English, which has increased on the spoil of other tongues. Another virtue of a language is to sound agreeably, and be easy of utterance, without being highly sonorous or prominently mellifluous. Music of speech is a great virtue in poetry, song and eloquence, but may become an obstruction in the business age of prose.

Next to oral is written Language, whose grand instrument is an alphabet, invented in the depths of unknown antiquity, and very little altered during the revolutions of three thousand years; and yet as regards of our own use of it, there is probably nothing in all our usages so much in need of improvement. In speaking English every principle of a sound alphabetical system is violated more than in any other modern tongue. Its characters do not correspond with the articulation, while the spelling of words stand unequalled for irregularity and whimsical caprice.

The next department of language is the right use and combination of natural and artificial speech, so as to communicate the thoughts and feelings of one man to another with the greatest exactness and the smallest possible expenditure of the instrument itself—that is to say, the rhetorical art divested of artistic intentions, and merely looked upon as teaching the best methods of attaining faithfully the end of inducing some given state of mind upon the persons addressed. This marvellous power was carried to a very great height among the ancient nations: but fell away in the middle ages amidst the difficulties of new languages, and has been gradually rising for the last two or three centuries among the European nations. The arts of expression (exposition, narration, description, oratory) have very much improved in these countries (Gt. B. and I.) during the past two hundred years, and are still susceptible of very great additional progress.

The second branch of the Arts of Social Intercourse includes the *Material Machinery of Social Operations*. First among those must be placed the immense instrument of the Press, whose progress is visible to our daily sight, next, the whole system of conveyance by land and water in course of improvement through railways, steamboats and the electric telegraph. Also must be included public buildings, and the perfect adaptation to all the purposes of congregated men—Churches, Public Halls, Theatres, Law Courts, Exchanges, Club-Houses etc., etc.; the perfect organisation of towns in regard to streets, squares, public walks, markets, shops, situation of public buildings, and so forth.

In all these matters the history and course of improvements in these countries is well known; but much has yet to be done especially in Ireland as also in England, ere anything like the progress that is manifest in American city-organisation is reached this side of the Atlantic.

The third of the Arts of Intercourse includes the methods or artifices by which we are directed to any place, person or thing we desire; as for example, almanacs, city directories, maps of towns or provinces, tourists guides, geographical and other dictionaries, and the like: also the facilities for finding out people of certain qualifications, such as register offices for servants, public advertisements, and the transmission of testimonials, open competition, etc. It is of prime importance to Society that every person should get the office he can fill best. But very little can at present be done to satisfy this condition: even where no partiality exists, the ways and means are mostly wanting. Very large improvements remain to be effected in this department.

A fourth branch under the same head regards the forms and methods of social cooperation. When people meet together for a common object, they choose a chairman, regulate the speech-making, and decide by majorities. When a company is organised the members contract obligations by the formality of signing their name. These things were devised early, and probably still admit of progress.

The last of the Arts of Social Intercourse is the large department of *etiquette* – manners or modes of external behaviour.

This, too, should present a history, a progress and a succession of devising minds. The essence of agreeable manners, is a constantly maintained expression of sympathy, attention, deference and respectful feelings in all the intercourse of life: the individual suppressing his own peculiar egotism, and acting with a view to the gratification of his fellows. To have the behaviour of men regulated according to this accommodating principle is probably an accession to the happiness of human existence. Education for this end is carefully attended to among very refined people. It must be added however that etiquette, as at present understood in "Society" is very often but a polish that enables worthless and immoral men to hide repulsive characters and sensual appetites beneath conventional manners. It has thrust nature one side and filled society with an artificial humanity. Progress is needed on this head—to make good breeding or etiquette *honest*. There are few things easier to discover or ascertain than the general methods of agreeable and respectful behaviour: since they are, or *ought* to be, accordant with Nature's instinctive expression of sympathetic and deferential feelings.

It is very interesting to observe what progress a people has made in the courtesies of life: to see their style of behaviour, not merely in general intercourse, but in the habitual relations where egotism and familiarity take a larger swing—in the family circle, in the intercourse of employer and labourer, among those engaged at a common employment, in the operations of buying and selling, with teacher and scholar, between "officiality" and "commonality", in deliberative assemblies and in social amusements. We require also to note the style of treating offences, feuds and animosities, whether by an appeal to brute force, by sinister cunning, by abusive language, pistol-dual, the "cut direct", refined sarcasm, or ready forgiveness. Nor should we omit the manner of criticising and commenting upon individual character and conduct either in private society or by public organs. The conventional ceremonies and modes of acting in the conduct of social entertainments, invitations, visits, marriages, births, deaths, congratulations, condolences, celebrations of victory, triumph, good fortune, popular festivities and demonstrations, behaviour of populace on holiday, character of popular recreations—are a portion of the external physiognomy of nations, and the historian or traveller who records them, render an important service to the study of progressive Civilization.

Such being a summary of the wide province of etiquette, we have only further to remark in what its progress consists, or the criterion by which its degree of advancement must be judged. The line of genuine improvement is from the pompous, ambitious, stiff, formal and insincere, to ease, delicacy, clear expression, and, above all, truth and sincerity. We require to reconcile more and more the pleasing of others with freedom to ourselves, and the testifying of good-will towards all with the expression of our own convictions, and the preservation of our self-respect. There may also be remarked the gradual perfection of the instrumentality of language and action for keeping out of view the disagreeable, and presenting the pleasing objects of thought and expression.

5. The *fifth* element of Civilization is *political institutions*. Of these and of their merits and demerits and the principles upon which they should be judged, and the stages that they pass through, it will be impossible to deal adequately in this essay. The main object it has in view is to bring prominently forward ten distinct elements of human progress and wellbeing that are often obscured by the prominence given to this single element.

Of political institutions the foremost is Government whose business it is to manage all interests that are common or general to the whole society. It ought to control and *steward for the Community* the material resources of the country—its land, water, mines, railways, telegraphs, roads, harbours etc. and secure them from becoming the monopoly of any particular class or being made subject to abuse by any individual, to the injury of the Nation—or the people. It should promote agriculture, mining, fishing, trading and manufacturing by wise provisions; it should regulate the material arrangements in building towns, public works, roads etc., as to aim at the general health and comfort of the citizen; it should frame laws for securing to every individual the fruits of his honest labour in the commerce of life, by restricting as far as possible the unjust exactions of Monopoly, preventing high rates of interest for money, extortionate legal expenses; it should institute true weights and measures and a decimal money coinage; should provide for a uniform and just interpretation of bargains, obligations and contracts; should see to the succession of property abandoned by death; it should superintend and promote public instruction and see to the eradication of ignorance from among its poorest subjects by special provision for the education of that class of society; it should of course be responsible for the maintenance of social order, and for defence against foreign aggression, and should also be the patron of civilization in all its departments.

Government has, moreover, to clear away the obstacles that may stand in the way of the execution of its regulations on all these points. The apparatus by which it does this, is

Law and legal administration. The obstacles are twofold—misunderstanding, and wilful resistance. For the former, a *civil code* is constructed; for the latter, a *penal code*; and for both there must be a system of *procedure*.

It is not very difficult to appreciate the goodness of a government, or the progress made by a people in bringing about good government, if we try its acts in all these heads, and ascertain how well it effects each distinct object; considering at the same time at what expense it works, what money it requires, how many lives it has to sacrifice, what is the severity of its punishments, and what its restrictions upon liberty.

The progress in Government has been generally from the despotic towards the responsible and the popular; from restriction towards freedom—from incapacity towards skill. There is still room for vast improvement in this department of civilization. Wars, or the reckless sacrifice of human life—often in pursuit of immoral ends, generally to attain questionable advantages for the people who have to pay for them, should be abandoned in favour of Arbitration. When the mass of all nations become educated and see the criminal folly of these wholesale murders of the human species, it will be an easy task to compel civilized governments to submit their disputes to the adjudication of an International Arbitration Tribunal instead of to the sword.[143]

Next in importance to government is the Organisation of Labour, which consists in separating the parts of complex operations, and assigning distinct portions to individuals, in creating a practical system of superintendence, and in putting the faculties of each individual to the best account.

By Labour, production or material industry is not solely meant, but every department of exertion from the tiller of the soil up through all grades and professions to the duties of government. The progress in this branch of Civilization has been very striking, especially since the advent of the Political Economy writers from Adam Smith[144] to our own day; but very much remains still to be done. This improvement will be facilitated by the correction of some errors into which Adam Smith has fallen—and which have been copied by subsequent writers belonging to the same school—in reference to the law of Wages, definitions of wealth, relation between Capital and Labour etc.

But the most important of all institutions is the *Family System*. The rearing of children is the universal element and essential feature of the family. But in its high state of improvement this institution performs many other valuable functions. It brings about an economical co-operation in procuring and enjoying the means of subsistence; maintains the old, the weak and the sick; develops the warm affections, and multiplies the feelings that enter into and enrich the current of life; and softens the blow of disaster or misfortune. On the other hand, it must be admitted that, it creates a new sphere of selfishness, and occasions quite as much of unfair play in the actual world as individual ambition.

The most instructive feature in the revolutions and progress of the family institution is the position of the woman. At first, bought as a slave to be a drudge, then used as a pleasant but silly companion; for a long time courted for her fascination, yet ruled with absolute power and deprived of independent rights, woman has come in these latter times to be more nearly the equal of man in the domestic circle, and to enjoy more of an independent existence. It is not to be supposed that a movement so persistent as this has been has reached its term in our own particular generation; and we may require to be prepared for still further alterations in the position occupied by woman in the world. The necessity of allowing them greater freedom of occupation has been practically recognised for some years in America, and is beginning to obtain on this sluggish side of the Atlantic, to some extent, at present.[145]

The next important element of Civilization is the *Spiritual power*, whose mode of organisation in any state is a feature which cannot be omitted in a survey of the progress of its people The definition of spiritual power that will apply to all history is, a body of men to dictate and enforce the moral duties of life, administer unworldly consolations to its ills, sustain the nobleness of human conduct, expound the nature of the supreme powers, and assist in serving and propitiating them. Much as the doctrines taught by the sacerdotal order have changed, its own political organisation has not presented many varieties of structure. In Greece and Rome the temple services were conducted by privileged families of distinguished origin, or by the leading men of the state; the other spiritual functions were not properly organised at all. Among the old Jewish Patriarchs, as well as in Egypt and in China, we find civil and spiritual power administered by the same persons. Again, among the Jews, in Persia, India and Assyria, in the Druidical times, and in modern Europe, the spiritual power was a separate order of men having a hierarchical subordination, and in most of these instances the offices were hereditary. The real progress has been from identity of civil and spiritual power to distinctness; not to say independence; from the hereditary to the elective system; and from impassable distinctions of rank to a free opening for talent. In Greece and Rome the spiritual functions were degraded into subservience to the base uses of the civil despots, who could also prop up spiritual tyranny by physical force.

The sixth and last of the leading Political Institutions is the *Organisation of Public Instruction.* This includes the primary schools for elementary education, the higher or grammar schools and academies for middle education, the universities and schools for the learned professions, schools for the fine arts, and institutions for the promotion of learning and science by original discovery. The scheme of such an organisation belongs to the middle and modern ages, and the leading European Nations are at work at present to realise it. France and Prussia—and later America—have moved first and done much in this direction—Gt. Britain and Ireland are doing something *now*.

6. Such are the main elements of political Civilization and from them we proceed to the next branch, which is *Morality*, or the theory and practice of the moral duties and virtues. This feature is so liable to fluctuate from age to age, that it is

difficult to recognise the particular thing in it that is permanent and progressive, and entitled to be called civilization. The largest half of morality has, in fact, more to do with Order than with Progress. To note the changes that have come over nations in this important element, it must be considered under the specific heads or divisions into which it resolves itself. In the first place there is Personal Morality, or the line of conduct by which each individual life is rendered, on the whole, most successful, happy, and great. This, like every other branch of morality, involves knowledge, intelligence or sound judgement, on the one hand, and the power of self-control on the other— an intellectual element and a motive element. The particulars of prudence are obviously such as, attention to health, diligence in business, living according to one's means, acting upon clear foresight in all operations and enterprises, laying up store for the time of need, availing one's self of all the circumstances of one's situation in attaining the highest possible cultivation of mind and character. This personal morality is vastly stronger in some peoples than in others, as is well known. The intellectual element of it increases steadily; the moral and active element has a tendency to grow from age to age, but all violent concussions of public affairs may subvert it for the time. The elevation of the individual or national character is clearly shown by what is the height to which the aim of personal prudence reaches, or what things are desired as the full and entire satisfaction of life and well-being.

Social Morality, the second branch, is much wider and demands more generous impulses.

Its foremost or predominating requisite is the subservience of private to public wellbeing; just as prudence requires the desires of every hour to be regulated according to the interests of the whole life. In the single point of acting to the highest perfection the parts assigned us in co-operative society, a great many particular duties are involved—as, for example, being ever ready to restrain all personal inclinations, desires, regards, partialities and interests; taking pains to acquire the skill needed in our occupations; rigorous truthfulness, or conformity of deed to word, and word to deed, without which all social operations would crumble to dust; justice and fair play towards our fellows; regularity and consistency of procedure, so as, not to disappoint reasonable expectation; not obstructing other men in their functions while performing our own; humility of deportment, and attention to the formal regulations of society.

Besides the steady performance of our own proper part, we have to look around us for a little way and assist those who are suffering from accident or ill-fortune, or the operations of inexorable general rules—that is to good service we must add compassion. We have also in the intercourse of life to treat men according to their real worth, without at the same time refusing a testimony of respect to those whom society has honoured for the performance of signal services to humanity or the state. We are to give active assistance in preventing social miseries, such as quarrels and breaches of social order; to promote schemes of public good, and labour according to our means for progress and posterity, preserving all the while the harmony and due subordination of the different duties. It must be obvious from a survey like this, that good intentions without common sense or cultivated intelligence, are worthless. In the department of *sympathetic* society, we have another range of duties, referring more to the sentiments, affections, and sympathies of others, than to their material interests, which last are the prime object of co-operative society. Domestic Morality, the duties of friendship, and kindliness of manner and conduct in general, are included in this great department.

In addition to personal and social duties, we recognise a class termed Moral Duties. The meaning of Moral, when distinguished from Social duty, is acting for conscience's sake. Some men have a strong feeling as such, or on its own account; while others—as for example Jeremy Bentham[146]— recognise no end of duty but the good of mankind.

The *foundations* upon which moral obligations are made to repose are very characteristic of an age, a nation or an individual. They may be such as—terror of punishment, temporal, spiritual, or eternal; the mere force of habit and education;

reverential submission to established authority; a prudence so elevated as to make the personal and social coincide, the promptings of inward conscience; the sentiment of social good; the perception of beauty, or the will of God. The revolutions of opinion that have shifted the foundations of duty have necessarily produced for the time, a moral anarchy; and in the present variegated state of the world, it is very satisfactory to know that the greater laws of morals may be made to rest on almost every foundation that men can respect or regard.

It is interesting, in connection with the moral development of a people, to observe what is their ideal of true, noble, highest manhood; who is the perfect gentleman, and who the admired hero of the time. This is a thing preserved us in the literature of all literate ages.

The career of progressive morality has been from the narrow to the wide view of "Who is my neighbour?"—to the almost general recognition of "Do unto others as you would wish to be done by" as a canon of moral law—from personal selfishness to patriotism and Christian Universal brotherhood. In this last stage we are now *theoretically* placed; but much remains to be done towards eradicating the anti-brotherly animosities of rival Christian sects and in banishing from controversial religion what has been aptly designated "hating each other for the love of God". We have also much to do in the way of effectively desiring the good of mankind at large, and of determining the means whereby it is to be accomplished.

There has also been some progress in the duties springing up in the interior of societies—in humanity, toleration, regard to human life, attention to human feelings, and the desire of elevating the character and circumstances of the least fortunate and most numerous classes of the community. There is vast room for further improvement in this last great work. While laws and systems are tolerated which render the most numerous the most unfortunate classes of society it will be impossible to elevate the standard of their morality or character, while both are at the mercy of those demoralising agencies of these countries—poverty, and its supposed refuge, the workhouse.

There has been a gradual improvement in the extrication of morals from casuistry and sinister evasions—except among lawyers and their kind—"the conservators of ancient barbarism".

7. *Religion* is the seventh elementary stream of Civilization. This involves, first, a system of doctrines relating to the nature of the supreme powers, the manner of divine interference in the world, the principles of the Divine Government, the religious duties and destinations of men; and secondly, a system of sacred rites—the temple, the offering, the sacrifice, the adoration, the prayer, the periodic observances, the personal rites. The great revolutions of religious belief are too well known to need more than a passing allusion. The present is probably the most irreligious of any age since Christianity obtained the ascendancy over the pagan *civilized* world. Profession and not observance of religious faith is the characteristic of most *soi-disant* Christian nations of the present day. In England, France and America "indifference" to religious belief or duty is the prevailing sentiment among nine-tenths of their respective populations, while infidelity and atheism are spreading daily and being openly professed by members of all classes. Ireland is probably the only country in the world where the Christian faith is sincerely and earnestly practiced by the whole people.

8. The element of *Science* holds a very prominent position in Civilization, and is at all times a most expressive feature. Science comprehends, first the group of fundamental sciences or those which expound systematically the distinct classes of phenomena that make up the world. These are Mathematics, or the doctrines of magnitude and number; the group of mechanics, astronomy and general physics; chemistry or the science of atomic affinities; vegetable and animal physiology and anatomy, or the doctrine of life; psychology or the doctrines of mind; and the science of society. These are [so] strongly related by a mutual dependence, that the human intellect cannot construct any one definitively till after the

construction of all that naturally precede it. Next to these great systematised keys to nature comes logic, or the science of method; after which we have many mixed sciences which can be presented apart, but which can include no other phenomena but those that have their laws more or less systematised in the primary sciences; such as natural history, geography, morals, education, jurisprudence, criticism, etc.

The primary abstract sciences above enumerated are the concentration and essence of what has been established as true in the operations of nature. They are the pride of human reason; an assemblage of doctrines snatched from the world, chaos, and made consistent with another—so much of certainty acquired in the midst of uncertainty. When sufficiently advanced to be directly applicable to the industrial and other arts, they convert the crawl of improvement into a race. They are always the greatest instrument of rational culture. In their maturity they convey to the human spirit in a short space an incredible range of insight and acquaintance with nature: the ready appropriation of them can invest the ancient superiorities of age and experience.

Giving to man the exact knowledge of his domain, they abolish the debilitating terrors of ignorance, and confer a power of foresight and control of almost boundless extent. In our own day, the scientific advancement must be ranked very high. The first three sciences (mathematics, mechanical and physical science, and chemistry) possess clearly-ascertained first principles, whose application has stood every test: and they have been the source of a very large portion of the industrial progress of the present. The other three (life, mind, and society) are less certain, but still so far advanced as to be at least in the way of explaining their respective phenomena by general laws, and of suggesting much practical improvement in medicine, education and politics respectively. The science of Society has been so far organised by M. Comte,[147] and placed in relation with those that go before it, that it may be safely said the key of politics, and the deepest understanding of social arrangements and changes, are henceforth to be the prerogative of scientific men. Not only has science itself improved vastly during the last three centuries, but the instrumentality of further progress is constantly improving. The science of method, or of sound procedure, is in a high state of advancement, and boasts of such authorities as Comte, Mill,[148] Herschel,[149] Whewell,[150] etc. The instruments of scientific research—telescopes, microscopes, balances, thermometers, etc.—have reached a high pitch of perfection, and the art of manipulation has become delicate and refined to a surprising degree. The communication between scientific inquiries has been facilitated by societies, books, periodicals, and encyclopaedical digests.

This is almost the only element of civilization that ought never to be controlled or resisted: which has only one course and will inevitably pursue it. It is the thing of all others to be encouraged, since its burthen is truth and certainty, the final dissipation of all delusion, deception, and hopes leading to disappointment. What we may actually and confidently expect from the march of time and the operations of nature, this science informs us of: it is the one word faithful and true to the sublunary scheme of things.

9. The *Fine Arts* constitute a distinct stream of civilization; and from its being their nature to put a face of *appearance* upon all things, to construct an exterior framework of life that shall cause a constant flow of lively and pleasant emotion, *their* ascendancy is prominently associated with the idea of progress.

The artistic or aesthetic character of things is an accident discovered in them, while we are merely in search of utility; but for the pleasure it gives, it comes afterwards to be sought for its own sake. Men raise a tower to be safe from the overflowing flood, or scoop out a rock, or search out a natural cavern for shelter and resting place; and they discover that even when the utility is departed, these objects stir the feelings of every beholder; that strangers come from far to see them and recite their description with excited countenance. The gigantic in nature or in human fabrication gives a feeling akin to Divine power and men make use of the identity to inaugurate a residence suitable to Him. Structures are built, not so much for any special convenience as for this mystic power of physiognomy that thrills the human heart. So the action and features of man or woman operating in the discharge of very humble duties, in some rare instances strike some onlooker with feelings so intense, delightful and enduring, that he disregards altogether the actual purpose of their activity, and stands gazing at their expression: he wishes the work or the speech which is the occasion of the effect to be renewed incessantly, or anything done that would sustain an action so impressive. All methods are thenceforth taken of multiplying and prolonging this appearance, according to the resources of the time, a line of activity is selected for the action which gives the best effect, incessant occasion is given for these, others are brought to imitate and diffuse the manner, its best attitudes are expressed by the cunning imitator of form, and a new element of the agreeable passes into life.

In the same way the sounds of the human voice, of the animal creation, of the winds and waters amid their primary service of indicating the things that are going on around, are felt sometimes, and by some persons, to have an accidental power of exciting strange and fascinating emotions. The more susceptible minds are led forth to search for the circumstances of this superadded effect, to dwell upon it, and with their own vocal powers to imitate it, repeat it, and teach it as a new pleasure given to man; and as there are occasions in human life that seem to call forth like emotions, or to mingle sweetly with them, the two are associated by the artist, who has thus found out strains of melody suitable to joy or woe, to victory or desolation. The accidental discovery of the moving and exciting influence is one step in art, the association of it with a harmonising circumstance of life is a subsequent process.

Whenever, therefore, the appearance and operations of nature, or works and ways of living beings, possess this power over the feelings, whether because of, or apart from their primary purpose, the genius of man tries all methods of prolonging the enjoyment of the effect; he imitates it whenever he can, either by literally constructing elsewhere copies of the original, or appearances to suggest the original, or by the still higher effort of educing the picture in the minds of men far away by the force of language. And once set on this vein, the superior minds of the race work up in their own fancy the elements of this super-sensuous effect, and strike out combinations and harmonies of such a complex order, that the original nature is so outstripped as to be denied even the poor merit of furnishing the alphabet of the artist's composition.

The Fine Arts may be reckoned up in the following order:— Architecture, Sculpture, Painting, Decoration and Design, Dancing and Bodily demeanour, Dramatic Representation, Music, Song, Eloquence, Poetry. They may produce the different effects of sublimity, beauty, the picturesque, and the ludicrous; and there is associated with these admiration of skill, and the pleasure resulting from the imitation of an original by a totally different medium. Beauty, however, must be the prevailing character of art, even when it is not the primary intention; fine harmonies of combination being essential in constituting any great production, and harmony and like-unlikeliness, whenever occurring are beautiful.

We have said that science has only one line of real progress. Art, on the other hand, can progress in many different lines, so as to be open to discussion and control by criticism. *Laissez-faire* does not apply to it. It has not infrequently disturbed the moral order of Society, and run many an individual career to wreck. For example, poetry, whether in the ancient epic and drama, or in the modern romance, or in the thousand ways in which it has beautified and bodied forth nature and life, has always taken the start of experience and sober reason in forming men's ideas of the world; and being so often untrue, it has been the means of causing many bitter disappointments and unavailing regrets. Among the different ways, therefore, in which poetry ought to improve, is that of being truer to fact and nature, discarding such fictions as the happiness of childhood, rural innocence, virtue its own reward, as well as purging out the super-sentimental, the horrible, the obscene, the vulgar, and the obsolete.

The mechanical improvements of the age have done a vast deal for art, especially the diffusion of pictures and designs, as well as in the fabrication of musical instruments. It is pleasant to reflect how humanity has advanced in the practice of removing out of habitual sight and contact the directly offensive, and substituting everywhere, along with the convenient and the useful, the beautiful and impressive in art, and to how great an extent we can now enrich the stream of life with emotions of every variety without sacrificing its pressing objects.

The arts are sometimes at a stand, as when the life of a people has little aesthetic physiognomy, and when subjects can only be had from the past. Our own age wants romantic and enthusiastic fervours, but has nevertheless much that can inspire the artist's genius. The absence of community of powerful sentiment is the death of song, but the life of the prose poem or novel. The most barren region at the present time is poetry.

10. The next great constituent of civilization is *Literature,* which when curtailed of all that has been included under other heads, reduces itself to the two great functions of Narrative and Criticism: that is it includes, first, the relation and description by language of the scenery and ongoings of the world, general and particular; and secondly, every sort of opinion, judgement, commentary, approbation or disapprobation, in regard to all that is related—the application of the feelings, instincts, beliefs, and first principles of individuals to appreciate whatever comes before their view. Hence, on the one hand, it contains histories, biographies, annals, records, descriptions, anecdote, gossip, stories, co-extensive with the domain of facts, magnified and multiplied in the minds of all onlookers; and on the other hand, the criticism of events, persons, systems, manners, daily-politics, as we see in the greater part of our periodic literatures and more transient compositions. In its first department it has something in common with poetry, and in the second, it brings in more or less of scientific exposition, in so

far as it gives reasons for approving or disapproving of men or manners.

Of all the intellectual efforts of man, the literary effort is the easiest to sustain. It is the only operation of thought that all men can usually improvise. To make scientific researches, or to compose highly-wrought pictures, is slow and laborious; but to describe what we have seen or heard, to give our opinions about it, to maintain a stream of talk on matters of fact, are almost universal accomplishments. Hence the subjects of literature are the common materials of the sympathetic un-business intercourse of men. Every person has a certain region of affairs that interests himself; he delights to hear and speak about their ongoings, about the people involved in them, and the merits and demerits that may attach to them. Written speech, by extending the sphere of communication with the world, greatly enriches the intercourse of life, as well as the current of solitary thought. The sources of a nation's talk, during all the hours of social reunion, are an important constituent of its wellbeing.

Literature progresses in many obvious ways. The mere course of time, with its new operations, and characters, and aspects, adds to its stock. In like manner the more careful investigations of the past produces enlargement and novelty. New arts, new dynasties, new institutions, new men, new fashions, new advances in everything, new incidents, have all to be related and commented upon. In the next place it advances with the progress of the general principles of the sciences on which judgements are founded. If our doctrines of morality, or politics, or character, or art, or education, or logic, are changed, all our judgements have to be renewed. Thus we have freshness in our literature, not merely by fresh events, but by new views of the past. A Voltaire comes and alters the whole face of universal history.[151] Johnson moralises on human life for the millionth time, and novelty is seen in his remarks.[152] Whether these changes constitute true progress or not, depends on the character of the new principles, which may probably be false in science, though believed for a time.

The third point in which literature advances is in the art of expression and illustration—this of course is the offspring of the genius of the individual litterateurs. Addison becomes an exclusive model in one age[153] and Johnson in another; but on the whole the choice of language and forms of expression, the copiousness of metaphor and aptly-associated phrases, are progressively extended. Variety is also provided for the varied tastes of men. Apart from poetry, philosophy, oratory, and serious history, the ancients had not a literature. It is only through the copious narrative and gossip of later ages that social parties can be pleasantly conducted by talk alone—the cheapest of entertainments.

11. The concluding division of the great complex stream of Progress is the *Art of Living*. There is a wide difference between the various arts above described and the one now mentioned, or between man's powers in farming, building, manufacturing, and trading, and his ability to apply the results of all these to his own life and wellbeing, which is the final intention of such manifold labours.[154] Because we have very much improved the Arts of Life, it by no means follows that we have equally improved the Art of Living. We may increase our abundance of the things that are useful and good, without acquiring the skill to apply them in proper measure, and in well-timed arrangement to the highly-complex structure of our living framework. There is even not a little ground for the insinuation that the multiplying of good things, or really beneficial agencies, is dangerous to our life, instead of helpful; such is the difficulty of rightly applying them to their proper use.

It is, beyond all question, desirable that each one of us should continue his arrangements and daily ongoings so as to make the very most of life, to render existence as rich and effective, and great and brilliant, as it can be made; to combine the choicest enjoyments with the most wide-ranging and beneficial activity. Our own nature prompts us to do all we can to prevent pains, distractions, irritations, and terrors from oppressing our daily existence. Moreover, we have to make sure never to compromise the future by the present; that the strength and vigour of the morrow shall not be exhausted by the business and pleasure of today. We need to learn to avoid all *avoidable* evil, and to support ourselves under the *inevitable* burthens of life. It is only by knowledge and skill going along with the adequate forces of resolution, that we can use the resources of the world on the one hand, and so control the impulses of our own nature on the other, as to maintain the highest possible pitch of vitality and arouse a constant current of our finest emotions and activities. In possessing the command of our own existence we have an important little world to rule, that may well employ the highest gifts of a ruler to govern it well, and if we run it to wreck and perdition, great indeed is the disaster to us. If our life go constantly halting and stumbling, if something about us is incessantly going wrong, if our Present is always uneasy, and our future frequently broken up, if we have neither enjoyment nor hope, if we are disappointed by all events and occurrences—it is plain that our existence is constructed in some fatal mistake, and that we are altogether out of harmony with the eternal law of things. It might be rash to say that any man could be happy and useful if he knew how to set about it, and were possessed of an ordinary degree of determination: but there is no rashness in declaring a vast mass of human ills could be avoided by a more intelligent arrangement of the scheme of life. It is a great misfortune to come home at night, weary and worn, and in our ignorance to resort to what makes us worse rather than better, to unstring our nerves in the hour when courage and hope are required of us; or to distract our energies when it behoves us to combine them for still greater efforts.

The Art of Living, therefore, is the method of stretching out the resources of the world, to the measure of human wants, desires, and capabilities. Each person has to consider his own peculiar situation and framework and to select from among his possessions and opportunities what will do most to yield him a contented, happy, and useful existence. We have all (saving the poor) a certain amount of what supports and gratifies both body and mind: we have our homes, city pleasures (if we dwell in or near a city) our companions, our books, our means of instruction and accomplishment, our walks and excursions, the beauties of nature and of art, the ongoings of the world, and many other things capable of influencing us to our very inmost being; while on the other side we are liable to burthens and trials, to violent shocks and slow miseries, to weariness and depression, to temptations and failures; and it becomes our task to dispose of all these things to the making our lives joyous rather than grievous, powerful and benignant, rather than empty or hurtful. We require to adjust ourselves to our situations, and, if possible, to get rid of contradictions and incompatibilities; to avoid attempting what is above our powers, to strike the balance between desire and gratification, and to observe the limit that our strength has placed to enjoyments and pleasures. If such a reconciliation be difficult of accomplishment, there is the more need that we should know of all the help that lies within our reach, and learn how far the good ordering of our daily and yearly life may be made to go towards rendering it harmonious and happy. Considering the boundless variety of human conditions and human characters, it looks at first sight a very hopeless business to construct an Art of Living, or a set of comprehensive maxims of life-guidance, that shall be useful to everyone, and injurious to none. What common prescriptions can be given to a man of pleasure and a man of ambition, to giddy youth and sedate old age, to a man struggling and a man victorious, to opposite temperaments and constitutions, to the recluse and the lover of social fellowship?

It is perfectly true, that the method of regulating each individual life cannot be exact without taking into account the character on the one hand and the worldly situation on the other. And hence if the literature of the future shall possess a perfect system of life-guidance, it must specifically allude to all the great varieties of human character and diversities of human conditions. There is such a very great similarity in man's nature in spite of all distinctions, and the outer world presents so much that is the same to every one, that we have room, in the first place, for a set of rules fitting to all places and times, and to every member of our common race. There is an anatomical and physiological identity in our frames; the earth, air, and water, light and heat, seasons and vegetation, are common to us all to an extent greater than the whole range of difference that separates man from man. And so far as this similarity holds we may have a set of universal doctrines—imperfectly understood, it is true, and still less diffused and made known—for regulating our lives to the best advantage.

To see how much there is common to all men in the necessities and requirements of life, apart from the obvious wants of food, shelter and sleep, let us reflect how extensive and ramified is the need of *support*, strength, or vigour in every human condition whatsoever. There is scarcely anything that any human being does—whether it be to work or play, to think or enjoy pleasure, to give or receive, to love or to hate, to sense or command—that does not tend to exhaust something about the human system, to bring on some weakness, or weariness. Although the varieties of exertion are innumerable, the fatigue falls upon nearly the same organs, and the modes of refreshment and sustenance and the cautions to be observed, are nearly alike for all. The same nerves, the same flesh, the same stomach, suffer from over-excitement, whether in business or in pleasure.

Men may be laden in many ways, but the counteractions and props, if we knew them, are very similar in all cases. Here, then, is one foundation for a general Art of Living. How valuable it would be to ascertain precisely all the things that can minister to the support of the human frame under fatigue, so that each one might apply to his own case whichever of them he could command! It is well known that a small increase of bodily vigour will often suffice to disperse a whole crowd of irritations and annoyances, and to renovate the entire tone and colour of the thoughts. In like manner, if the Art of Living were rested on a scientific and systematic basis, it would have to enumerate the various causes of depression and exhaustion, not merely the obvious influences known to every one, but many that are utterly unsuspected by most people. We should thus know to avoid all of them that are not involved in the performance of our indispensable duties. A full and detailed exposure of all false stimulants, opiates, and undermining excitements, would be a treasure of wisdom to the whole human family.

We have already said that the Art of Living is quite distinct from the various Acts of Production, although these must in general be determined by what is useful to man. But it is also distinct from the Arts of Education, social and moral duty, and religious observance. It must, for example, often prescribe things to be learned or required and thus, interfere to control education. It is necessarily subservient to our duties, and should aid us in the fulfilment of them. Still, it has a field exclusively its own: its purpose is peculiar to itself, and the knowledge on which it proceeds is a distinct branch of inquiry. It is prudence enlarged, so as to include the uttermost compass of our being. Bodily preservation is the primary department of it, the highest possible range of mental elevation and power, rendered consistent with tranquillity and enjoyment is its highest end. It is, in fact, Wisdom, in the sense most universally understood in all countries and times. The lowest animals have this art for the most part included among their instincts. We too, have instincts, some of an inferior and others of an elevated order, to guide us a certain way. But our chief monitor is Experience, or repeated trials, conducted under the guidance of our rational judgements, which lead us to adopt or reject according to the issue of each various scheme. In this way a great store of useful facts and maxims have been accumulated and handed down through the successive generations of men. We are duly told to labour diligently at our callings, to control our passions, to acquire useful accomplishments, to be regular in our modes of life, to lay up store for the future, to be content with our just share of the world's goods; and we are introduced into the games, pastimes and recreations, that exhilarate human existence. We find institutions and manners set up in the world, with a view to gratify and improve our lives, and we are taught to take our part in working under them. There is no lack of devices for sweetening the flow of man's earthly career; and these have actually accomplished their end with a degree of success that would astonish any poor creature launched naked into a primeval forest to act out his drama of life there.

But that the Art of Living has not yet come to great perfection, is testified by the deplorable experience of the human race. The perplexity and discord, and difficulties of life have been the theme of complaints that ring through all ages; yielding Cynic and Stoic philosophers,[155] self-inflicted tortures and immolations, voluntary banishment from the World, gloomy speculations, suicides and crimes. It is surely worth while trying whether a better knowledge of the actual course of things, and of the beneficial agencies wrapt up in the womb of nature, may not help, among other causes, to stem such a torrent of despair, and prove the possibility of a great and harmonious existence for man.

Like the Industrial and other Arts, the Art of Living has owed much of its recent improvement, and in a great measure rests its future prospects, upon the advancement of the Exact Science.

The Arithmetical and Mathematical Sciences have now reached an amazing perfection, and they carry their usefulness into all the arts and ongoings of life. They have also been valuable to the specific act of Living. Even the small range of arithmetic requisite for enabling each individual to balance his means with his expenditure, fulfils an important function. But the most notable application of Mathematics to our present case is its serving as the foundation of the great device for improving the tenure of human existence, which is peculiar to this age—namely, the system of Insurances as now practised. This wonderful instrument for alleviating, to some extent, the load of human cares, and quieting feverish terrors and sleepless nights, could not have been set up until the Greek had perfected his geometry, till algebra had come from the Arabs, and the system of logarithms had been constructed.

Physical Science (which comprehends the laws of the aggregation of bodies into solids, liquids and gases; the laws of movement, rest and resistance to movement commonly called Mechanics; and the doctrines of the four natural powers—gravity, heat, electricity and light,) has attained a very high degree of perfection, and its various branches have been applied, more or less, to the improvement of the Industrial Arts. Several of these branches have also been highly useful to the art now under consideration. For example, *Mechanics,* in the hands of scientific men, has furnished our modern time-keepers, and made their construction so simple that they have come to be distributed over the whole face of civilized life. Besides facilitating the business of Society, these timekeepers are a very great help to our individual existence. They mark out the divisions of our day and the alternations of our employments, with rigid accuracy; rendering us independent of the illusions of our own feelings in knowing when to work and when to rest—when to eat and when to sleep. They are the handmaids of reason in controlling our life; and we ought to feel grateful for a power, out of ourselves and infallible in its indications, serving to keep our actions right. We must add other mechanical helps to the economy of life, such as thermometers, hydrometers, barometers, etc. Especial mention must be made of *Chemistry* in connection with this present subject. Besides creating entire new fields of industry, and multiplying the diffusion of useful commodities, this science first explained to us exactly our dependence on a pure atmosphere, and specified the change that comes over the air in passing through our lungs. The settled indifference of the human race to such a prime element of existence as pure air, proves how long it would take to perfect even our bodily condition by the experience of the general multitude. The immortal discoveries of Lavoisier,[156] Priestly,[157] and others, on the different kinds of air, took the lead in the movement for the improving of human habitations. Chemistry has also helped to more satisfactorily explain the laws of digestion, from which it will gradually proceed to render an exact account of all the changes connected with the absorption, and expulsion of material substances from the human system. The Arts of eating, drinking, and cookery, universally associated with living well, will one day owe their perfection to this beautiful region of scientific truth.

The science of Animal Physiology ought naturally to be the most fertile in applications to the art of maintaining high bodily vigour and enjoyment, seeing that it is the principle [*sic*] foundation of the art of healing; and this will certainly be the case when it is further advanced. But even as it stands, it has made some very valuable contributions to the Art of Living. It has pointed out the relation of the different organs of the human body to one another, as for example, the connection of the muscular system with the nerves, of the stomach with the skin, of the heart and the head. We are thus taught how we can act upon one organ through the medium of another. We may affect the stomach by purifying the skin; and by regulating our motions, and activity, maintain the vigour of the circulation and the clearness of the brain. This allows us a choice of resources in supporting the weaker part of our frame: he that cannot eat and drink as he ought, may bathe or walk, and by such means support or regain a healthful system. Physiology also explains the doctrine of the alternation of exercise and rest, which is perhaps the most comprehensive of all the conditions of health and well-being.

Mental Philosophy, professing as it does, to expound the peculiarities and proceedings of the human mind, ought to abound in useful applications to the art of existence. As Physics, Chemistry, and Physiology have to teach us all the sources of strength and support of a material kind, the science of mind, ought to point out clearly all the supporting sensations, associations, and emotions, as well as all that are annoying and hurtful. This has not yet been done in a way to be practically useful. There are many important maxims, however, which owe what clearness or distinctness they have, to the labours of a few scientific men who have as yet applied themselves to the study of the human mind; for example, it is ascertained that the happiness and satisfaction of a human being may be directly secured by gratifying his strongest sensibilities and tastes on the one hand, and on the other by giving full scope to the exercise of his greatest powers and capacities; that is to say, *passively* or by what he feels most, or *actively* by what he can do best: This is a general doctrine, which would, if carried out, very much simplify a great many of the questions and proceedings of daily life. The general experience of men has made them always in some degree aware of facts falling under this principle. We are accustomed to speak of a person being in his *element*, when he has his finest and favourite susceptibilities gratified, or when engaged in pursuits that call into play his highest capabilities; but the comprehensive statement of this principle, simple and almost obvious as it may seem, could not have been arrived at without careful and exact inquiry.

The doctrines relating to conjugated human beings, or masses of men living together in societies, including the principles of government, law, social duties, political economy and civil history, have been proposed to be consolidated into one grand branch, to be termed the *Science of Society*, or social science, to follow up the science of the human mind, which very much restricts its attention to the individual. Much good would arise if such a science were to attain any degree of certainty or precision. The society that we live in influences our life as much as the light of heaven or the air we breathe; and an exact appreciation of the effects of all our varied contacts with the world of human beings is as desirable as to know the virtues of what we eat and drink. We are liable to be very much mistaken in our judgements of the good and evil we desire from companions and societies, from being masters or servants, teachers or scholars the givers or receivers of benefits, from mixing with the multitude, or retiring to solitude. The action of Society upon the individual is mixed and complicated beyond the power of ordinary sagacity to unravel. And yet, if it were explicitly defined, there is nothing in the whole range of the sciences that would be more useful to them that are desirous of sound guidance to their lives. Our sympathies, affections, admirations, and general enthusiasm, in presence of our fellow men, are of unbounded effect in elevating and widening the current of existence; but besides that, in this mixed world, the opposite emotions of hatred and antipathy occur to depress and irritate the spirit. These very enlivening influences have their evils and their drawbacks, and it would take more knowledge than we have yet acquired of human nature, to control them to our greatest advantage. It is even a disputed point on many occasions how far the assistance that we receive from others in getting through the labours of life, is for our good—as in the matter of Education, and in taking care of ourselves generally. There is therefore much need for introducing the accuracy of scientific determinations into this important region of human knowledge.

Such are the things whereby we may test the advance of a people, and from whose characteristics we would deduce the methods of encouraging in our separate spheres the progress of humanity. In regard to many of the acquisitions now sketched, much has to be done in merely extending to the many what is as yet but enjoyed by the "better to do" portion of Society.

At the end of this review of what should constitute the practical education of our people, and what the tests by which a country's Civilization may be judged it can, I think, be safely asserted on the first of these heads, that the intellectual training which the National School system is affording to the mass of our people is lacking in many of the essential requisites pointed out in the foregoing pages; and on the second, that Ireland is far behind her contemporary nations in most of the points that indicate their progressive civilization. The remedies for both these shortcomings are not far to seek. The beggarly stipend of £40 a year for a National School Teacher is no inducement to the induction of such talent into that important class of our citizens, as would insure the better education of our boys and girls. When the yearly salary of those employed in the Art of Teaching is made more than the "three R's" rate at present fixed by the National Board, something more than these rudiments will be taught—but very little more until then. The remedy for the backward position of our country in the march of Civilization is simply the removal of those restrictions that impeded the progress of most continental peoples until enlightened statesmanship swept them after the other antiquated and barbarous systems of bygone ages. Land Monopoly must be abolished, better houses for the people provided, manufactures encouraged, and full stimulus given to the industrial powers of the people of Ireland, ere they can be expected to compete with other nations in those arts and accomplishments which have mitigated so many of the ills incidental to humanity and which are destined yet to raise mankind to a happier and more perfect state of earthly existence. [end of essay]

. . . [Traits of Criminal Life and Character] . . .

Had I been arrested forty days earlier than the 2nd of Feb last, this would make the *ninth* Christmas which I would have passed in Prison out of a total of thirty five that have as yet fallen to my lot in this weary world of struggle and suffering. Had my release from Dartmoor on the 18th of Decr 1877 been delayed for one week this would make the 10th of the still progressing number! A trifle less than *one fourth* of an *additional* unlucky life passed within the precincts of stone walls and iron bars is not a very cheering fact to look in the face when just turning the corner of the half-way house to man's long pilgrimage of three score years and ten! Heigho! That was an unlucky star which shed its baneful rays over Straide on the 25th of March 1846. Twas an unfortunate epoch in which to come into existence (in Ireland) anyhow, and had I been consulted upon the matter I would have selected a later period in which to make my *debut* on the world's great stage of life and strife. Tis a most singular thing, that same Life! To some it is but another word for the possession and enjoyment of almost everything that contains the essentials of earthly happiness— to others—to most of mankind, it is just as prolific of all the elements of human misery; while to all the rest it seems to be at best but a three-quarter period of anxiety, toil, pain, and fear, to purchase a little ease and comfort for the short remainder. With three more Xmas Days to add to those already on Prison record,[158] it is not an easy task or a pleasant one, to guess how much of ease or happiness the next thirty five years has in store for one who has yet to experience *one* year's unclouded enjoyment of either—if that length of time be fixed by Fate for *my* sublunary wanderings. Nothwithstanding these not my pleasant reflections I would be much happier than I am were I convinced that there was nobody else in the world today any more miserable *in heart* and *in mind* than myself.

"There is no help for misfortune, but to marry again," as the widow said when being condoled with on the death of her husband; translated to apply to my situation, there is nothing for it but, "to bate no jot of heart or hope"[159] in the service of Justice and Humanity, in prison or out, and to increase my love for the Landlords and the Whigs while I have such an uninterrupted opportunity of dwelling upon the good which the former have done to Ireland and the handsome manner in which the latter have treated myself.

That would be a devilish bad position in which a man should be placed where there was no room for any the least consoling comparison with the situation of the remaining portion of the human family—although that *very fact* might, if he were of a charitably philosophic turn of mind, bring him what mental comfort is to be found in the enjoyment of an hitherto inexperienced "fix" and the particular advantage which belongs to *my* present location, i.e., that it renders the keeping of a diary a matter of the easiest possible exertion of memory. Who is he, among the sons of Adam, that is now in the enjoyment of plum pudding, revelling in the anticipation of kissing some old maid beneath the mistletoe, and looking like a pleasure-glutton through all this delight at the store of other seasonable joys that shall commence on Boxing night, who can say, without referring to his diary, where he was on each of *Eight* Christmas Days!—what he had for dinner on each and all of them, what he was doing, saying, thinking, planning, and dreaming? Outside of a prison there is no such fortunate being in existence today. So shake hands old Father Christmas, long life to you old boy, and may every visit which you have yet to pay this silly world bring more happiness to the poor, the weary and the afflicted—not on *any* account forgetting "Dear old Ireland, Brave old Ireland, Ireland, Boys, Hurrah!"

So good bye until I have the pleasure of seeing you again, and if you have to make the round of the other planets may you have luck in all your adventures between this and Saturn and back again, is the wish of your old friend, W.822.

. . . [Impressions of Criminal Life—*continued*] . . .

On January 1st 1871 I was "doing bread and water" in Dartmoor. As I am privileged to write this in the Prison Infirmary, Portland, I have, in the space of ten years, passed— in prison language—from the "Chokey" to "The Farm". It's a sign of *Progress*, anyhow. If I were to be offered my liberty on condition of being able to say where, in Ireland, I spent *last* New Year's Day, I could not purchase that priceless treasure even for such a trifle. All I know *positively* regarding my special whereabouts and particular doings on that most prominent of all dates of the year, is of a negative kind of information: I was *not* the guest of a landlord, nor did I attend the Castle levee. Wherever I may chance to be twelvemonths, five, ten, or twenty, years hence—if alive—I will be at no loss to say where and how I passed the first day of 1882. In the important matter of recording one's personal movements for the convenience of memory, Liberty has to cede the position to Imprisonment. May this year which recalls a bright little chapter of Irish history, bring Peace and some prospect of prosperity to poor, distracted Ireland; and may it see Tyranny and Injustice humbled throughout the world, to the exaltation of Justice and the Cause of Humanity. Amen.

Some of my movements during portions of the past year, even though associated with a certain amount of liberty are better remembered than those with which I commenced that singularly eventful year, and are easily recorded for the benefit of old age—providing I ever reach that uncertain stage of human life.

Feb 3rd While crossing O'Connell Bridge Dublin in company with Tom Brennan[160] and Matt Harris[161] of Ballinasloe with no other intent against the peace of Society than what might be found in a resolution to subdue (temporarily) an appetite at a place of luncheon, I was met by an "old acquaintance"[162] who politely invited me to come and have a few words with a gentleman owning apartments in the Lower Castle Yard.[163] Under the circumstances, to refuse was impossible—to say nothing of the discourtesy that would be shown in declining, so away I went with my o. a., aforesaid. Upon arriving at the office of the gentleman alluded to I was further informed that two *very* old acquaintances[164] had come all the way from London to see me and so full of desire were they to have me in their company that they were prepared, if necessary, to use force in order to take me with them on their return journey— presenting to me in the meantime a written invitation from one of the most important personages in that wonderful city.[165] In face of all this solicitation for the honour of my society how was it possible to resist such flattering importunities. So on to England I went for the second time *that* week.[166]

Feb 4. Arrived in London early in the morning. Quite a number of gentlemen to meet and escort me, whom I had not the pleasure of meeting previously.[167] Thus welcomed to the metropolis the whole party proceeded to the residence of some dignitary whose name I did not learn—nor yet the name of the particular location of his residence.[168] However, as he also claimed an acquaintanceship with me it would have been an evidence of bad breeding upon my part to appear inquisitive, so I accepted the situation and awaited his pleasure. This was shown in a tenderly anxious manner by his addressing himself to the gentlemen who had travelled all the way to Dublin to see me and invite me over, and requesting one of them to give some evidence that I was *really* myself and not somebody else. This, one of my attached conductors readily consented to, and actually took an oath that I was introduced to him ten years previously in that same city and that he could not possibly be mistaken in my identity. This appeared to give every one immense satisfaction, not omitting myself, as indeed the strange events of the preceding twenty hours had somewhat staggered my faith in my own personality. I was then bowed out with what I fancied was a trifle colder manner than my introduction, and informed that I was to take up my quarters in an old West End Establishment that had formerly been placed at my disposal in an equally generous and hospitable manner[169]. I was very soon made at home in my own quarters.

Feb 5. Very early in the morning of this day I was awoke from a somewhat disturbed sleep by the entrance of two of the servants of the establishment who brought me some breakfast, and—what I must confess was even more satisfactory—intelligence that I was to get ready for another journey. Somebody else in some other part of England is evidently anxious for my society, also, I reasoned with myself, and indicated, of course, my readiness to oblige the party whoever it might be. Some five or six hours drive brought me to this, my present abode,[170] where I have ever since enjoyed the conversation and society of my most intimate and I may say inseparable friend, or rather alter ego, "Reg. No. W. 822."[171] We have been occupied since my advent here in the delightful occupation of gardening, our companions the birds; (and a most interesting lot of "chums" they are and no mistake), our canopy (in day time) the blue vault of Heaven, or scenery made up of sea and land, coast line and wave-beat shore, chalky cliffs and dim distant views of the Isle of Wight. We have not as yet been introduced to *the Governor*, but a gentleman named Mr Clifton has never ceased to treat us in a most kind and gentlemanly manner since the hour of our arrival to the present date.[172]

As if the fame of this, our Retreat from the noisy world, had spread therein, we have been visited as follows since our advent on this Island—once the seat of a Roman Colony. Dr Joseph Kenny[173] of Dublin two visits. Mrs A. M. Sullivan[174] two visits in one of which she was accompanied by Mrs Dr Kenny;[175] and upon Sept 7th a visit from His Grace the Archp of Cashel[176] accompanied by Dr Fitzgerald Bishop of Ross.[177] What procured *us* the honour of this visit we know not. His Grace gave us a summaried detail of the new Land Bill[178] and seemed desirous that we should have a favourable opinion of it as an *Instalment* towards a settlement of the Land Question. From what we learned of the measure it seems to us that *some* relief or protection has been afforded to the class of *large* farmers, or those who are best able to take care of themselves, while the whole of the poorer class—constituting the majority of Irish Holdings—are left to the mercy of *Arrears* and the old helplessness of their impoverished existence.[179] Among the Sub-Commissioners appointed under the Act is John George McCarthy.[180] The Bill is a good one for *one* Irishman anyhow— and he a miserable sample of a class of miserable office hunting lawyers. *All* the other Commissioners are lawyers and land agents, it seems. A nice lot of rogues into whose hands both farmers and landlords have been placed by Mr Gladstone's *second* attempt to patch up a peace in the agrarian war of Ireland!

Heaven help the country or people for whose "welfare" the lawyers legislate. Our opinion is that this Lawyer-Agent Commission will simply turn the whole country into litigation for the benefit of their own profession, and leave the main difficulties of the Land Question where they will add to, and perpetuate, such litigation. How simply just it would have been to have declared the Land of Ireland to be national property with the State as only Landlord; to pension off the *ten thousand* individuals out of the revenue of the land whose interests only constitute the one grand evil that afflicts the people and arrests the prosperity of Ireland; to give security from wrong and disturbance to the tillers of the soil by the removal of every other power that stands between them and the protection of the State; and finally when landlords should be compensated and the Treasury reimbursed for its expenses in the process of settlement, to abolish Rent, fix a reasonable tax upon the land, and allow the revenue from this tax to be employed in developing the general resources of the country and in defraying the expenses of its civil administration, public education, etc., etc. Such a final and satisfactory settlement would be possible did it not threaten the spoils of litigation ad the plunder of the legal profession.

This comprises a very brief history of our movements and doings during the year of our Lord one thousand eight hundred and eighty one.

Signed M. D.
and W.822

SYNOPSIS OF OUR IRISH PARLIAMENTARY REPRESENTATION

1st—*National* constituencies, or those who have returned Home Rule or Advanced Land Reform Members to the 22nd Parliament, elected March and April 1880:

Alphabetically arranged

CONSTITUENCY MEMBER AND DEFEATED CANDIDATE	NUMBERS POLLED	NO. OF ELECTORS ON REGISTER	POPULATION	RATIO OF NATIONAL TO OPPOSITION VOTES	PREVIOUS COMPLEXION OF REPRESENTATION	GENERAL REMARKS UPON CHARACTER OF CONSTITUENCY AND PRESENT MEMBER OR MEMBERS, ETC
Carlow 1-*Dawson* Col. H.I. Butler C.	149 145	302	7,842	Very small majority	Opposition	*Member* Honest but *Eccentric* *Constituency)* Wants careful nursing to keep it out of opposition ranks. Not *very* national
Carlow Co 2 { *Gray* *Macfarlane* Kavanagh Bruen	1,218 1,138 710 630	2,212	45,124	Nearly double	Landlord and bitter opposition	Gray able adroit & ambitious. Macfarlane weak & questionably honest politically Intelligent but needs occasional rousing to keep it in national ranks. Priests very influential and inclined to go with people.
Cavan Co 2 { *Fay* *Biggar* Capt. Maxwell C.	3,097 3,061 2,233	6,090	140,734	Safe majority but vigilant opposition	H.R.	Fay thoroughly worthless. Biggar staunch. National. Landlords party very active. Priests & Nationalists must keep united to retain hold of country.

CONSTITUENCY MEMBER	NUMBERS POLLED	NO. OF ELECTORS	RATIO OF VOTES	POPULATION	PREVIOUS REPRESENTATION	GENERAL REMARKS UPON CHARACTER OF CONSTITUENCY AND MEMBERS	
Clare Co 2 { O'G. Mahon / O'Shea } Cap. Vandeleur, C.	3,283 3,133 912	5,443	3 to 1	141,361	Landlord & sham H.Rule	No great gain either to National party—Need watching	National but requiring stimulus of popular enthusiasm to keep up to "scratch"
1- Clonmel A. Moore S. Moore, C.	244 89	430	3 to 1	10,036	Uncertain	Ambitious, weak and not reliable.	Capable if *carefully* tended of returning a finer & more reliable man
					If Archbp of Cashel would not feel inclined to protect him, Moore should be put out next election. If *otherwise* it would be unwise to attempt to disturb him		
Cork City 2 { Daly / Parnell } Goulding C. Murphy C.	1,923 1,505 1,279 999	4,680	Safe majority when opposition is divided	100,518	Divided. Local interest strong	Daly reliable but subject to prejudices. Parnell sans peur et sans reproche[181]	Nationalist and *conservative* feelings strong. Great care needed to keep *both* seats as priests are inclined to side *against* national party.
					If Conservatives put forward only *one* man & he be a strong *Local* man & a *Catholic* they would make a close fight at next election		
Cork Co. 2 { Shaw / Colthurst } Kettle	5,354 3,584 3,430	14,745	No chance for opposition	393,263	HR	Shaw able and ambitious. No real nationalist sentiment. Colthurst thoroughly unreliable	National and capable of returning two more advanced men. Priests very active. Part of them strongly opposed to National Party & in favour of Clothurst [*sic*].
					Intelligent farmer voters and indoctrinated with new ideas on Land Reform. Priests need handling very carefully.		

Dundalk 1-*Russell* Callan Davis, C.	263 214 9	553	Little or no fear from opposition	11,327	HR	Russell lawyer but honest as a lawyer looking for promotion can be —	National. If Russell continues to adhere to the Whigs and refuses to adopt programme of the National Party he should not receive *same aid* again as on last

I should be unwilling to oppose Russell owing to his many good parts & services but a National Constituency should be *so represented*

Dungarvan 1- *O'Donnell* V. Stuart	139 87	273	Strong majority	7,753	HR	A most accomplished Fraud. Dishonest, treacherous and aiming for office	National if well handled. Would *kick* O'Donnell out.
Ennis 1-*Finnegan* O'Brien	124 95	252	Only small majority	6,503	Weak National	*Reliable*	Advancing in National sympathies. Wants handling with care—*Non-Electors* and *Ladies* carry the election for Finnegan
Galway 2 { *Lever* *O'Connor* Tarpey	503 487 481	875	Only small majority but safe from former kind of representation	19,838	Hostile	*Lever* a worthless humbug *O'Connor* able, ambitious, *needs care.* English Radical more than Irish National opinions	Uncertain. Like Drogheda is easily taken by projects of "Doing something for the place". If carefully handled would reject Lever next election

CONSTITUENCY MEMBER	NUMBERS POLLED	NO. OF ELECTORS	RATIO OF VOTES	POPULATION	PREVIOUS REPRESENTATION	GENERAL REMARKS UPON CHARACTER OF CONSTITUENCY AND MEMBERS
Galway Co 2{ *Nolan* *Henry*	No opposition	4,911	Quite secure from landlord or anti-national opposition	228,280	Landlord	*Nolan—An Army officers* should be permitted to keep to his military duties. *Henry*—False deceitful treacherous & mean	Healthy National constituency. Both present members can easily be replaced by better men. Henry—especially should be kicked aside. Parnell partial to Nolan. *N'importe*
Kerry Co { *Blennerhasset* *Sir Blennerhasset*	No opposition	5,326	Safe from landlord influence	187,094	Half hostile	Both present members unreliable & hostile to Land Reform	Rather doubtful. But if two *strong* men were put forward next election they would be returned.
Kildare Co { *Meldon* 2 { *Leahy* O'Ferrall Jem Harris	1,245 1,004 684 295	2,793	Safe from landlord influence	83,614	Luke-warm	*Meldon* Office seeker, unreliable *Leahy* weak & ignorant	Intelligent containing crowd of disguised *Whigs*—especially among Priests. Still capable of returning two better men.
Kilkenny 1–*Smithwick* Doherty	318 204	675	Safe from anti-national influence	15,748	Whig	Local man—non-national	Scarcely capable of returning stronger man.

Constituency / Members	Votes			Opposition	Character of Members	Remarks
Kilkenny Co 2 { *Marum* { *Martin* Lord Jim Butler C.	2,707 2,674 913	4,854	Safe from landlord influence	93,274	Opposition	*Marum*—not over strong—will take cue from tone of public. *Martin*—"nice boy" of an office seeking lawyer—thoroughly unreliable	Progressing favourably towards national & land reform sentiment. Will shunt Martin if stirred up. Bishop & most of clergy non-national. Needs careful handling.
Kings Co { *Sir P. O'Brien* { *Molloy* H.V. Jackson C.	1,893 1,712 801	3,262	2-to-1 secure from land-lords but not from Sir Pat O'B	74,983	Hostile—*save* Sir Pat!!	Sir Pat is a Sir Humbug & unreliable. *Molloy* new man worth a trial.	Improving to the extent of Molloy. Would require a *strong* man to shut Sir Humbug.
Kinsale 1-*Collins* McOstrich C.	112 42	194	2 to 1	6,955	Same as present since '74	*Collins* worthless both as a member & in political character	Local influence constituency.
Leitrim Co 2-{ *Tottenham* { *O'Beirne* Quin Nelson	1,038 737 668 593	2,383	Only small majority over enemy who has gained one seat	95,562	Weak H.R.	*Tottenham* landlord & dangerous enemy. *O'Beirne* hostile, mean. Army officer	Retrograde—owing to hostility of priests and *Division* in National present Ranks. Both members could not be beaten *only in detail.*
Limerick 2 { *O'Shaughnessy* { *Gabbett* Spaight C.	1,109 989 620	1,934	More than 2 to 1	49,853	H.R.	*O'S* adroit. *Gabbett* unreliable	Cautiously national. Partial to local men.

CONSTITUENCY MEMBER	NUMBERS POLLED	NO. OF ELECTORS	RATIO OF VOTES	POPU-LATION	PREVIOUS REPRESENTATION	GENERAL REMARKS UPON CHARACTER OF CONSTITUENCY AND MEMBERS
Limerick Co. 2 { *O'Sullivan* { *Synan*	No oppo-sition	6,085	Secure from landlords	142,071	Same	*O'Sullivan* weak but afraid to go wrong. *Synan* unreliable. Healthy constituency & capable of doing better. Synan at least should walk.
Longford Co 2 { *Errington* { *McCarthy*	No oppo-sition	2,626	Safe from enemy but not too national	64,501	Lukewarm	*Errington* renegade. McCarthy reliable but not enthusi-astically national. Progressing. Capable of shunting Errington. Priests not favourable to national party.
Louth Co 2 { *Callan* { *Bellingham* Sullivan Kirke	902 830 688	2,168	Safe from all enemies but "Honest Phil"	57,447	H.R.	*Callan* low unscrupulous and altogether untrustworthy. Bellingham new man but unreliable Advanced Nationalists & Priests control elections. Two strong men who would be Land Reformers and not objectionable to priests could put Phil & Bellingham out. But A.N. ugly enemy to encounter.
Mayo Co 2 { *Power* (Parnell) Brown { *Nelson*	1,645 1,564 628	3,221	Nearly 3 to 1	245,707	Weak national	*Power* Renegade to former nationalist principles. Unscru-pulous, ambitious & untrustworthy. *Nelson* honest but too old for effective work Most Radical & inde-pendent in Ireland. The Nationalists *when united* can carry both seats. Priests jealous of N. influence, but numbers of them go with N.

Power a counterpart of O'Donnell. *Self First* Ireland and principles after. If opposed by strong Land Reformer priests would not support him.

Constituency / Candidates	Votes	Total	Ratio	Electorate	H.R. status	Remarks	General character
2-*Meath Co* (Parnell) Metge (Bourke) A.M. Sullivan[82]	2,283 2,253 514	3,877	4 to 1	94,639	H.R.	*Metge* young, honest but not very national. *Sullivan* Able, impulses national, but cautious to a fault.	Thoroughly reliable. Priests control electors but act in accord with prevailing national sentiment.

AMS strong individuality. Might be termed a conservative Nationalist. Too *serviceable* a member to be pushed beyond where he is willing to go.

Constituency / Candidates	Votes	Total	Ratio	Electorate	H.R. status	Remarks	General character
1- *New Ross* Foley Tottenham	165 77	267	2 to 1	6,738	H.R.	*Foley* weak	National and reliable.
2- *Queen's Co* Lalor O'Connor Cosby C. Digby	1,686 1,545 899 109	3,190	2 to 1	76,666	Worthless pair of H.Rulers	*Lalor* honesty personified. O'Connor able, adroit and reliable	Advancing in spirit & independence. National & reliable.
2- *Roscommon Co.* Commins O'Kelly O'C. Don Mapother	1,585 1,479 1,107 933	3,602	3 to 2	137,319	Hostile	*Commins* Able, honest but slow. *O'Kelly* crotchety but reliable, honest & able.	Democratic and independent. Bishop & priests *all* hostile.

CONSTITUENCY MEMBER	NUMBERS POLLED	NO. OF ELECTORS	RATIO OF VOTES	POPULATION	PREVIOUS REPRESENTATION	GENERAL REMARKS UPON CHARACTER OF CONSTITUENCY AND MEMBERS	
2- *Sligo Co* Sexton O'Connor R. Harman	1,550 1,500 1,250	3,266	5 to 4 But strong & vigilant opposition	104,477 Next election O'Connor must shunt	Hostile	*Sexton* Honest, reliable & promising. *O'Connor* worthless humbug	National majority & democratic. Opposition conservative strong & active. Bishop hostile.
2- *Tipperary Co* P.J. Smyth Dillon	No opposition	9,134	No landlord or enemy need apply	201,687	Half H.R.— half opposition returned by a 'fluke'	*Smyth* Our Irish National Don Quixote eccentric, rhetorical & most thoroughly impracticable. *Dillon* slight overdose of sincerity.	National & reliable. Archp of Cashel controlling influence Nationalists next power in elections.
		Dillon thoroughly honest & unselfish but wanting in habits of reflection & calculation. Liable to make mistakes & regret them.					
1- *Tralee* O'Donoghue Hussey C.	187 135	355	Safe majority only	9,498	Same—less a public profession of repentance.	Adroit and not very reliable— once a traitor to the National cause	Has faults of all small Irish constituencies. Can however be relied upon for a national member

Constituency / Candidates	Votes		Total	Opposition	Electorate	H.R. status	Character	Description
2-Waterford Power Leamy O'Gorman	661 494 430		1,452	Safe from all opposition	29,988	H.R.	*Power*—Honest & reliable. *Leamy*. New man & reliable	Modestly national not subject to enthusiasm ordinarily but can be counted upon as safe from opposition.
2-Waterford Co Stuart Blake Beresford	1,757 1,625 870		3,135	National and opposition almost equal	85,502	Hostile	*Stuart* Whig & hostile. Blake unreliable. Ex-Office Holder	National party might with two strong men carry county. Local influence strong & Bishop next door to Hostile.
2- Westmeath Sullivan Gill Gowing	1,621 1,609 141		3,381	Opposition nowhere	75,146	Weak H.R.	*Sullivan* courageously cautious and reliable. *Gill*, Honest but weak—reliable.	National & safe from all landlord opposition. Priests strong and people radical
2- Wexford Co Barry Byrne Gibbon O'Clery	3,075 2,879 846 457		5,773	3 to 1	113,173	Rotten H. Rule	*Barry*. Strong Honest & Reliable. *Byrne* Weak & unpromising	National and Democratic. Farmer voters mostly peasant proprietors. Most of priests side with national party.
1- Wexford Redmond Hughes—L. *Healy no contest*	292 95		479	3 to 1	13,112	H.R. weak	*Healy* Earnestness run riot. Honest without judgement or discretion	National. Democratic and reliable.

CONSTITUENCY MEMBER	NUMBERS POLLED	NO. OF ELECTORS	RATIO OF VOTES	POPU-LATION	PREVIOUS REPRESENTATION	GENERAL REMARKS UPON CHARACTER OF CONSTITUENCY AND MEMBERS
2- *Wicklow Co*		3,311	Majority only through division of opposition	78,697	Landlord & hostile	*Corbett*—weak fashioned by public sentiment. *McCoan* an adventurer. Needs watching. English Radical more than Home Ruler. Office seeker & lawyer. / Hitherto in hands of Landlords. Will require *care* to keep it out of their hands. Priests non-national. Farmers intelligent and taken by Land Reform ideas.
Corbett	1,433					
Mc Coan	1,240					
Dick C.	1,233					
Cunninghame C.	450					
Mahony L.	366					
1- *Youghal*		289	Uncertain	6,039	Same	Local Influence Constituency
McKenna	133				Whig in Home Rule Disguise	
Taylor Arnott C.	120					

IRISH REPRESENTATION

2nd—Whig constituencies

CONSTITUENCY MEMBER AND DEFEATED CANDIDATE	NUMBERS POLLED	NO. OF ELECTORS ON REGISTER	RATIO OF NATIONAL TO OPPOSITION VOTES	POPULATION	PREVIOUS COMPLEXION OF REPRESENTATION	GENERAL REMARKS UPON CHARACTER OF CONSTITUENCY AND PRESENT MEMBER OR MEMBERS, ETC
1- *Athlone* Ennis Shiel H.R.	163 162	360	More than half	6,566	H.R.	*Ennis*—a worthless anti-national Whig. He is believed to have "bribed" himself in.	Like the rest of our small constituencies rather rotten. Still National Party could retain seat with a strong man.
		This Bribery Whig can easily be kicked out next election.				
2- *Donegal Co* Lea Kinnear Hamilton, C.	2,274 2,015 1,954	4,612	About 1/3	218,331	Landlord and Tory	Both moderate land reformers but Anti-National. Preferable to former landlord representatives	Growing independent of landlords. Presbyterians control elections. Nationalists weak because unorganised.
		National vote can turn balance between Whigs & Landlords.				
1- *Drogheda* Whitworth	No contest	743	Over one half	16,165	H.R.	Anti-Irish & hostile Whig—one of the Grand Jurors who found "True Bill" against Allen, Larkin & O'Brien in Manchester	Like Galway taken by promised work for place. National vote strong enough to retake seat with a strong man.
		National disgrace to allow this English Whig to keep seat with more than half the voters national.				

CONSTITUENCY MEMBER	NUMBERS POLLED	NO. OF ELECTORS	RATIO OF VOTES	POPU- LATION	PREVIOUS REPRESENTATION	GENERAL REMARKS UPON CHARACTER OF CONSTITUENCY AND MEMBERS
2- *Dublin City* *Brooks* *Lyons* Ardilaun C. Stirling C.	5,763 5,647 5,446 5,059	13,599	Over ½ Both Whigs could be put out by allowing a Conservative in. National party by aid of Publicans might even carry both seats with two *Honest Moderate* Men.	267,717	One C and one Whig	*Brooks* Whig under guise of Home Ruler. Renegade from *Public* professions. *Lyons* New man and not over promising.	Being Headquarters of the Garrison has large percentage of English & Scotch voters. National vote of an uncertain character but in a majority. Publicans' influence very strong
2- *L'Derry Co.* *Law* *McClure* Alexander C.	3,012 2,912 2,107	5,853	About 1/5 No chance of turning Whig flank except through Land Reform Candidate unconnected with National Party.	142,553	Whig & Landlord	Anti-Irish	Strong Scotch complexion. London companies' influence very great. National sentiment weak.
1- *Mallow* *Johnson* Webb C. Kelly H.R.	189 72 52	293	Uncertain	4,165	H.R.	Office seeking Lawyer & anti-Irish	One of the most rotten boroughs in Ireland. Might still be won by a strong National candidate.
2- *Monaghan Co* *Givan* *Findlater* Leslie C. Shirley C.	2,818 2,545 2,173 2,099	5,496	Nearly ½	114,970	Landlord & Tory	*Givan* new man, able but Lawyer & of course office seeker. Findlater [nothing entered here]	Tenant Farmer & National vote growing stronger. Landlord influence declining.

IRISH REPRESENTATION

3rd—Tory or "Landlord" Constituencies

CONSTITUENCY MEMBER AND DEFEATED CANDIDATE	NUMBERS POLLED	NO. OF ELECTORS ON REGISTER	RATIO OF NATIONAL TO OPPOSITION VOTES	POPULATION	PREVIOUS COMPLEXION OF REPRESENTATION	GENERAL REMARKS UPON CHARACTER OF CONSTITUENCY AND PRESENT MEMBER OR MEMBERS, ETC
2 - *Antrim Co.* Macnaughten Chaine Wilson L. Black L.	4,936 5,124 4,789 4,542	11,701	Small & uncertain	228,376	Same	Both Anti-Irish and Orange in sympathy Scotch and Orange complexion. *Liberal* vote growing stronger.
1 - Armagh Beresford	No contest	657	About ¼	8,953	Same	Orange with sprinkling of Liberal & National votes.
2 - *Armagh Co.* Richardson L. Close C. Blacker C. Verner C.	2,738 2,614 2,275 1,781	6,937	About ¼	164,964	Landlord & Tory	*Richardson* sincere Irish Liberal but non-national. *Close*—Orange Majority—Orange, Liberal & National growing stronger. Land Reform ideas gaining ground among farmer voters.
1 - Bandon Bernard Allman L.	200 185	430	Insignificant	6,131	Tory	Indigo Blue Tory Liberals gaining ground. Always strongly anti-Papist & anti-Irish.

CONSTITUENCY / MEMBER	NUMBERS POLLED	NO. OF ELECTORS	RATIO OF VOTES	POPULATION	PREVIOUS REPRESENTATION	GENERAL REMARKS UPON CHARACTER OF CONSTITUENCY AND MEMBERS
2- *Belfast*		21,188	About 1/5	174,413	Same	Most orthodox Orange. Mixture of Orange Presbyterian-Liberal & Catholic-National. Two latter uniting could carry one seat. Bitter and shameless religious animosity entering into all contests.
Ewart C.	8,132					
Corry C.	7,683					
Seeds C.	6,119					
Brown L.	5,122					
1- *Carrickfergus*		1,414	Insignificant	9,122	Same	Orange etc. Liberals—gaining ground. Will probably win seat next election.
Greer	591					
Dalway L.	554					
1- *Coleraine*		472	Insignificant	6,522	Same	Tory. Divided between Orange majority & Scotch Liberals—gaining ground.
Bruce	222					
Taylor	193					
2- *Down Co*		13,085	About 1/4 can turn balance	263,292	Half Landlord & Whig	Landlords both. Strong Democratic tendency since last election & independence among Farmers. Two Land Reformers would stand a good chance of carrying both seats next contest.
Hill	5,873					
Castlereagh	5,599					
Crawford	5,579					

1- *Downpatrick* Mulholland 176 Frazer L. 99	304	About 1/3	4,156	Same	Orange etc.	Union between Presbyterian & national voters would carry seat with strong Local Land Reformer.
2- *Dublin Co.* Taylor No contest Hamilton	4,867	Nearly 1/2	137,545	Same	Landlords of the purest water, and religiously anti-Irish.	One of these seats could be wrested by a strong Tenant Farmer candidate next election.
2- *Trinity College* Plunket No contest Gibson	3,548	Insignificant	—	Same	All landlord advocates	Hopelessly anti-national—and yet this is the chief seat of *Irish* learning!
1- *Dungannon* Dickson L. 132 Knox C. 128	283	Very small	3,887	Tory	*Dickson*—Honest Irish Liberal and promising young member favourable to moderate Land Reform.	Close division of Orange and Liberal votes—national & Presbyterian being comprised in latter.
1- *Enniskillen* Cole 204 Collum L. 183	416	Insignificant	5,836	Same	Landlord Orange	Liberals gaining on Orange party
2- *Fermanagh Co* Archdale 2,479 Crichton 2,443 Porter L. 1,835	4,778	About 1/3	86,959	Same	Landlord Orange	Union between Catholics & Presbyterians would secure one & threaten the other seat with strong Land Reform candidates.

CONSTITUENCY MEMBER	NUMBERS POLLED	NO. OF ELECTORS	RATIO OF VOTES	POPU-LATION	PREVIOUS REPRESENTATION	GENERAL REMARKS UPON CHARACTER OF CONSTITUENCY AND MEMBERS	
1- *Lisburn* Wallace	No contest	768	Insignificant	9,283	Same	Landlord	Landlord pocket borough
1- *L.Derry City* Lewis Hogg	964 876	2,005	About ⅓	24,830	Same	Bitter Anti-Irishman	Union between Presbyterian & National sections of constituency could kick Lewis out.
1- *Newry* Thompson Carvill	587 557	1,201	About ½	14,213	Tory	Anti-Irish	Nationals vote growing stronger. W[ith] Presbyterians could c[apture] seat. [corner of folio missing]
1- *Portarlington* Fitzpatrick Clay L.	118 18	147	Insignificant	2,706	Same	Anti-Irish, &c.	Strong anti-Catholic and unIrish feeling predominating.
2- *Tyrone Co* E. *Macartney* *Litton* L. C. Hamilton C.	3,808 3,500 3,452	8,573	About ⅓	211,857	Landlord Tory	*Macartney* Bitter Orange man. *Litton* Liberal Lawyer—probably looking for place—like all lawyers.	Farmers growing more independent of Landlord influence. National and Presbyterian votes can keep one seat secure.

64 constituencies of which

    38 are National

    7 Liberal or Whig, and

    19 Tory, Orange & Landlord

Returning

103 Members, divided into 65 National Representatives

    13 Liberals or Whigs

    25 Tories, Landlords, etc.

Of the 65 Returned on the National Ticket at the last election the following *have deserted the National Party*, gone over either overtly or covertly to the Whigs or otherwise proved recreant to their constituencies & pledges:

Fay (Cavan) *O'Shea* (Clare) *Moore* (Clonmel) *Shaw & Colthurst* (Cork Co) *O'Donnell* (Dungarvan) *Nolan & Henry* (Galway) the two *Blennerhassetts* (Kerry) *Meldon* (Kildare) *Brooks* (Dublin City) *Martin* (Kilkenny Co) *Sir P.O'Brien* (Kings Co) *Collins* (Kinsale) *O'Beirne* (Leitrim) *Errington* (Longford) *Power* (Mayo) *Denis O'Connor* (Sligo) *P.J. Smyth* (Tipperary) *McCoan* (Wicklow) and *McKenna* (Youghal). In all the sickening number of 22, or just ⅓ of the whole turned traitors! Any one of whom it would be a pleasure to kick out next General Election.

RANDOM THOUGHTS ON
THE IRISH LAND WAR

I learned from Mrs Sullivan on yesterday that the Arch[bisho]p
of Cashel had reported me to the outer world as having
expressed *an approval* of the new Land Act, on the occasion of
his interview with me 7th of Sep[tembe]r last.[183] His Grace or
my own inability to communicate my correct opinions has
placed me in a somewhat contradictory position. If I can trust
my memory for a recollection of what I *really did* say, I must
conclude that my language must have been misunderstood.
Upon hearing from him that one of the provisions of the new
measure provided for the payment of *all arrears* of rent (or only
three years' arrears?) I pointed out the impossibility of a compliance with such a provision on the part of *the majority* of Irish
farmers who are unable to pay the *ordinary* rent, their inability
to meet the yearly demand for which had been one of the
principal causes of the land movement, and the chief ground
upon which the demand was made for a reduction to Griffith's
valuation. As the 300,000 holders of small farms would be thus
called upon to practically *increase* their payments to the
landlords until all arrears were wiped off, I would be placing
myself in a very inconsistent position indeed if I expressed an
approval *of that*. What *appeared* to me from his Grace's account
of the Bill to be *an improvement* upon the *previous* existing
relations between landlord and tenant I of course admitted to
be such: but I distinctly remember adding that the same
sanguine hopes (as those expressed by his Grace in ref the
benefits that would follow from the Act) were held immediately

after the passing of the Land Act of 1870 in reference to the good that was expected to result from the passing of *that* measure, which time has since shown to be a complete failure. His Grace told me that both himself *and Mr Parnell had* (publicly) *consented to give the Bill a fair trial; but told the people to keep on the agitation for a final settlement in accordance with the programme of the Land League.* Now it was to *this policy* which I expressed approval, and *not to the new Bill*—hence doubtless the mistake into which His Grace has fallen as to the opinions I gave expression to in regards to that measure. As I am even yet entirely ignorant of the *full scope* of the Bill and know little or nothing of the *real* powers, machinery or constitution of the Land Commissions or Land Courts, I could not at that time be—nor am I at present—in a position to offer anything like a correct opinion upon the Bill or the benefits to be derived from it.

What I "approve of" re the Irish Land Question is what I have advocated and upheld, from the beginning of the agitation and must be in the direction of the *complete* removal of landlordism from the scene of its crimes and the social ruin of Ireland, and the Nationalisation of the Land substituted in its place. Every other plan save this for terminating the agrarian strife which landlordism has maintained in the country since its introduction among our people, will fail if they seek to reconcile the two elements of Irish social discord—a rent-extracting landlord who produces nothing, and a rent-paying tenant farmer who produces everything. The time for perpetuating landlordism in Ireland by improving the terms of partnership between those two is gone by—the time for a dissolution—complete separation of a "union" between one who grabs all and does nothing, and he who creates all and enjoys about as much of it as the other earns—must now be looked for.

1. Why should English Statesmen or English public opinion be anxious to continue the existence of Irish Landlordism?
2. Upon what grounds of either justice, social or political morality, state policy, or expediency, can they justify

their support of this system of land laws against the wishes, interests and happiness of the Irish people?

3. Are some ten or twelve thousand individuals who comprise the landocracy of Ireland the sole object of English government and parliamentary legislation for a population of five and quarter millions?

4. What valid objection should be offered in England against a settlement of the Irish Land Question which more than *four-fifths* of the people of Ireland demand, and which reason, logic, common sense and justice must necessarily sanction when it is the *only* remedy for a desperate social disease?

5. Whether would a pacified Ireland at the cost of landlordism, or a continuation of the existing state of things, as the consequence of upholding the admitted cause of discontent, be the more desirable situation from an English point of view?

6. What has England gained in Ireland through the means of landlordism?

7. What would Ireland *lose* by its abolition and how would the relative political relations of the two countries be affected by the Nationalisation of the land of Ireland?

Landlord, Conservative and Nationalist objections to the State becoming the only landlord.

(1) "Why should English statesmen or English public opinion be anxious to continue the existence of Irish Landlordism"?

A policy of exasperation is the most costly and impolitic that could be pursued by any government towards a subjugated people; yet the history of English rule in Ireland from the period when its conquest was deemed complete down to the present year is but a record of seeming systematic exasperation. Putting aside all other questions that have irritated and aroused the angry passions of our people in their efforts to gain some measure of liberty, such as their struggles against the Penal Laws, opposition to the Union, movements for Catholic Emancipation, Repeal etc., and dealing only with the social evils that have resulted from the English connection, we shall find sufficient cause for popular discontent independent of the national and religious injuries that have swelled the measure of Irish disaffection. No people having a national record of independence, civilization and enlightenment has yet been found submissive enough to their conquerors to tamely forego all claim to the soil of their country, willingly accept a state of social vassalage for one of comparative agrarian independence, or submit to a perpetual life of semi-mendicancy in order to gratify their rulers and minister to the insatiable greed of a caste that has seized such land as its own and grown rich and insolent upon the spoil of the country. A people that would *not* protest, plan, contrive and unceasingly endeavour to rid themselves of a system that should entail such consequences as landlordism has inflicted upon Ireland—would be a unique spectacle indeed and fit only for the most abject of slavish existences among struggling and progressive mankind. In face of all the *admitted wrong* which landlordism has caused our country, and of an increasing, desperate and sanguinary opposition to its deeds and exactions on the part of our agricultural population from its introduction to Ireland to the present hour, English Statesmen have employed every resource known to government to uphold these obnoxious agrarian laws, and English public opinion has invariably supported every such effort towards maintaining them against the will and the interests of the Irish people. Why should this be continued? Is landlordism worth what its support is costing England, and the troubles and misery which it is entailing upon the people of Ireland? No rational Englishman knowing the history of Irish landlordism, and acquainted with the treasure of blood and money that has been wasted in defending it against the assaults of its victims, would hesitate one moment for a reply to this simple question.

The only grounds upon which anything approaching to a rational defence of this anti-Irish policy and system can be based, are, that it is English—that it has always been deemed essential to the existence of England's power in Ireland, and that those whose interests would be affected by its abolition are the portion of the population of Ireland that is known to be the most loyal and devoted to the government. Surely such reasons as these ought not to outweigh those which can be advanced by Irishmen and supported by history, experience and facts on the other side. That these feudal land laws are of English origin is true, but this does not necessarily constitute them good laws or such as are adapted to the genius, customs and wants of the Irish people. They are moreover unsuited to the requirements of a progressive age and have consequently been long ago repudiated and abolished in every civilized country outside of Gt. Britain and Ireland. Even had this not been their fate in other parts of the world and were they still capable of being pointed to as suiting the feelings and social conditions of one or more civilized nations, this would be no argument for their continuance in Ireland in face of their career of disastrous failure in that country and in opposition to the will of the Irish people.

The assertion that landlordism is essential to the supremacy of English authority in Ireland, that it constitutes "the garrison" by which the country is held in subjection, is one of those popular English fallacies in regard to Ireland which only needs examining in order to be thoroughly exploded. Its origin is easily traceable to those who find security from the consequences of their acts in proportion to the extent of credit which it obtains in the English mind; but if the landlords of Ireland were really its garrison, and constituted the only force, power, or influence for the upholding of English authority there, about how long would the country remain a portion of the British Empire? If the *real* garrison of 20,000 soldiers and 12,000 military police which is deemed necessary *to protect the property of the landlords* were withdrawn tomorrow, how long would this "sham landlord garrison" be able to maintain *itself*—not to speak of English supremacy—against the people whom it has wronged and outraged in every variety of misdeed known to an insolent and merciless caste? Not for a single week! Of all the institutions or laws bearing an English complexion in Ireland and making part of the machinery by which it is governed, landlordism presents the weakest point of attack, has always been and will always continue to be the most obnoxious factor of English rule, and would alone in the absence of every other exasperating agency keep the country in an unsettled state, fan the flame of social discontent, and inspire a national sentiment of disaffection towards the power that could sustain such a monstrously ruinous system. Instead of being England's stronghold, it is just the reverse; as it renders the name and authority of English government responsible for every and all the injuries which it has inflicted upon the county and our people, and makes England a sharer in the hatred and antipathy which its manifold wrongs enkindle in the breasts of its outraged victims. The next argument that is adduced to sanction the support given to Irish landlordism by England, is calculated to appeal even more strongly to the sympathies of Englishmen than those just reviewed, as it is made to represent a loyal section of the population of Ireland as occupying a helpless situation in the midst of a disloyal majority, and in need of that protection which is chiefly required *because* of its loyalty. This is one of the trump cards of the Irish landlords and has always been played in a skilful and effective manner by them.

But is it a true or honest argument? It is quite true that they constitute what is known as "the loyal section of the Irish people," because they hold the land that formerly belonged to the Irish Nation and could not be otherwise than grateful to the power which guarantees them in its possession; but would their boasted loyalty be equal to the test of a government confiscation similar to those by which the land was wrested from the people in the days of Elizabeth, James and Cromwell?[184] I scarcely think it would. They are loyal because it is their interest to be so; but they know as well as their plundered tenants could tell them that the laws by which they have succeeded in reducing the country to beggary and chronic discontent are unpopular and detested not because those in whose interests they are maintained are loyal to England but from the fact of their being the root of every social evil under which the country is groaning and the chief cause of the poverty and misery that burdens the lives of our people. Is the selfish loyalty of a class a justification for upholding a system which constantly invites twenty times its number to be discontented? Can a boasted attachment to English rule be construed into a privilege of pauperising an Irish nation?

Let England by all means sustain what is just and proper to defend in the interests of her Irish ultra-loyalists; but let her not uphold and threaten to perpetuate by all the influence and powers of the Empire an antiquated and obnoxious system that has proved itself to be a complete failure as a land code, the deadly enemy of Ireland and merciless scourge of its people solely in the interest of a fraction of her subjects; such a policy is as unjust to the population and social welfare of the country as it is impolitic and ruinous to the popularity of English government and should never receive the sanction of a people who claim to rule their dependencies in accordance with popular principles and the spirit of constitutional law.

(2) "Upon what grounds of justice, state policy, political or social morality, or even of expediency can Englishmen justify their support of Irish landlordism against the interests and wishes of the people of Ireland"?

The more closely the Irish land question is examined into and all the phases of its contending interests in relation to the government of Ireland is investigated, the more difficult is it to avoid the conclusion that the power which should always stand in the position of an impartial umpire among contending domestic interests is the most culpable factor in the Irish land war. Had Irish landlordism been left to the fate of its merits or demerits to be adopted or repudiated as it should improve or injure the social wellbeing of our people, a system more conformable to the wants and ideas of the country would have been selected long ago, the landlords be compensated for what they might have to relinquish in the settlement, the government be credited with having had a due regard to the interests and convictions of our agricultural classes, and Ireland allowed to benefit herself by an unrestricted development of her natural resources and the healthy influences that are born of agrarian peace and contentment. Oceans of blood would have been spared, outrage and crime prevented and all the fierce and deadly passions that have been called into play during the past one hundred years have been peacefully obviated, by the adoption of what must yet inevitably be conceded when every other expediency to prop up a doomed system, shall have failed. A persistency in adhering to laws or customs that are associated with certain events or phases of English conquest but which time and the march of social progress have proved to be unsuited to the necessities and ideas of the people upon whom they have been forced, has been the source of not a few calamities to the cause of British Empire involving the prestige and name of England in more than one defeat and disgrace.

If blind conservative stubbornness will continue to disregard the consequences that have invariably resulted from unbending opposition to the just demands and social necessities of a people, the support of landlordism may yet prove a more costly mistake in Ireland than did the imposition of unpopular taxes on the North American Colonies. Historical blunders like historical facts often repeat themselves, and similar results may be predicted of the political blindness of our own times, as those that have followed from perverse and shortsighted statesmanship in days gone by. If the support of Irish landlordism by England could be justified upon *any* valid grounds whatever, social, political or economical, instead of having to defend it on the untenable theory of its English extraction and identity with the interests of a small section of Anglo-Irish, there might not be less cause for complaint on our part, but there would be at least more rational ground for the encouragement given by Englishmen to their political parties in the task of backing it up. Judged by the only tests that should determine the existence or continuance of any law affecting the most vital interests of a people, namely its justice, social worth, political advantage or economic utility, how will the maintenance of Irish landlordism bear impartial criticism? A system which everyone conversant with its history knows to have been born of violence, confiscation and fraud and owing its present vitality to scarcely less reprehensible and immoral means, cannot be credited with much inherent right or the possession of titles or attributes that could confront the accusations of its enemies, or inspire its victims with any reverential ideas in its regard. Its criminal origin might have proved no very great argument in favour of its abolition *now*, if it had adapted itself to the requirements of social Ireland and become a success, as an agrarian code, but as the reverse is exactly the case and that it stands today a huge, complete, unmitigated failure with a criminal career added to its sanguinary and fraudulent inception, we are justified in including its original guilt in our indictment of it before the tribunal of public opinion. Viewed from the next critical standpoint, what is its record considered as an institution affecting the social life of Ireland? Diminishing population, widespread destitution, increasing pauperism, periodical famine, complete stagnation of trade, miserable and unhealthy one roomed mud cabins as the habitation of a million of our people, inferior diet inducing palpable physical deterioration among our working classes, incitement to agrarian crime and universal discontent! Most of its feudal kindred systems have been long ago kicked from the path of a progressive age by other nations for one tenth of the social wrong which landlordism has done to Ireland and its people, and yet Englishmen appear to have made up their minds that if there be any offense at all in connection with its continued existence it is on the part of the people of Ireland for demanding its abolition! Going no further back in its history than the present century we are confronted with facts concerning its ruinous effects upon the social life of our country that should alone damn it to unceremonious extinction and silence all talk about remedying its "admitted evils" or prolonging its career an hour beyond the time necessary to legislate it out of existence. Putting the average annual rental of the land of Ireland during the past eighty-one years at £10,000,000 (which will not be above the actual figure)[185] we have the enormous sum of £810,000,000, or $4,050,000,000 extracted from the soil and the labour of the country, by some ten or fifteen thousand individuals! As landlord investment, care, enterprise or super-intendence cannot be credited with having contributed anything to the production of at least seven-eighths of this enormous wealth, they have been enabled to walk off with it, to spend most of it out of Ireland without the people who earned it by their sweat and toil or the country in which it was produced being benefited to any appreciable extent whatever in return. No outlay to improve the generous soil which has given forth such treasure to a handful of favoured beings—no expenditure to lighten the daily toil of those who earned it by aiding them to apply mechanical arts to the labour of cultivation. No encouragement to methods of improved agriculture—no outlay in the providing of better houses for the people—no concern about their education—no expenditure for schools, colleges or hospitals. Nothing, absolutely nothing worth placing on record has been returned to redeem this annual plunder from being as vast and undiluted an act of public robbery as was ever perpetrated in the form of a "requisition" by an army in an invaded country. I contend that rent for land that is cultivated by labour alone or by labour and the capital of him who tills or works it, independent of all landlord outlay, superintendence, or risk, is nothing but theft by law, and is defensible only upon the supposition that

> The good old rule the simple plan
> Let him take who has the power
> And let him keep who can[186]

is still a moral code sanctioned by civilized custom wherever the ignorance and weakness of the industrial orders invite the application of its plundering precepts. The levying of ten millions a year of a tax upon the industry and resources of a country by a non-labouring and non-investing class having power to unhouse and to practically banish from the land those who are unable or who refuse to contribute their portion of such tax, is as pure and unmitigated an act of "day light robbery" as was ever perpetrated in the days when society was honest enough not to disguise the "good old rule" under the more complicated "plan" of landlordism. A people who can sanction a system of laws which operate in this manner, can, at least, say that they are governing Ireland for the least good and greatest misery of the greatest number of its inhabitants.

Side by side with this vast drain of Irish wealth during the present century and as a seeming necessary concomitant of such a national loss, no less than five famines are on historical record, that have swept away for want of the bare necessaries of existence upwards of 2,000,000 of our people, and this in a land from which nearly a thousand million pounds have been abstracted by a few thousand individuals while holocausts of human beings starved to death were being offered by law as sacrifices to their rapacity. And yet Englishmen cannot understand why we Irish are demanding the abolition of this system the handywork of which in numerous other deteriorating ways is operating at the present hour in a distracted country, presence of an immense army, suspended constitution, prisons crammed with public men, and the prevalence of agrarian outrage and murder! None are so blind as those who will *not* see nor as unjust as those who punish Irishmen who can no more help seeing the evils of Irish landlordism and combating their cause than could the citizens of London be oblivious of danger during an epidemic of small-pox.

Considered from a political point of view Irish landlordism is perhaps a greater failure than in any other respect. If its baneful influence upon the social life of the Irish people has been marked with general ruin and disaster, its effects upon the attitude of the country towards English law and supremacy—the support of which was contemplated as the chief end of landlordism—have been scarcely less emphatic in their unpropitious results.

A system that is made to supplant another belonging to a conquered people must have two qualities that are essential to the permanency of all laws substituted for those that are abrogated by a dominant power: it must either equal or surpass in utility or popularity that with which the people upon whom it is imposed was familiar, or it must possess sufficient inherent force or authority to command that attachment or respect which its shortcoming or unpopularity might fail to elicit. Wanting in the quality of intrinsic merit or favourable comparison with a superseded system in the estimation of those whose wellbeing and interests are at stake, the new code must necessarily be defective; deficient as well in the power to enforce its behests, it becomes a complete failure. Tried by these tests how does Irish landlordism stand as a political institution? Instead of reconciling the people of Ireland to the loss of the national system which obtained among them for ages previous to the English invasion, and winning them over to a willing acceptance of the new law, and a willing submission to the power that upholds it, landlordism has had to sustain itself against an incessant agrarian war from its very introduction into Ireland until the present hour, while the Government is under a constant necessity of guarding its own existence.

Never has landlordism succeeded in obtaining a moral recognition from the Irish people—not for a single hour has the Irishman ceased to look upon the landlord as an enemy and the law by which he was compelled to part with most of his earning in the shape of rent but as the detested instrument by which himself and family were impoverished and his country ruined.

Illustration or evidence are unnecessary to sustain these facts as they are patent to all and stand uncontradicted by every Englishman who has studied the Irish land question and published or spoken his views thereon. As for the force or influence by which Irish landlordism might retrieve its moral abasement in the opinions of our people, I have already shown, what is patent to all the world, that this politico-social system needs the constant guardianship of 12,000 military police and an army of 20 or 30,000 soldiers to protect its very existence; and without the aid of which external power, as has been truly remarked by an English writer, "the property of the landlords of Ireland would not be worth a month's purchase".

Examined by the next and last of the three major tests by which the value of Irish landlordism can claim either national sanction or support from Englishmen, we shall find its economic defeats as pronounced as its social and political failure. In addition to the obstacles which the landlord system *per se* places in the path of industrial progress and the full development of the land (through the baneful influence of monopoly in the ownership and insecurity in its cultivation) as compared with what obtains in those countries where this feudal code has been swept away, we are confronted in Ireland with extra ruinous consequences to the soil and rural economy of the country, which are not experienced in English agriculture and which, *a fortiori* make landlordism still more a burden and curse to our people. The richness and fertility of the soil of Ireland are proverbial and if left unfettered by restrictions that discourage the industry and thrift of those who till it, by depriving them of security for the fruits of their labour and capital, would, in the opinion of all competent authorities, be capable of supporting a population of from 12 to 15,000,000 of people.[187] In the year 1821 the united population of England and Wales was 12,000,236, and that of Ireland 6,801,827 or 1,603,418 *more than half that of the former;* in 1871 E[ngland] and W[ales] had 22,712,266 (having nearly doubled in the space of fifty years) while Ireland, instead of figuring as 12,000,000, (which would be its relative proportion to the increased population of Eng. and W) had actually *1,389,450 less* in 1871 than in 1821, and will exhibit a *still diminishing* population in the census returns of the present year! In the space of sixty years during which England has more than doubled the numbers of its people, Ireland shows a *diminution of a million and a half!* The difference between 6,801,827 (its population in 1821) and 13,603,654, (which no. should be its population this year if it had maintained only the same influences as that of England) *or close upon seven millions of people*, represents *what the extra destructive* effects of landlordism in Ireland has cost our country in the short space of sixty years![188] There is not on the records of modern history a more astounding fact than this or evidence of any country ever having experienced from any scourge in the power of man to inflict anything approaching to the loss of population which Irish landlordism has cost the ill fated land upon which it has been thrust as if to banish from its shores or destroy every vestige of our Celtic race. Continuing still the *extra* or peculiar evils that landlordism inflicts upon the rural economy of Ireland—which do not manifest themselves under the same system as administered in England—we find further evidence of its ruinous influence upon the social happiness of our people and the prosperity of the country. In England where the landlords are not absentees the wealth which land and labour produces if not justly divided among the producers is at least spent in the country and thereby performs some part in ministering to the wants and necessities of the English nation. Some return is made to the population for the enormous wealth which the landlords are enabled by law to extract from the industry of the agricultural classes; while the soil itself receives some care and attention at the hands of those who are enriched by its annual treasures. Yet under these relatively favourable conditions and methods of improved cultivation from expenditure of landlord capital and comparative security to farmers' outlay an eminent English Agriculturist has declared that the land of England does not yield *one fifth* of its proper production![189] Or what it would be capable of yielding under the stimulus that would necessarily result from a feeling of complete independence from landlord exaction of disturbance! If this vast amount of cereal wealth is thus lost to the people of England under a state of landlord monopoly of the national property which is ten times more favourable to production, to the labour and investments of farmers, and to the land itself, than what obtains in Ireland under the same system more recklessly and ruthlessly administered, what must the reign of landlordism cost our people in the shape of food and land in productiveness, by its extra destructive customs and influence? The annual wealth that is drained out of the country by means of absenteeism and other causes incidental to Irish landlordism is comparatively small when compared with the treasures that its soil and other kindred resources are capable of producing if left to the creative agencies of labour and capital freed from the deadly grip of unscrupulous monopoly. The total value of all the crops grown in Ireland in 1879 was but *£22,743,006* or *£4.9.0* average value per statute acre of the 5,121,833 acres under cultivation of Wheat, Oats, Barley, Bere and Rye, Beans and Peas, Potatoes, Turnips, Mangel and Beet Root, Flax and Hay. These figures show that but *one fourth* of the land of Ireland is under cultivation and that the gross value of its produce is but little over £1 per year for each acres of Irish land and about £4 per each head of population!

As the year 1879 was very bad for crops and as the value of the total cereal produce of the country in 1876 was over £36,000,000 we may put down as the average yearly value of the crops above specified the sum of £29,000,000, which would still be only a little over £5 gross produce per each acre cultivated, and about the same per each head of population. Assuming that twice the amount of land at present under cultivation, that is in round numbers ten million acres, is capable of production equal to that at present under tillage— which no one acquainted with the fertility of three fourths of the land of Ireland will deny—the annual cereal wealth now yielded by the country, would be doubled or be made above £58,000,000 gross production and £10 per head of population while still leaving ample provisions for purposes of pasturage.[190] The influence which this increase of food and wealth would exercise upon the rural life of Ireland and upon the social well being of the whole country in the multiplication of creature comforts and in the diminution of pauperism and misery, would be immense, and no one will deny but that the indirect consequences through the means of better clothing and better and healthier dwellings would still add to the blessings which would flow from the augmented wealth and industry that could be thus created. I am proceeding upon the proposition that the present backward state of cultivation and consequent poverty of cereal production is a direct consequence of the *extra* evils of landlordism in Ireland and apart from those which affect Irish in common with English agriculture. Putting the annual loss last specified along with what the landlords take from the country in absentee rent, we suffer at moderate computation *no less than £36,000,000 national, or over £6 per head of population of a dead loss each year from the manner in which the land and labour of Ireland* is treated by Irish landlords! If we now proceed upon an argument of equality with England in the evils of landlordism and apply Mr Mechi's[191] estimate of the difference between the existing and the possible productiveness of English land, or call in the testimony of travellers, publicists and political economists as to the increased production of cereal wealth that has followed the abolition of the feudal system in Continental Europe, we shall arrive at something like a true knowledge of the full extent of the wrong which the landlord system is inflicting upon our people, and shall find another overwhelming argument in support of our national demand for its compete and final abolition. The standing argument resorted to by landlord apologists in defence of the existing land laws, and against the opposite system, is really too ridiculous to be quoted, and shows the straits to which land monopolists are driven in efforts to sustain an untenable argumentative position. "Irish Farmers would not plant or sow nor Irish agricultural labourers work if not compelled to do so by the necessity of producing rent for the landlords!" A similar mode of reasoning was made use of by South American planters in favour of slavery, and might in fact be applied to the defence of a state of society in which all civil rights should be abolished and political privileges abrogated except in the case of the aristocracy, lest an indulgence in the blessings of social and political liberty might beget *slavishness* in the enfranchised masses! What an Irishman is capable of doing in his own behalf when freed from the influence and rapacity of a legalised idler who devours his substance and treats him like a dog, he has

shown by his industry and thrift in almost every clime under
the sun to which his enemy has driven him; and the
imputation that he would fail to do the same in his own land
to which he is as passionately attached if freed from the deadly
incubus of landlordism, is in keeping with the other injuries
and insults that have been heaped upon Ireland by that class
that has ground our people to the dust and that affects an
inability in the year 1881 to comprehend *why* we are so resolved
upon ridding ourselves of them finally and for ever. Le Comte
Chaptal (quoted by Kay, in his *Free Trade in Land*)[192] writing of
the difference between the productiveness of the land and
condition of the people under the old regime (landlordism)
and the division of land which followed the Revolution, says:
"Formerly there were estates in France of very great size, the
produce of each of which scarcely served for the nourishment
of a single family: circumstances have caused their division,
every part of them has been brought under cultivation, and
their produce *has increased tenfold*. Proofs of the truth of this
assertion may be found in all parts of France. When one
compares the present cultivation of the land with that of 1789,
one is astonished at the improvement which has taken place.
Harvests of all kinds cover the land, a more numerous and
stronger race of cattle labour and manure the land. Healthy
and rich nourishment, clean and comfortable dwellings, and
simple but good clothing have been acquired by the inhabitants of the country; misery is banished, and general prosperity
has arisen, out the power of disposing freely of the land."[193] If
such a vast change for the better had manifested itself in
France at the period when Chaptal wrote his work *De l'industrie
française* (in 1818)[194] what must be the advance at the present
time upon the condition of the people and the country while
under the feudal system? The same progress from rural misery
to rural plenty from national poverty and discontent to national
prosperity and contentment, from wretched cultivation and
scanty harvests to improved agriculture and increase of cereal
wealth, has followed a similar change from the old to the new
system in every other country in which it has been effected—

in Prussia, Saxony, Bavaria and the other parts of Germany, the Tyrol, Switzerland, Holland, Belgium, Denmark Norway, etc. Why should similar results not be looked for in Ireland under the happy influence of a similar change? A clear-headed and impartial Englishman will answer this question better than I can. "Many countries" (observes the author of *Free Trade in Land* p. 291 et seq.) have now tried the experiment, and in all it has signally succeeded. Before the division of land in France among the peasants, they were, according to the accounts of Arthur Young[195] and many contemporary writers, *in as bad a condition as that of the Irish peasant of the present day.* The same may be said of the peasantry of many parts of Germany before the great statesmen of Prussia, Stein and Hardenberg,[196] persuaded the late King of Prussia to annul all the laws which enabled the old proprietors to prevent their successors from selling any portion of their lands. Since these great men have effected that change, the peasants of Prussia have risen from a condition *analogous to that of the Irish at the present day* to the prosperous and happy one which I have endeavoured to describe; and it is but reasonable to conclude, that if a change were made in the land tenures of Ireland, similar to that brought about in Prussia by Stein and Hardenberg, an equally happy result would follow; and I am convinced that it can be effected by no other means."[197]

But if the abolition of landlordism in Ireland would produce the social and economic changes in the condition of the people and country which have accompanied the abolition of similar laws in other lands, how vast would be the gain in a moral point of view from the state of things induced by land monopoly and which now unhappily exist in Ireland, to one under which all incentive to agrarian outrage and crime would of necessity disappear along with the system that engendered them? A war of antagonistic interests that has lasted from the introduction of landlordism until the present hour would cease as surely as day follows night, and with it the scenes of murder and the play of deadly passions that are now of such frequent occurrence.

"Nothing" says De Barante[198] (quoted by Kay) in his work *Des Communes et de l'Aristocratie[199]* makes a people calmer or more moral, than the great subdivision of the land, a regulation against which persons who have more envy than intelligence have raised a sort of opposition. By means of this division the whole population become sharers in the public interests: all are made to love peace and order which are so necessary to their prosperity; the poor man is made economical and saving; he works harder because he works for himself: his life becomes more regular; and he acquires respect for property, because he himself is a proprietor." If all the other good that would unquestionably result from the abolition of landlordism were but a doubtful conjecture, the effect upon the life of our country by the removal of the cause which keeps it in a state of chronic moral disorganisation, would justify a national demand for so envious a condition of social peace and harmony.

Continuing the enumeration of the principal evils of land-lordism that militate against the rural economy of Ireland, we shall obtain an insight into the injuries which it never ceasingly inflicts day and night and year by year upon the domestic life of our agricultural classes. Although the phrases "Irish poverty, squalor and misery" and "Irish hovels" are familiar to all who have made themselves acquainted with the literature of the Irish Land Question, very few Englishmen are to be met with who have acquired, through observation, anything like a true knowledge of the conditions under which at least a million of our people, are compelled to exist. Facts that would supply such correct information when offered to English public opinion by Irish writers or speakers, only too familiar with their too objective reality, are looked upon with a suspicion of exaggeration or accepted at a rate of *ex parte* evidence; while the clear perception which travelling in Ireland would beget with the conditions of progressive hardship and absence of all homestead comforts peculiar to so large a portion of its inhabitants, is seldom aimed at, except to a little extent, by an occasional Special Correspondent of some London paper. Even in this latter case there is generally too much hurry to get through a disagreeable task and away from localities where there are anything but agreeable hotels, to enable the literary itinerant to make close and consecutive observation of mud-walled cabins and turf-built huts and their respective interiors.

It will scarcely be denied, I hope, by Englishmen that few influences operate so powerfully in shaping the moral and intellectual character of a people than those that spring from comfortable, clean, and orderly homes; or the truth of the converse be questioned as to the debasing tendencies of cheerless, squalid, and untidy dwellings. Under the elevating influences of the former man must, generally speaking, as necessarily put on the qualities that are essential to the part which he has to perform in the duties of life, and woman assume those attributes by which alone she can exercise the full extent of her beneficent power upon society through the medium of her domestic sphere, as must a flower shoot forth all its beauty and fragrance when enjoying the conditions of friendly soil, genial atmosphere, sunshine and shower, under which its charms are developed in obedience to the law of Nature. The same never-erring and bountiful Nature in adapting this earth of ours to the varied requirements of our animal being—in stocking it abundantly with everything that can minister to the necessities and comforts of life—has performed for man all that enables the flowers to blow and the birds to sing through their bright and joyous existence, and if he revels not in the possession of all that Nature has so beauteously placed within reach of his industry, he has but to blame modern society for having placed a law between him and the enjoyment of his natural rights. Of all the iniquitous obstacles which the feudal principle of Modern Society has succeeded in throwing between humanity and earthly happiness in order to retain a monopoly of what most conduces to its enjoyment—the conditions imposed upon labour hungry for employment yet restricted by the exactions of a class, and upon the inmates of a hovel yearning for the possession of a home, to which landlord rapacity could not reach or insolence and tyranny of agent molest yet doomed to remain in an abode of poverty and a state of virtual slavery—the law which places it beyond the power of millions of human beings to rise above the social degradation to which it has abused them and which prevents tens of thousands of families from emerging from the damp, dark and cheerless dens into which it has driven them—and even of the shelter of which from the winter's blast if often deprives them—is the most infamous and constitutes the very embodiment of "man's inhumanity to man", a blasphemous interference with the providence of God, and a contravention of the eternal ordinances of Nature in behalf of mankind.

What power has given to Society or to a fraction of Society the right to make man miserable for no other crime than that of having come into being in obedience to the law of Nature? From whence the authority to make his life a burden, to starve him within reach of plenty, hover over his existence as if to snatch from his dreary path every semblance of hope and dash from his lips every draught of pleasure—to herd him or cast him forth shelterless like an animal, hunt him from off the land from which and upon which Nature intended him to live, and finally sends him to the prison a criminal or to the grave a pauper? If society or fraction of society that is alone responsible for such nefarious crimes against human nature, were a thing with a soul that could be damned "hell would not be hot enough nor eternity long enough" in which to prolong in expiation of its guilt, its accursed immortality. A law that prevents a man who is willing to employ his labour upon the natural agencies or opportunities that Providence has placed around him but can only do so upon condition that an idler shall share in the fruits of such labour, recognises such a man as half a slave and would only have to undo a few enactments forced by popular combination from unwilling legislation in order to forge again for the industrial class the links of social slavery. The same law which exercises daily throughout these countries the right of depriving families of the roofs that cover them—of driving a man forth from the house that he has built by his own hands upon God's green earth for the protection of his wife and children from winter's biting blast, has but one step farther to advance to claim the right of inflicting death upon all who shall refuse to labour unmurmeringly in pain and poverty for the pampered drones of society the landlords. Yet such is the power claimed by Irish landlords and this the law that sustains them in their warfare against the domestic happiness of our people and the peace and prosperity of our country and which is supported by English statesmen at the present hour and sanctioned in the exercise of its naked iniquity by English public opinion!

The Census Commissioners (Ireland) for 1841 divided the dwellings of the people into four classes. *The fourth class comprised all mud cabins having only one room*; the third class consisted of a better description *built of mud*, but varying from two to four rooms and windows; the second were good farm-houses or in town, houses having from five to nine rooms and windows; the first class included all houses of a better description . . . In the year 1841 there were 574,386 families living in houses of the *third* class (or those built of "superior mud" having two or more rooms) and 625,356 families (*over three millions of human beings!*) living (or rather herding) in houses of the fourth class or those built entirely of mud and having only one room in which to eat, *sleep,* and perform all domestic duties!

In 1871 the number of families inhabiting the third class was *432,774*—those of the fourth class *227,379* or close upon *one million and half* of people. These figures show a considerable falling off from those of 1841 tis true, but this is not on account of the better class of houses having absorbed the difference, but from the murderous fact that in the space of thirty years, no less than *405,141* families *or over two millions of our people*, not including the total increase from births in the meantime had *disappeared from Ireland* most of them starved to death and buried like dogs during the artificial famine of 47-8! And all this human misery—this herding in mud hovels—this holocaust of human beings—this decimation of our population—this one million and a half of the Irish people doomed to live *at the present hour* in these homes of misery, poverty, squalor and cold, because

Englishmen *will* that it shall be so in the interests of some ten
or fifteen thousand Irish landlords! I can offer no more fitting
conclusion to this short summary of the evils and complete
failure of Irish Landlordism and brief argument in defence of
our national demand for abolition, than by quoting the
following remarks from Mr Kay's admirable and conscientious
work on *Free Trade in Land*, already laid under contribution in
these remarks upon the Irish Land War: "The condition of
the peasantry is something none but those who have actually
witnessed it for themselves, *can possibly realise*. At the mercy of
sub-agents of agents of the landlords—with no interest in the
soil—liable to be evicted from their holdings by the agents—
they live more wretchedly than any other people upon the face of the earth.
Everywhere, even in the most prosperous of the eastern counties
of Ireland, a traveller, as he passes along the roads, will see,
on the roadsides and in the fields, *places which look like mounds
of earth and sods, with a higher heap of sods upon the top, out of which
smoke is curling upwards; and with two holes in the side of the heap, next
the road, one of which is used as the door and the other as the window,
of the hovel which exists beneath this seeming mound of earth. These are
the cottages of the peasantry! Inside there is scarcely ever more than one
room, formed by the four exterior mud walls; and in these places, upon
the mud floor, the families of the peasants live, often without a single
piece of furniture, excepting a kettle, in which they boil potatoes, a plate
or two, a wooden bench, and a heap of straw in the corner of the hovel.
In this hole human beings—men, women, boys and girls—all live and
sleep together, and herd with the pigs they fatten!* Gaunt ragged figures,
whose clothes hardly hang about them so as to hide their
nudity, crawl out of these sites, and plant the ground round
their cabins with potatoes, which generally constitute the only
food of the inmates throughout the year, or infest, as beggars,
the thoroughfares or swell the rebellious gatherings of the
peasantry."[200]

"But horrible and shameful as this state of things is, it is by
no means the full extent of the evil. Not only are the majority
of the Irish condemned to exist in such hovels, but even their
tenure of these disgusting cabins is insecure. If they do not

pay their rent for them at the proper time, they are liable to be turned adrift, even in the middle of the night, in the bleak road, without shelter, and with their helpless wives and children. The miserable tenants are subject to the tender mercies of a bailiff, without any remedy or appeal except to Heaven. *More than 50,000 such evictions took place in 1849! More than 50,000 families were, in that year, turned out from their wretched dwellings without pity and without a refuge! Is it a wonder that fathers, and husbands, and brothers, should often be driven to madness, desperation and revenge!"* (*Free Trade in Land*, pp. 303,4,5). This is the language and indignation of a *moderate* English Reformer who had visited Ireland himself, and who cannot be accused of exaggeration or Land League sympathies, as unfortunately for the cause of land reform, he has been in his grave, deeply lamented by thousands of English political friends, these last three years.

Would that the rest of his countrymen could see the incurable evils of Irish landlordism as he did! And were actuated by a similar honest desire to have them swept away for ever by the removal of their cause. When prejudice shall pass away and English public opinion shall return to a calm and rational consideration of the Irish social problem, its decision will not differ materially with that pronounced by this noble-hearted and generous minded English man: "Such is the frightful, the appalling result of our long misgovernment of Ireland, and we wonder that the Irish should rebel against such a system of misgovernment! *Hitherto we have done nothing to effect a change.*"[201] Memorable words written after quoting a speech of John Bright on the state of Ireland[202] and printed after the passing of Mr Gladstone's Land Act of 1870.

RANDOM THOUGHTS ON
THE IRISH LAND WAR

DIFFICULTIES IN THE WAY OF A
SOLUTION OF THE IRISH SOCIAL PROBLEM

I sought, in the last lecture, (1) to summarise the chief injuries permanently inflicted upon Ireland by Irish Landlordism; (2) to examine upon what grounds, social, political, or econo-mical, its continued existence can be rationally defended by Englishmen; (3) how upon each and all of these grounds it stands convicted of complete and disastrous failure; and (4) how justly and reasonably all its crimes, defects, failures, and continued antagonism to the prosperity and peace of our people, amount to an unanswerable argument in favour of the national demand for its abolition.

In the following short discourse I shall endeavour to point out (1) some of the accidental difficulties that have prevented the English public from appreciating the full extent of the ruinous effects of landlordism upon Ireland—or the consequent reasonableness of our people's demands for its abolition; (2) how Englishmen would be exhibiting more consistency with principles of just government and sound policy if, instead of feeling a prejudice against four millions of people for their efforts to overthrow the system that has worked and is still working such evil to themselves and their country, they demanded from Irish Landlordism an account of its stewardship in Ireland, and of Irish Landlords some better return for all England has done for them than involving her in perpetual conflict with the people of Ireland; and (3) how this agrarian war that has

existed in Ireland for three centuries can be finally and satisfactorily settled without bloodshed or revolution with every
advantage to our people, peace and order to the country and
credit to Englishmen.

The party or the man, whether English or Irish, that would
be instrumental in terminating the social troubles of Ireland
and in bringing peace, order and contentment to its distracted
people, would merit, not only the everlasting gratitude of our
country and thanks of England, but would earn, in addition,
the obligations of the whole civilized world. Irish Famines
have appealed for charity, Irish grievances have resounded in
the ears of, and Irish movements for redress have solicited
sympathy from almost every nation in the world which the
press has brought within reach of our voice and a cognisance
of our misfortunes. If this is annoying to Englishmen—and it
cannot possibly be otherwise, being, from an English point of
view, a scandalous domestic brawl in sight and within hearing
of "damn good natured" friendly powers—and begets an
irritation of English public opinion that proves anything but
favourable to a calm or an unprejudiced consideration of our
claims, it tends likewise to lower the character of our cause in
external estimation, as well as to induce political and party
demoralisation among our people.

We have therefore involved, in this Irish difficulty, almost
everything that could possibly combine to render its solution
a legislative necessity—the peace and welfare of Ireland, the
constitutional reputation of England, and the patient interest
of an on-looking world. Nothing could well be more decidedly
within the "domain of practical politics" than this vexed Irish
Land Question; yet no question ever submitted to the arbitrament of public opinion—and public opinion alone is capable
of deciding it—in these its days of omnipotence, has been
more unfortunately presented under circumstances unusually
favourable to a radical settlement of a long standing and generally unquestioned wrong. The land agitation, by aid of which
this social grievance of our people was again brought forward,
was originated in anticipation of one of the chronic evils of

landlordism, Famine; was continued during and after its
visitation, while the charity of foreign nations was performing
what Irish landlordism refused, with its usual brutal selfishness,
to perform; and during the existence of an organisation which
embraced the manhood and the intelligence of Ireland and
the services of two-thirds of her public men and representatives. I have said "unfortunately presented," not however in
reference to time, opportunity, or modus operandi, *in Ireland*;
for, as I have just remarked, there existed a combination of
circumstances unusually favourable to public discussion, large
meetings and popular combination, seldom before presented
to our people; but from *the total* want of tact which the leaders
of the movement exhibited in neglecting, overlooking or
despising the second, if not the most powerful and important,
factor in any settlement of an Anglo-Irish difficulty—*English
public opinion*. If filling the English press with accounts of imposing
demonstrations in Ireland, speeches, resolutions, facts, figures
and declamation, *from Irish platforms*, could be called educating
English public opinion upon Irish landlordism, Irish misery
and peasant proprietary, there would be no reproach of opportunity lost or want of judgement in not assailing our enemy's
position in its most vital point of attack; but unfortunately we
overlooked the fact that while we had driven landlordism as
it were out of most of its intrenchments in Ireland by public
meetings and organisation, we allowed the landlords to take
up their *old position* in England and to turn the whole battery
of English public opinion first against us, next against our
movement, and finally against that which was *their* vulnerable
point, the question proper at issue. It matters not that the
character of the Land League leaders given by the landlords to
the English press was a false one, and that the whole agitation
was misrepresented and maligned to the English people; *we*
were not considered over tender, on our side of the Irish Sea,
of the reputation and misdeeds of our opponents; and should
have understood English prejudice well enough to know, that,
while devoting all our time and spending all our resources
against the system that identified with the ultra-loyal Irish class

in Ireland, the English people would not take *our* part or lend *us* their sympathy *in preference* to those who represented themselves as driven from Ireland by our movement and as placing the justice of their cause in English hands. Instead of anticipating a recurrence to the old tactics by the Irish landlords—"an appeal to Englishmen to defend them, their property, and *English Rule in Ireland from Revolutionists*, etc."—and taking all necessary measures to place a proper and dignified representation of our aims, character of the Land League, and the justice of our people's cry for abolition, before the English people; as well as a proper representation of the injury done to the name and reputation of English law in Ireland through the misdeeds of landlordism; and by this means showing the real extent of our design and nature of our motives, we simply ignored the direct importance of English public opinion altogether until it was too late to retrieve our position in its judgement of our acts and intentions; and, by this neglect allowed the Irish Landlords to become solidaries with English prejudice, and thus invited the customary press denunciation, suspension of Habeas Corpus, imprisonment and temporary defeat.

What we *might* have won by means of the grand opportunity we possessed, can be conjectured from what the Government felt *compelled* to attempt in the direction of a settlement of the Land Question, notwithstanding the storm raised against us in England by the old tactics of misrepresentation, and our own cavalier treatment of the people of this country. We had a splendid case, but failing to put in an appearance before the tribunal which was to decide upon its merits, we were non-suited—with costs.

It may be objected by Irishmen that it would have been at once non-national and undignified for the leaders of a popular Irish movement to have recognised English public opinion as arbiter in the question at issue; that seeking for English sympathy would be tantamount to appearing as a suppliant where prejudice was certain to decide against us; and that as the question to be decided was one between the Irish people and the Irish landlords, its settlement was an exclusively Irish national affair, and its consideration a matter affecting Irish public opinion only. If the two last propositions could be sustained by fact, I would feel no reproach for having performed my part of the big blunder which I have indicated; and if the objections above mentioned were founded in truth, instead of being the offspring of a jealous national conceit, I am of opinion that I would be about the last Irishman alive who would insist upon their infringement. In neither of the objections just supposed, however, can it be reasonably proved that the procedure, which they are made to repudiate, would, if carried out, amount to anything like what they affirm. The recognition of public opinion in this country as the only power that can decide the fate of Irish landlordism is simply the recognition of a fact, and would be no more an abandonment of the national claims or dignity of Ireland than would an Irishman discard his national opinions or principles by the act of addressing an English audience upon an exclusively Irish topic. Going to England before the Irish landlords in order to forestall their alarmist designs upon English popular feeling, would be no more a petitioning or begging attitude than would the precaution of occupying a strong position in an enemy's territory, be a surrender to the foe, who had calculated upon making it his principal *point d'appui*. But in perpetrating the great blunder I have pointed out we, by omission, committed a huge mistake in addition, which we endeavoured to rectify when it was too late to recover the ground which we lost by it. Any one conversant with Continental and American papers will not need to be told how much they are influenced, in their opinions of Irish questions, by the tone and representations of the London press, the chief, if not the only source from which their information is derived. A French or American journal seeking correct information upon Irish matters from an Irish national paper is something seldom or ever met with; and the conclusions that are to be drawn from events or occurrences in our country, by foreign public opinion, must therefore be more or less complexioned by the usually prejudiced medium through which it obtains its facts and information—that of the great London Dailies—English public opinion, therefore, reacts upon that of other countries, through London being the greatest centre of press-association in the world; and the amount of sympathy which Ireland can expect to receive from France, Germany, Italy or America, in her political or social movements, will depend, in a great measure, upon the tone of the principal English papers, regarding such movements.

The Irish Landlords and the newspaper writers in their interest were well aware of the foregoing fact; and while seeming to abandon Irish public opinion to the Land League and the Agitation, set themselves to work to counteract the influence of both upon external opinion and sympathy. This they completely succeeded in doing in England, and, to a considerable measure in France and America, also, by constantly supplying the press in these countries with pamphlets and publications in their own defence and in denunciation of the Land League, as well as with copies of the three Dublin papers that are printed in their interest. They also had at their service all the Dublin correspondents, or agents of the London Dailies and English and American press associations with, I believe, one exception. The Irish agent of the *New York Herald*, was, I believe, actually in their pay.[203] Writers and Reporters belonging to the (Dublin) *Daily Express*, *Evening Mail*, and *Irish Times*, were the "Dublin correspondents" of *the Times*, *Standard* and *Daily Telegraph*, as also of most of the large Scotch and English provincial papers, and of course coloured their communications to the same complexion of landlord feeling as that which characterised the views of the Dublin landlord press to which they were attached. By this simple but thoroughly effective plan, together with the special attention paid to the position of the English public in the struggle between themselves and the Irish people, the landlords succeeded in exercising more influence upon English and Foreign public opinion than the Land League succeeded in doing, with all its meetings, organisation, agents, and resources.

Had we, at the commencement of our movement recognised the vast importance of external opinion and judgement, upon the question we had undertaken to bring forward, and paid due regard to the value of English popular feeling especially, the issue of the agitation, would have been, in my humble opinion, very different, to what it has turned out to be. Had we established an Agency in London, organised public meetings there and in all the great centres of English population, submitted the justice and practicability of our demands and constitutional character of the Land League to the criticism of English papers and English audiences, and distributed our pamphlets and publications among the English people, we would have disarmed all suspicion as to ulterior designs, caught the ear of English popular interest, and have placed our movement in such a light before the people of this country that landlord misrepresentation would have found it much more difficult to have raised such a storm of popular feeling against us, as our culpable neglect of a common sense action has enabled them to do. And yet we could have performed this work without materially interfering with the agitation in Ireland. Another of the accidental causes operating to prevent the people of England from forming an impartial judgement upon Irish landlordism and upon the justice of our demands for its abolition, has, unfortunately, been increased by the foregoing reasons, and is never wholly absent from the consideration of Irish questions in this country, namely *English prejudice.* Englishmen will of course, always deny that any such feeling is entertained towards us or our country, by them, but an argument to establish the contrary would be about as unnecessary as to adduce proofs that the river Thames flows through London. If no other evidence of its existence could be mentioned or met with than what is presented by the cartoons of *all* the English comic papers—in which we are constantly represented to the world as if we constituted, in physical conformation, a nation of the "missing link" type of being in the evolution of species—it would be an ample refutation of the Englishman's disclaimer of prejudice against our country and its people. It is needless to discuss the causes that have given birth to and still keep alive this English dislike to us. It is enough to insist upon its but too objective reality and to point to it as a powerful obstacle in the way of a just or impartial consideration of any subject which may concern the best interests of Ireland. To this, it is but truth to add that the people of Ireland and their popular leaders while alive to and indignant at this "Saxon prejudice" against them, seldom or ever make any attempt to conciliate this adverse feeling. Englishmen cannot brook anything approaching to independence on the part of those whom they hold in political subjection. Irishmen (holding national opinions) cannot and will not stoop to a suppliant attitude towards those who have derived them of their liberty, and who treat this country with injustice and themselves with contempt in the bargain. From whence it very naturally follows that a section of the people of Ireland, intimately associated with the power of England in that country, and being identified with the (English) system that is at the root of Irish poverty and discontent, are looked upon by our people as doubly inimical to them, while from the first of these reasons cooperating with the seemingly innate English aversion to "the Irish", this same section of our population is rendered popular in English estimation and supported thereby in its monopoly of land and of the administration of law and government in Ireland.

This condition of affairs gives rise to something very near akin to the following situation—from which the Irish Landlords, and not the peoples of England or Ireland, are deriving benefit:—

The Irish, addressing England, say: "Landlordism is the curse of Ireland. It has depopulated and impoverished it in the past and still continues to make it the most miserable country in the world. Those in whose interest you are supporting it, are not of us—they are our social and political enemies, and never disguise their dislike of everything in this ill-fated land except our money and the power which you enable them to wield over us. We therefore demand the abolition of landlordism."

Ere England makes reply to this demand the Irish landlords say to her people: "We are your garrison in Ireland, and your loyal and obedient subjects. The Irish people have an invincible hatred of both you and your power and would cut the connection between the two countries if our influence were withdrawn. The charges which the Irish bring against us are untrue. No people in the world are better treated by their landlords, but no people are so ungrateful and hence their desire to be rid of us. In supporting Irish landlordism you are simply upholding your own supremacy among a disaffected people. Withdraw that support and you invite the separation of England and Ireland, the ruin of both, and a disruption of the British Empire". This appeal to English popular prejudice dictates England's reply to our rational and just demand: "We will always be ready to remedy the admitted evils of Irish landlordism, but the system itself we will not abolish. We respect the rights of property and will defend the vested interests of the landlords. They and their dependents are loyal to our authority administer our law, and are necessary to our policy of anglicising Ireland. Within the terms of this reply you must look for all the change we are willing to make in your social system. If you persist in demanding more, you know the consequence."

Until Englishmen shall investigate how much of truth there is in the allegations of the Irish landlords respecting the political worth of landlordism in Ireland—until they discover, what is palpable to every Irishman, that the system which is pretended to be the connecting link between Ireland and England, is, on the contrary, a never ceasing incentive to disaffection, disorder and disregard of law, a final and satisfactory adjustment of the Irish social difficulty, will not be arrived at. When the discovery is fully made however, in this country, and light is at last thrown upon the worthless character of the system, law and the class that have so long trampled upon the interests of our people, and invited periodical uprisings against English law, landlordism will march bag and baggage out of Ireland forever.

Another of the difficulties standing in the way of a popular English impartial view of Irish landlordism and a right opinion upon the attitude of our people towards it, is a doubly unfortunate one in as much as it tends to strengthen the existing prejudice against us, while it is calculated at the same time to seriously injure the moral character of our country. I allude to the unfortunately but too prevalent occurrence of agrarian outrage.[204] As to the cause of this blot upon the name of Ireland, no two opinions can be held. No deduction could be more convincingly made from any cause producing effect than that the murders and outrages resulting from the Irish land war are the direct offspring of Irish landlordism. Still, as if our unfortunate country should, in her deeds of despair, be doomed to injure not her enemy, but herself, these crimes are made to tell against our people and their cause instead of branding with infamy and detestation the very name of the system which is alone responsible for their perpetration. While almost every other species of crime springing from the evil passions, poverty and temptations of man, with which the law and the public of every other civilized country are daily familiar, are almost unknown amongst our people—exhibiting an almost unparalleled aspect of moral rectitude in a notoriously immoral age—this foul pestiferous social rinderpest of landlordism can add to its seemingly exhaustless [*sic*] power of injuring the land upon which an evil destiny has fastened it, the stigma of assassination and the obloquy of crime.

There *have* been Englishmen familiar with Ireland who could justly attribute these deeds of violence to their legitimate cause, and to strengthen the foregoing remarks upon this saddening topic, I will quote the opinions of two whose names will command respect from the positions they held for the judgements which they have given. Captain Thomas Drummond, Under Secretary of State for Ireland (from 1835 until his death 1840)[205] in replying to a public letter which was addressed to him by the Magistracy of Tipperary in reference to the murder of a Mr Cooper in that county, made use of those now memorable words: "Property has its duties as well as its rights;

to the neglect of those duties in times past is to be mainly ascribed that diseased state of society in which such crimes take their rise."[206]

The Right Honourable John Bright in one of his great speeches upon the State of Ireland, has said:

> But there have been recent outrages committed in Ireland. A respectable gentleman was shot in open day, on the Sunday morning at eleven o'clock, whilst on his way to Church—shot, too, while two men were within two or three yards of him; one, in fact, with his shoulder against his saddle. And the man who fired was seen going through the garden and escaping; while two men were walking rapidly over a bog, supposed to be the assassins making their escape. Why were not these men apprehended? *Because of the rottenness that there is in the state of the society of these districts;* because of the sympathy which there is on the part of the great bulk of the population with those who, by these dreadful acts of vengeance, *are supposed to be the conservators of the rights of the tenant, and supposed to give him that protection which imperial legislation has denied. The first thing that ever called my attention to the condition of Ireland was the reading an account of one of these outrages. I thought of it for a moment, but the truth struck me at once; and all I have since seen confirms it. When law refuses its duty*—when government denies the right of a people—when competition is so fierce for the little land which the monopolists grant to cultivation in Ireland—when, in fact, for a bare potato, millions are scrambling, these people are driven back from law and from the usages of civilization to that which is termed the law of nature, and if not of the strongest, the law of the vindictive; and in this case the people of Ireland believe, to my certain knowledge, that it is only by these acts of vengeance, periodically committed, that they can hold in suspense the arm of the proprietor and the agent; *who in too many cases, if he dared, would exterminate them. At this moment there is a state of war in Ireland.* Don't let us disguise it from ourselves; there is a war between landlord and tenant; a war as fierce, as relentless, as though it were carried on by force of arms. There is a suspicion between landlord and tenant, which is not known between any class of people in this country; *and there is a hatred, too, which I believe under the present and past system, has been pursued in Ireland, which can never be healed or eradicated!* Of course, under a state of things like this, industry is destroyed, the rights of property are destroyed, and at this moment landlords

in Ireland of the most excellent character, and of the most just intentions, cannot make those dispositions of their property which are necessary for even the advantages of the tenants themselves in some cases, because of the system of terror which prevails through many of the counties." (quoted by author of *Free Trade in Land*, pps 306–7).

"Don't let us disguise it from ourselves, there is a war between landlord and tenant." Yes, there *is*—there has *always* been, and there will continue to be a war so long as *its sole cause*, Landlordism, exists in Ireland. Is it any wonder, then, that under such a state of society, that murder and violence should be perpetrated?

One of the means resorted to by the landlord government of Ireland to "repress" agrarian outrages, is, of itself, the greatest incentive to the commission of that class of crime, known as the mutilation of cattle, as also the destruction of property, in other ways. Under what is known as the "Whiteboy Acts" (passed in the reign of William the 4th?)—which acts it is in the power of the L[or]d. L[ieutenan]t of Ireland to impose upon any "disturbed" county—the owner or owners of any injured property or *mutilated cattle* can present their demands for compensation (to the full value of their damaged property) to the Grand Jury of the county in which the outrage has occurred, which is, by this exclusively landlord tribunal, *levied as a fine upon the whole locality in which the outrage shall have been committed.*[207] Here, in the first instance, there is a premium set upon the commission of these horrible deeds—the maiming of cows, horses, sheep, etc. by heartless unprincipled men; and secondly a manifest injustice done to the people who chance to reside within the district thus doubly injured; and whose only offence consists in living in the neighbourhood of some undetected ruffian and under the protection of an inefficient police.

It is the supremest asinine stupidity to pretend that these Whiteboy Acts operate to the *prevention* of these crimes. If not to *encourage* them, why are they allowed to be put in force? Anyone conversant with the weakness of human nature—with the unscrupulous means which avarice and criminal selfishness will employ in order to gain their ends, will easily comprehend the inducements which such regulations must hold out to desperate and unconscionable men who see in them a means of obtaining money for property which they may not be otherwise able to dispose of, or to obtain so full an equivalent for. It is simply the application to agricultural stock of the frauds and tricks that are common to the class of beings who set fire to houses or other such property after having insured the same for a large amount in one or more Insurance Societies.

It would, however, be shutting one's eyes to most disagreeable but objective facts to attempt to account for *all* their abominable outrages upon the ground of these Whiteboy Acts suggesting their perpetration for dishonest pecuniary ends; but I do assert that numbers of them—especially in times of popular excitement, are committed under the *inspiration* of these antiquated and mischievous enactments, *for political purposes.* The only remedy to which Irish landlordism ever resorts in a contest between itself and the people of Ireland—apart from the suspension of the Habeas Corpus and such like methods, is to raise a storm of prejudice in the English mind against the particular movement, party, or men which it may dread. In the accomplishment of this purpose no scruples are permitted to interfere—no act is too low to stoop to—no calumny too foul for invention in the work of preventing a calm and unprejudiced discussion of the consequences of the Irish land laws, between our people and English public opinion. At one time, we are represented as aiming at Revolution under the pretence of asking for land reform; at another we are compassing the general massacre of the "loyal subjects" of Her Majesty, in Ireland; while very lately we had become Socialists and Communists bent upon destroying society and exterminating both property and aristocracy. These and other kindred charges, born of landlord fear of English investigation into the causes of the land war, and of an implacable hatred of the people whom they rob, are usually first discussed at a "Meeting of County Magistrates"—*all landlords*—next taken up by the Grand Juries—all ditto—and then regularly commented upon by the landlord organs in Dublin, in which English public opinion is invited to consider the danger to the United Kingdom that manifests itself in this movement or agitation, and the Government is solemnly charged with every species of culpable neglect that falls short of a suspension of the Habeas Corpus Act, suppression of popular meetings and the investiture of Dublin Castle with full powers to enable it to cope with "the enemy".

Any real occurrence in Ireland which may be calculated to arouse this sleepless English prejudice to an unusual degree of ascerbity is a Godsend to the Irish landlords—it turns popular feeling from prying into their system or their conduct, places a false issue before newspaper critics and tends to earn for the country in which such occurrences take place the obloquy which should attach to the infamous land code from which alone they can spring. The mutilation of cattle is one of these lucky events for Irish landlordism. An outrage of this description would far outbalance half a dozen Land Meetings in the scale of English sympathy. Anterior causes seldom influence English popular feelings; they are the offspring of recent or present events and incline always to the side of what seems to be English interest and theoretic humanity against what, if inquired into calmly and impartially, would generally claim from the same critics the award due to the claims of manifest justice and to the dictates of humanity in its most exalted exercise. If the houghing of cattle and other kindred atrocities against our dumb and defenceless domestic animals enkindles the animosity of Englishmen against both Land Reformers and the Irish generally, why should not this most effective means of arraying English public opinion in opposition to the former and their demands for remedial legislation, be resorted to by the creatures of Irish landlords? As England would concede nothing to the settlement of a question that appeared to have its loyal and "humane" Irish subjects on one side and the disaffected and *brute-torturing* Irish on the other, what more powerful weapon could be wielded by the enemies of the latter—in defence of an otherwise doomed system—than occasional outrages that wound alike the most sensitive feelings of every humane breast and the character of the people who are represented as guilty of such crimes. I say it deliberately from my intimate knowledge of the forces that have been marshalled against each other in the Land League movement—the people strong in the justice of their demands and the mercenary instruments employed by the landlords in what was to them a desperate game—that the *majority* of the outrages perpetrated upon cattle were the work of those whose interest lay in fanning the flame of English prejudice against the Land League movement— whose policy it would be to keep alive by periodic wounding of cows, etc. the indignant feelings which any such inhuman act might have awakened in the public mind of this country. Who so well able to perform those dastardly acts with impunity as the herds and bailiffs employed to look after cattle? What earthly interest would, say, a victim of landlord injustice have in performing a deed that could entail *no* pecuniary loss upon a landlord or other owner of cattle—owing to the facility of obtaining full compensation for all such damage under the Whiteboy Act—that would inevitably impose *a fine* upon the locality—that is *a tax* upon each farmer near where the outrage would occur—that would damage the cause of the tenantry of Ireland in the estimation of public opinion; that would earn a disreputable name for the tenant farmer class, and worse than all these to any being claiming to have a heart within his breast, a deed that would inflict pain upon a poor harmless inoffensive beast?[208]

These devilish outrages will yet in my opinion be brought home to felonious and unscrupulous Irish landlordism, and the stigma which they now attach to the peasantry of Ireland will recoil with tenfold more crushing infamy upon that system that has added the torture of animals to the crimes committed against the interests, the homes, the peace, and the reputation of our country.

As for the *individual instruments* of these horrible brutalities— whether actuated by the incomprehensible motive that would prompt a *tenant farmer* to their commission, or the infamous *ruse de guerre* of landlord hangers on, or the criminal plans of a compensation-seeking owner of otherwise indisposable property, no difference of opinion would exist in Ireland and England as to the punishment which such crimes deserve. The wretch who could be capable of such monstrous barbarity places himself beyond the pale of human sympathy and merits being branded with some indelible mark of public execration that should point him out for ever as detestable and infamous.

The Whigs—according to Mrs Sullivan—are incensed because the people of Ireland have practically refused to give "a trial" to their new Land Bill.[209] This attitude of our people will also tend to shape public feeling in this country against us. It is not, however, a refusal to give Mr Gladstone's second attempt at Irish land reform a fair chance of proving itself (a success or) a failure, like his first of 1870; but a refusal to give *Landlordism another* trial after all its crimes and failures. Ireland did not ask for an improvement in the conduct of her deadly enemy, but its complete removal—the *only* remedy for her desperate social condition—and hence the want of enthusiasm for a Bill which aims at *perpetuating* (under the guidance of lawyers and an apparent reform of some of its abusive powers)—our enemy of three hundred years standing and ruin.

Irish Landlordism is like an incorrigible thief—no attempt at reformation will cure it. Its instincts are plunder and its very existence depends upon the amount of the earnings of labour which it can abstract from the industry of the farmers and the wealth of the country.

English Statesmen—and Englishmen generally—view the Irish Land Question from a standpoint of local issues, or as if the difficulties which it presents to the work of remedial legislation are referable only to the particular agitation which compelled English attention to be turned to it and calling only for efforts of statesmanship in keeping with this circumstantial consideration. Whereas Irish Reformers are constrained to consider it in connection with a train of retrospective ruin— social, economical and domestic; present poverty, discontent, and crime; with a but too certain tendency to move in "a circle of reproductive wrong," to the peace and best interests of their country, so long as any vestiges of the system shall be allowed to rear its head in Ireland. They are therefore compelled to place little value upon temporary expedients which experience has shown to be really valueless to our people, and to insist upon such a radical reform as reason, experience and commonsense indicate to be the only logical and final settlement of the Irish social difficulty, by which a warfare of selfish and conflicting interests can be permanently arrested and the natural resources of the country freed from the restrictions that have so long retarded their full development.

Instead of having grappled with this festering social cancer in a courageous and effective manner, which his previous failure to cure the evil should reasonably warrant—instead of having made an effort in the direction of a thorough eradication of the evil itself which would have won respect even did it fall short of popular expectations, Mr Gladstone has proceeded upon the lines of his former mistake and has produced another experimental measure by which landlord and tenant, instead of being legally divorced, are both turned over into the hands of the lawyers, the country invited to place all its prospects of peace and prosperity in universal litigation, while the tenant farmers are expected to see their interests "protected", their happiness insured and their security guaranteed in the existence of a land Commission or Court, composed of "conservators of ancient barbarism" and land agents! The spider inviting the fly into his parlour is about equalled in seductive disinterestedness by Mr Gladstone introducing the tenant farmers into a mixed gang of Irish lawyers and Irish Land Agents, *in order to be protected*! Unless Mr Gladstone has acted on the principle of *paritur pax bello*[210] it seems to me impossible to comprehend how the Irish tenantry are to see the end of their troubles and a security for the results of their labours in a bill which compels them to seek redress at the hands of lawyers and agents.

Even *this* much of legislation could not be given to Ireland without being spiced with the customary vindictiveness by which Irishmen are deprived of their liberty and their country flooded with troops because England has been put to the inconvenience of recognising the existence of a wrong in Ireland and the necessity of attempting to remedy it. Those whose complete vindication from the charges of their enemies is established by an enactment in the direction of the remedy which they called upon the people to demand, are nevertheless flung into prison in order to gratify the vengeance of Irish landlords and the instinctive hatred with which Irish Reformers are regarded by the governing classes of England! Yet doubtless there is increased indignation and wonder on the part of English public opinion at the still disturbed state of Ireland. England and her legal instruments in Ireland have never yet failed in showing our people a way in which to violate English law and English precept and it appears ridiculously unreasonable to find fault with us for improving upon the teaching and practice of our alien rulers.

COPY OF LETTER IN REPLY TO
THAT OF AUNT ELLEN'S

IF I OBTAIN *PERMISSION* TO WRITE IT

Dear Aunt Ellen[211]

Your very kind letter of 13th April last has but come to hand within the past few days, owing to its having been addressed to Mr Sullivan[212] and reaching its first destination while that gentleman was lying dangerously ill. It became mislaid afterwards, and yet amidst all her troubles and anxieties my kind and good friend Mrs Sullivan has searched it out, and here I am enjoying the privilege of writing you a reply.

Now I beg leave to take "epistolatary exception" to the imputation implied in your sympathetic concern about my "not being strong *or hearty*." Very strong I may not be, but I was never before accused of bearing such a resemblance to the Knight of the Sorrowful Countenance[213] as you credit me with possessing. Doubtless in my hurried passage through Washington eighteen months ago,[214] I may have worn, what in Ireland is called a "Wirrasthru" expression of face; but a heavy domestic loss a few weeks previous,[215] and a crowd of other cares—and *not* a tendency to sad or melancholy disposition—must be credited for such an unfortunate appearance.

But even if the external world and the trials and strifes that are incidental to one's life therein, produce habitual dejection of spirits in some individuals it does not follow that they must therefore cling to an existence under circumstances the reverse to an inducement of such unenviable companionship. Judged by the standard of cause and effect there is no place in the economy of imprisonment for troubled heart or care-worn brow. The agencies that beget such drawbacks to the enjoyment of life are found where a thousand and one objects and pursuits appeal to the necessities and aspirations of our ever craving, restless, selfish nature; and not under a condition of mental idleness and physical repose where all yearning, wishes and desires are comprised in and reduced to *one single want.*

The absence, then, of the disturbing influences of life that belong to your outside world must conduce to a state of negative happiness, if not to actual, content here, and would conspire to make this an existence suitable to an Epicurean philosopher,[216] were it not that an excess of quiet and too much of "nothing to care for", engendered more selfish indulgence in the luxury of idleness than is good for the higher attributes of our being. Unalloyed pleasure consists chiefly in the satisfaction of heart resulting from efforts to make others happy, and the purest delight of life is curtailed in proportion to the circumscribed action of our affections in seeking the complement of their own felicity by means of "something attempted something done" towards lessening the pain and misery that surrounds us. In this respect I am somewhat unfortunately situated and to this extent I am "not hearty"; but I am not altogether bereft of the gratification arising from scenes of reflected happiness. You will be surprised to learn that I have got a very large family to look after and one that commands a deal of my otherwise unoccupied attention. Perhaps you don't like sparrows? Few people do, but I am not [*sic*] among the few, I am happy to say, and there are few birds of which I am so fond as the self sufficient saucy little "street arab" of the feathered world. I am on the most intimate terms of friendship with about one hundred of the happiest, noisiest, most playful and most love-making sparrows that were ever yoked to the car of the lovely Aphrodite.[217] No wonder indeed that Jove's favourite daughter should have made them her favourite bird. Never have I witnessed such scenes of love-making successful wooing and conjugal felicity as fall beneath my observation almost every day. I have made two discoveries of sparrow life that exercise my curiosity very much, one of which fortunately for the limited amount of happiness in your big world has no parallel therein, while unfortunately for its better conduct and government, neither has the other. In my sparrow society there are at least two of the male to one of the superior sex, while, as if in the exercise of this superiority, Madame Sparrow is in the habit of soundly thrashing her husband or lover occasionally, but whether as proof of her affection or as merited chastisement for flirtation with the better halves of others, I am as yet unable to determine. This unfortunate disproportion of the sexes very naturally leads to a great deal of amorous contention as well as to jealousies and pitched battles. I find however that a chosen crumb given to a chastised husband or defeated and disconsolate lover restores the ruffled plumage of the one and appears to heal the wounded affections of the other. (What a pity it is that similar troubles and heart aches are not as easily cured among men!). Thus in the midst of this lively society where Nature seems to have provided everything essential to the enjoyment of unclouded happiness (by sparrows) most of my time is spent, and I assure you most truly that there is no occasion for feeling of "solitary" ennui or room for "not being hearty". I am very grateful to Mary Ellen[218] for her prayers on my behalf and thankful to all my friends in Washington for thinking of me sometimes in their leisure moments. You will confer another favour upon me by writing to my sister[219] (Main St, Manayunk, Philadelphia) to the effect that I have changed my mind since having written to her about coming to see me this year. I will consider the matter again next year. I am very much grieved at the news which she communicated about the serious illness of my cousin Joe.[220] The remedy which she hints at as likely to be tried by the doctors would have cost me my life if I sanctioned its application when suffering from a similar complaint, and I am of decided opinion that the *certain effect* of such a remedy *if applied* to Joe will be *death*. Please say this to my sister and that I am very anxious to help him pecuniarily if in any way wanting such assistance. I am very thankful for your kind offer of books, but permission would not be granted to you to send or me to receive them. I am fairly well off in that important item of prison life, and on the whole am as well, as contented and as "hearty," as any other mortal could well be under the circumstances while in addition I am

Your affectionate nephew

Michael Davitt

. . . [Secret Societies John Henry Foley R.A., William Lloyd Garrison, miscellaneous poems] . . .

RANDOM THOUGHTS ON
THE IRISH LAND WAR

Abolishing landlordism—and with it Rent—and substituting a Land Tax upon all land values, say to the extent of 10 per cent estimated annual produce (about *half* of what is now paid to the landlords in rent) would save the farmers half the amount which they are now taxed by a favoured class, and supply all that would be needed to carry on the administration of Irish civil affairs. It would do more. Ten per cent of the annual agricultural wealth of Ireland would be sufficient to meet not only the charge of civil government, but those for which all taxes, Poor's[221] and other local rates are now levied upon farming and non-farming classes alike. Thus the Nationalisation of the Land would be a direct gain to the non-agricultural and agricultural classes alike. All very well theoretically but *how* could this be accomplished? Put down £7,000,000 as representing the annual revenue now contributed to the English exchequer by the people of Ireland.[222] Add to this 10 per cent of the annual agricultural produce of the country as a land tax—which would amount to say, £7,000,000 more[223]—in all £14,000,000 per an[num]. Out of this sum allow £5,000,000 for the administration of civil affairs: and £2,500,000 more for purposes for which poor rates and county cess are now levied, and there would be a balance of £6,500,000 left each year with which to pay off the debt to be incurred in the compensation of the landlords. How would you compensate them with this amount? I start with the proposition that in accordance with strict justice they should not obtain their fares from Kingstown to Hollyhead; but as *conventional* justice or the claims recognised as belonging to prescriptive right, is that which governments only deal in, the question of compensation to Irish landlords must be considered on that ground—if ever a final settlement of the land question is to be satisfactorily arrived at. Well, according to even conventional or political justice those who have given the present value to the land of Ireland are surely entitled to a share of the market value of such land as it now is—in other words the farmer's property in the land which he alone has improved by his labour and capital should be equal to that of the "sleeping partner", the landlord. Leaving this property to the farmer (whom nobody wants to disturb) we should only have to deal with the landlord's share. To purchase off the landlord's interest to the extent of seven millions annually, would require, at the rate of 20 years purchase, the sum of £140,000,000. This sum I would propose to raise by public loan at 3 per cent per annum—interest and principal to be chargeable to the Imperial Revenue now collected in Ireland—the land tax of 10 per cent upon all land values supplying the expenditure now to be met by this revenue. Thus An. Revenue £7,000,000. Interest upon £140,000,000 @ 3 per cent £4,200,000, leaving annual balance of £2,800,000 for sinking fund with which to clear off the principal of debt. This is would do in about 50 years. After the liquidation of the debt *all taxes and rents* now levied for civil and local government could be abolished and everything allowed to be duty free, as the tax upon land values or rather upon the nation's property— the land—would produce all that would be required to carry on the government of the country as well as what would meet the charges for maintaining the poor and keeping the country "in repair". What a change from the present state of the country to one by which the farmer would be perfectly secure while only paying half what he is now robbed of while *all* classes would be free from taxes, duties and rates, now imposed.

. . . [Religions of the Japanese; short list of "Works I must read'; Estimated Annual Expenditure of Ireland; Arguments in Support of Nationalisation of Land; Centenary of the Voluntary Convention in Dungannon; John Ruskin's opinion of Irish character; letter to Mr Hugh King[224]] . . .

HOW IRELAND WAS ROBBED
OF HER PARLIAMENT

There is probably no event in the history of England's rule in
Ireland to the discussion of which Englishmen have so decided
a repugnance as to that of the Act of Union: yet there is no
other event in the dark and sanguinary record of that rule,
the study of which would throw more light upon subsequent
discontent towards the power and law of England, on the part
of the Irish people, if we except the confiscation of the land
and the establishment of the fatal system of landlordism.
Although Nations cannot be said to experience any sense of
shame at the remembrance of their dishonourable actions, as
is the case with individuals, there is, still, a feeling akin to
shame experienced by their popular minds which causes them
to avoid, as much as possible, all allusion to such actions, and
to consider it as an affront when they are dwelt upon by
unfriendly or even impartial criticism. As the people of Ireland,
however, are not remarkable for the charity of silence upon
the crimes or wrongs that have been perpetrated against their
country by England, the world has not been kept in ignorance
of the infamous manner in which their right to self government was stolen by English statesmanship eighty and two
years ago; and Englishmen, during this commemorative year
of Irish legislative independence, will have to listen to and read
the oft-told story of one of the most discreditable transactions
in civilized history. Where indubitable facts are more than
abundantly sufficient to make out a case against an adversary,
the least use there is made of one-sided comment or opinion,

the better for the cause at stake as well as for the conclusion
that is desired to be drawn in its favour. The facts that can be
gathered from the Castlereagh[225] and Cornwallis[226] papers,
regarding the means by which the Act of Union was carried
in the Irish House of Commons, and the atrocious manner in
which the people of Ireland were butchered by English soldiery
in the carrying out of martial law part of the general plan by
which Ireland and Gt. Britain were henceforth to be united,
would damn to everlasting infamy the most unconscionable
and sanguinary despotism that has ever trampled in riotous
ferocity upon liberty, justice and humanity. It would, in my
humble judgement, be well-nigh impossible for any fair
minded Englishman to read the story of fraud and treachery,
of terrorism and blood which these *published* papers (official
correspondence)[227] disclose, and ever after find fault with or
condemn those Irishmen who, as inheritors of that liberty the
right to which their country has never forfeited, and of those
wrongs by which its political servitude and social misery were
consummated, seek, by every means that an honourable cause
will justify, to regain, for themselves and their fatherland, the
priceless right of self-government—of legislative separation
from England. It is the duty of Irishmen, therefore, to lay these
facts bare to the scrutiny of English opinion, as often as possible;
in order that the now almost universally educated "Britisher"
may understand certain phases of Irish political discontent,
which are both explained and justified when deducted from
those acts of English statesmanship to which they are politically and historically referable. Ere reproducing a resumé of
historic data connected with this transaction, it will be well to
glance at and answer a few of the argumentative "extenuating
circumstances" which English apologists for every act of British
statesmanship might advance in justification of Pitt's plan of
the Union[228] and the actions of the tools by which it was successfully carried out. I[st] it will be maintained that the existence
of an Irish parliament would always be a source of weakness
to the British Empire as it would remain a standing incentive to
Irishmen to effect the complete political separation of Ireland

therefrom, whenever a suitable opportunity might present itself.
Under certain contingencies, such as unjust and unwarranted
interference on the part of the English legislature, for instance,
a desire for actual independence would be both rational and
natural on the part of Ireland; but then England would be
affording the justification for a step which no people could be
blamed for taking if compelled in self-defence to its adoption.
No such unjust actions of the English parliament offering the
necessary inducement to the alternative of complete separation,
we are left to judge what an Irish parliament would be likely
to do ordinarily from the conduct which it pursued when, previous to the accomplishment of its independence from that of
England, it could have wielded an army of 60,000 men to
whatever purpose it pleased; or after being flushed with the
victory of Grattan and the Volunteers,[229] it stood almost in the
position of a dictator to the government that had openly
confessed its inability to defend Ireland. Surely if ever a subject
nationality should dream of throwing off the yoke of political
servitude imposed upon it, it would be while experiencing the
plenitude of misery and wrong resulting from its subject
condition, and when circumstances should so conspire as to
leave its political masters without an army to support their
right of supremacy, while at the same time the subject people
would be in possession of one that could so easily accomplish
their final liberation as ever did a conquering force possess
itself of an abandoned or defenceless city. Yet, mark the outcome to an exactly similar situation to this in Ireland a century
ago. An invasion or attack was talked of as possible from
England's enemies. The English Government, when applied to
for troops with which to meet the invaders should they touch
on Irish soil, replied, that it had no troops to spare for such
purpose, and that Ireland should depend upon its own
resources for a defence of its shores. What was the conduct of
the Irish parliament in face of such an emergency, and while
in the act of agitating for the restoration of its legislative
independence? And what the action of the people of Ireland,
ground to the very dust under the penal laws—scarcely

recognised by English law—that is the Celtic portion or three-fourths of the population—as anything better than dogs to be shot down or trampled upon as the "mere Irish"?

"Then arose" says Mr Lecky,[230] speaking of this period, "one of those movements of enthusiasm that occur two or three times in the history of a nation. The cry to arms passed through the land and was speedily responded to by all parties and by all creeds. Beginning among the Protestants of the north, the movement spread, though in a less degree, to other parts of the island, and the war of religions and of castes that had long divided the people vanished like a dream. Though the population of Ireland was little more than half of what it is at present, 60,000 men soon assembled, disciplined and appointed as a regular army, fired by the strongest enthusiasm and moving as a single man: they arose to defend their country alike from the invasion of a foreign army and the encroachment of an alien legislature. Faithful to the connection between the two countries, they determined that that connection should rest upon mutual respect and upon essential equality."[231] Instead of seeking that complete separation (which could have been as easily accomplished at that time as was the repeal of Poyning's law[232]) the dread of which constitutes the chief English argument against the existence of an Irish parliament, the then parliament and people of Ireland concerned themselves *first* with the defence of the King of England's authority against a threatened French attack,[233] and *then* demanded from England the repeal of an obnoxious act that had for some two hundred years rendered all Irish legislation dependent upon the sanction of the English parliament.[234] Having obtained the latter concession, and, failing to win further necessary reforms for their country without coming into open conflict with England's authority in Ireland, the Volunteers were dissolved and the Irish people fell back into their normal state of passive expectancy! There is not on historic record an example of such loyalty from an infamously governed people to a defenceless dominant power that had for centuries exhausted every means known to a remorseless policy of extermination to stamp out both the nationality and faith of a conquered people, as that shown by Ireland when under the sway of Grattan, Charlemont[235] and the Volunteers. This very example, in my humble opinion, shows the leaders of that period to have been very little in patriotic stature—simply so many naturalized Englishmen in Ireland playing the part of Anglo-Irish nationalists, and the people who thus flew to arms to defend the yoke that had been placed upon their necks from a threatened severance by a friendly power, as a nation of poltroons— particularly for having laid down those arms when once in possession of the means by which every right could have been honourably and safely won: And I am convinced that this would be the opinion of every candid-minded Englishman that would read the history of that period along with that of the manner in which the Irish people had been treated by England during the previous three hundred years. Let us suppose for instance that England had occupied towards, say France, a similar dependent position to that which Ireland occupied towards her a hundred years ago and that France should have found herself compelled to withdraw all her troops from this country, and constrained to tell the English people that they should depend upon themselves in the task of guarding their shores from any other invading power: Is there an Englishman living who would not say that both national honour and "British Interests" would have been *betrayed* if their countrymen could have acted towards the supremacy of France under such circumstances as ours did towards that of Gt. Britain under precisely similar ones?

The flag of France would have been hauled down from the Tower of London within a week after such an admission of weakness from the power that would have planted it there over the liberties of Englishmen, and the first foeman that would be hurled from the shores of England would be him who had first subjected her people to his sway. As no such opportunity as that which occurred during the existence of the Volunteers, is likely ever to present itself to Ireland again, the only argument that can fairly be drawn from the then strained relationship between England and the Irish parliament, is altogether opposed to the standing English objection against a repeal of the Union. An Irish parliament with the right of framing such laws as are needed for the social progress and material interests of the Irish people, and without the inclination or the privilege of meddling in the concerns of that which directs the affairs of Gt. Britain, would, instead of being a source of weakness or danger to the latter, be, on the contrary, a security against that dismemberment which is now and always must be dreaded from the discontent and disaffection engendered in the minds of so many Irishmen from the Act of Union and other English enactments of misrule which have inflicted so many injurious consequences upon the welfare of their country. A concession of the right of self-government similar to that which Ireland enjoyed a hundred years ago adapted to the requirements of a more liberal and enlightened age would simply settle the Anglo-Irish Question for good and put an end to Irish risings and English coercion acts for the future; while it would, at the same time, relieve the English House of Commons from that obstruction which arises there from the neglect and mismanagement of Ireland's business by an Assembly that will neither trouble itself with their proper consideration or permit our Representatives to make it their sole duty to do so. On the other hand a persistency on the part of England in maintaining the system of rule which she has imposed upon us in lieu of that which obtained under the parliament which she suppressed—a system that has already involved Ireland in three attempts at insurrection and necessitated the passage of over *fifty* coercion acts in eighty years for her disaffected people—must inevitably continue to breed the same discontent and call forth the same repressive measures that even at this present moment disturb the peace and inflict injury upon the country, while compelling England to the adoption of a policy that can only find a parallel in countries ruled by despotic governments.

2nd: It may be likewise pleaded in behalf of the way in which Pitt's plan of the Union was made to succeed that, the measure, having been determined upon by the English government as a necessary step to the safety of the Empire, it was to be carried out in whatever manner might best meet the difficulties which surrounded the operation, the wishes of the Irish people and the morality of the means to be employed in depriving them of their parliament being subordinate considerations to the principal object in view.

Such an apology for the tactics employed by Castlereagh is I believe implied in Mr Froude's views upon the carrying of the Act of Union;[236] but an abler and far more impartial critic, Mr Lecky, has passed a juster sentence upon Pitt and Castlereagh's *modus operandi*; where he says "The Union was emphatically one of that class of measures in which the scope of statesmanship lies not in the conception but in the execution. Had Pitt carried it without offending the National sentiment—had he enabled the majority of the Irish people to look back on it with affection or with pride—had he made it the means of allaying discontent or promoting loyalty—he would indeed have achieved a feat of consummate statesmanship. But in all these respects he utterly failed. There was, it is true, no small amount of dexterity of a somewhat vulpine order displayed in carrying the bill; but no measure ever showed less of that enlightened and farseeing statesmanship which respects the prejudices and conciliates the affections of a nation, and thus eradicates the seeds of disaffection and discontent. The manner in which it was carried out was not only morally scandalous: it also entirely vitiated it as a work of statesmanship."[237] It was in fact one of those *coûte que coûte*[238] projects in which after-consequences were as little considered as the morality of the means by which it was to be carried out; and was in thorough keeping with the unprincipled spirit that has always characterized the action of Englishmen when "British Interests" are to be advanced by trampling upon the rights and liberties of nations or states from whom a formidable resistance is not to be expected. If this mode of dealing with the obstacles that have stood in the way of the extension of the British Empire has its advantages in rapidity of conquest and the pushing of English trade interests, it has also its "bad bargain" side as well. Englishmen conquer but they seldom or ever conciliate a subjugated civilized nationality. Their selfish, grasping, instincts in all dealings with those whom they force beneath their rule, are but the continuance of the unscrupulous acts and artifices by which they have become the masters of the people or country which are deemed to be their legitimate prey, and hence arises the circumstance that all England's dependent subjects from India to Ireland are ever more or less disaffected and keep her in consequence in a state of dread at the possibility of separation.

Pitt was not the first English statesman who looked with a jealous eye upon the existence of an Irish parliament. The ease with which the Scotch submitted to have their nationality merged in that of England and allowed their parliament to be abolished must have encouraged the various after governments of England to plot the destruction of that of Ireland also. In 1759 such a project was mooted in England, but it created such excitement in Ireland especially in Dublin, that it was abandoned for the time. Lucas the intrepid champion of Ireland's nationality—the link between Swift and Flood—roused the citizens of Dublin by his pamphlets and harangues against the obnoxious project: and to such an extent did the excitement provoke the Protestants of Dublin that a mob forceably [*sic*] entered the House of Lords where, to show their contempt for that assembly of hereditary Irish traitors, they seated an old woman upon the throne.[239] From this period until 1782—from Lucas to the days of Flood and Grattan, rather—the contests which England waged with France and America favoured the cause of the Irish parliament so much that its independence was achieved, and took it out of the power of the former to carry out the policy that had united the Scotch with the English legislature. The triumph of the Volunteers, the parading of so many armed men in Ireland and the general enthusiasm manifested by the entire people at the victory which had been gained over England, together with the part which the expatriated Irish had played in the war of

American independence, and the avowed sympathy of the Irish parliament and people with the revolted Colonists, must have aroused all the latent prejudice of English nature against Ireland, and have caused English King and English statesman to take up again the postponed project of Union, with the double view of abolishing for good a legislature which *might* become a danger to the political connection of the two countries, and of humbling a people that had profited by an English difficulty to win a concession repugnant to the pride and feelings of the people of England.[240] Two events which occurred in 1784 and 1788 respectively by placing the two parliaments in direct opposition to each other upon questions which Pitt was most anxious should be treated with unanimity, further incensed that statesman against the Irish Commons and strengthened his resolve to effect its destruction. The attempt which was made to induce the Irish parliament to sanction a commercial arrangement between England and Ireland by which the latter would be compelled to contribute a quota for the protection of the general commerce of both countries at the discretion of the English Legislature, was virtually defeated by the action of Grattan and his party after the measure was returned from Westminster with additional propositions by Pitt, tending to still place the Irish parliament in a position of subserviency towards that of England. The measure of his wrath at the attitude of uncompromising independence of the Irish Commons was finally reached, when the Regency question came up for discussion in both Legislatures during the year 1788. The English parliament adopted Pitt's proposal of constituting the prince of Wales (afterwards the "virtuous" George IV) Regent with certain restricted powers; but the Irish House ignored both Pitt and the action of the English Commons altogether, and Grattan's proposal that the prince should be invested with full regal powers was carried in the Irish parliament.[241] These events, together with the after-recovery of the King, from his temporary insanity fixed both Pitt and his master's determination on the work of abolishing what they had failed to bend to imperial policy and projects; and from this to the consummation of the design twelve years afterwards, the history of English government in Ireland is but a revolting record of unveiled corruption in the maturing of its plan of infamy, and of systematic and inhuman goading of the people to desperation in order to produce an excusatory plea for carrying that plan to the accomplishment of the Union. Every attempt at a reform of the Irish representation, every effort made to pass such measures as the then state of the country demanded, were alike strenuously resisted by the Government. Side by side with this policy was pursued a kindred one towards the people at large. The Demon of Religious Strife was unchained in the north,[242] and sanguinary contests between armed protestants and their (by-law) unarmed Catholic adversaries, filled that part of Ireland with crime and bloodshed , while engendering a feeling of mutual animosity among rival sects which unhappily has been transmitted to our own times. In the south the rapacity of the "Tithe Mongers"[243] goaded the people to violent resistance against the monstrous law which compelled a Catholic to contribute from his scanty earnings to the support of a Church to which he did not belong. Repeated efforts were made by Grattan, during these disturbances, to obtain some relief for the persecuted peasantry in the matter of tithes—but to no avail. In 1788 he drew a deplorable picture of the condition to which the agricultural classes were reduced from a variety of causes, and declared the tithe exactions to be "an odious contest between poverty and luxury—between the struggles of a pauper and the luxury of a priest."[244] He asserted the Whiteboy to be the least of the peasant's foes and charged "the precept of the Gospel, and the example of the Apostles" with being the great enemy of the toiler's home and happiness. To such an extent had the corrupting policy of the Government made itself felt in the Irish Commons, but six years after its emancipation from subserviency to that of England, and so fanatically opposed to all proposals tending to some mitigation of the wrongs suffered by the Catholics, were the members of that House, that Grattan's measure was rejected by a vote of 121 to 49.[245]

Along with the rapacious acts of the "successors of the Apostles"—"Harpies," observes a writer of that period, "who squeezed out the very vitals of the people, and by process, citation, and sequestration, dragged from them the little which the landlords had left them,"[246] the major curse of Ireland— that social rhinderpest that has desolated our land and decimated our people in acts of ceaseless, sleepless, plunder and infamy during three centuries—landlordism, rioting in the exercise of legal robbery, added new infamies to its already intolerable outrages, as if to swell the measure of its victims' wrongs to a degree of maddening intensity that should drive them to frenzy and despair. The landlords throughout most of the south of Ireland, had, some years previous to the outbreak of the tithe war,[247] raised their rents far above the value of the land, on the pretense of allowing their tenants certain rights of commonage for pasture purposes, a make-believe compensation for the extra rent levied upon them. These pasture-commonages were subsequently fenced in by the landlords thus making it next to impossible for the tenantry to subsist; and the law of course sanctioned the proceedings in its courts and defended such "property" by its penalties and soldiers! It was in connection with this species of legal fraud and ruffianism that the "Whiteboy outrages,"[248] as they were termed, first made their appearance in the agrarian strife of our country. The people, roused to fury by this dastardly action of the landlords, assembled by night and demolished the fences wherever erected. These "outrages" could not of course be tolerated. They were so many attacks upon "law and order" and the unhappy "Whiteboy" who was caught in their perpetration, or peasant who was suspected of such "crimes" against "the majesty of the law," were treated to a taste of the gallows. The heart literally sickens in dwelling upon the crimes and murders that were committed in the name of law during this period, in the interest of the hell-born system which still rears its monster-head in Ireland, almost as prolific of misery, outrage and murder as ever. It almost weakens one's faith in the existence of such a thing as Divine Justice taking any cognisance

of the transactions of human society when we see "Ministers
of God" exhibiting the rapacity of a licensed banditti in the
name of religion and with impunity; when we see "God's poor"
as the robbed and plundered are very piously termed; subject
to every wrong which it is in the power of an unscrupulous
class to inflict; while over all this outrageous contravention of
Divine precept and callous indifference to human suffering,
we see "the powers that be" towering in the plenitude of
unbridled infamy as a protection to those who outrage every
principle of justice in defiance of every precept of Christian
morality; and as a scourge only to those who claimed but the
right to live where their Creator had placed them in the peaceful enjoyment of the food which their sweat and labour brought
forth from the soil. In the conflicts which the people of Ireland
have had to sustain from the period of Adrian's Bull[249] down to
the present, we see a triumphant vindication of almost *every wrong*
that is capable of being arrayed against those universal rights
that both religion and the generally accepted code of human
morals guarantee to a Christian and civilized people, inhabiting
its own soil, and guilty of no crime against any other nation
in the world: Religion (from the invasion to the Reformation
made more or less subservient to the greed and criminal
appetites of the invaders—and from thence, during the penal
laws, to within the last generation, in the attitude of a Divinely
Missioned plunderer and exterminator) appears in Ireland in
the garb of an enemy coming to violate almost every cannon
of the Decalogue,[250] instead of bringing that promise of peace
and good will which the Saviour intended to be the herald of
Christianity, event to the Gentiles. The "Nobility,"—"Aristocracy", "Upper Classes,"—or by whatever other jargon of
names are designated the licensed idlers of Society, whose
mission or social functions in other lands show, as a rule, something more "noble" than the mere plunder of industry, as well
as some other return for its wealth to the people from whom
it is obtained, than persistent efforts to retain them in social
and political servitude—assumes in Ireland the character of the
most rapacious and tyrannical caste that ever scourged an

Eastern people. Not a single feature of the Irish Aristocracy, can, when even viewed from the most unprejudiced standpoint, be made to exhibit one redeeming virtue, morally, socially, politically or nationally as a class possessed of almost every acre of land in the country and thus monopolizing all its wealth, wielding all its civil power, and invested with more governmental privilege than any section of a country's population ever obtained from a ruling power. They abstract from twelve to fifteen millions a year from the soil and the labour of Ireland, and in return expend scarcely a fraction upon the one, while they treat the other as if it were but a feudal service due from a serf to his legal lord and owner. The country which supplies them with this enormous wealth, they have ever slandered and betrayed, and would, tomorrow, if 'twere possible, wipe out its very name and efface its nationality as willingly as if it were a land from which they reaped nothing whatever in the way of income, and its inhabitants but a people who were a tax upon their patience and generosity. They have systematically ground the industrial classes to a state of almost abject mendicancy and then banished them in hundreds of thousands from their homes and country: and yet when but a decimated population remains from a ceaseless policy of eviction and extermination, they still cry out "over populated" and embrace with rapture every scheme of emigration which promises to remove the Celtic race from its native plains and mountains. The tenantry who supply them with enormous incomes they reduce to semi-pauperism and compel to herd in hovels which are a disgrace to civilized society, and then reproach and stigmatise them before the world as a people whom nothing will redeem from misery and discontent, and whom it is hopeless to endeavour to extricate from habits of squalor and unthrift. The "nobility" of Ireland in word, is, in religion fanatical; in morals dissolute; in intellect contemptible; in politics the deadly enemy of the national cause and name; in the social economy of the land, an unmitigated curse; to the material progress of the country an impassible [*sic*] barrier; to the intellectual and moral improvement of the people indifferent or hostile. In the defence of what they claim as their own they are cowardly; in the administration of the law, unblushingly partial and unjust; while, as the chief factor in the government of Ireland, they are the constant advocates of despotic and repressive measures; and as such, and in conjunction with their whole anti-Irish, grasping, inhuman and ruinous conduct in every sphere of social action and political "emergency" they constitute the standing incentive to national discontent, and the primary cause of the people's contemptuous disregard of the law that is entrusted to their merciless and polluted hands. Of the third great power the Ruling Authority that has combated, during the same period, against every interest and almost every right of the Irish people, it may be said to have been but the centralised embodiment of the other two, without a single redeeming feature that could snatch its name of government (even for a brief space of time) from the stigma of a sanguinary and unmitigated tyranny. Against these three great powers which should be the protection of the people and the safeguard of their interests, the people of Ireland—that is the Celtic or four-fifths, part of the population—have had to be content for their very existence—to defend their lives and homes from a scarcely ever-ceasing series of merciless persecutions and proscriptions on the part of Government, Aristocracy, and Religion, from the invasion down to the time of the Volunteer Movement of 1782. No sooner had this ephemeral exhibition of martial patriotism dissolved into meaningless holiday reviews and the government had recovered from the fright under the influence of which it had conceded the Irish demand for Legislative Independence, than the three great scourging powers, whose career of extermination had been suspended somewhat during the reign of patriotism under Grattan and the Volunteers, recommenced the old policy of systematic exasperation which was the customary preliminary to wholesale hangings, imprisonments and expatriations. From 1785 until the outbreak of the Insurrection of 1798—excepting the brief period, in 1795, during which Earl Fitzwilliam was Lord Lieutenant[251]—everything which Castle rule, landlord oppression and the rapacity of the Tithe Mongers, could perpetrate upon the unfortunate peasantry seems to have been resorted to. Under such circumstances and with the example of the American Colonists before them, and the course of events in France such as to lend a hope of liberty from an unbearable yoke, is it any wonder that the terrible weapon of Revolution should have presented a tempting inducement to a people suffering such unparalleled wrongs? The English and Irish settlers, in what had been British colonies, invoked the arbitrament of revolution and finally threw off, by its aid, the supremacy of England, because the latter had presumed to tax them without their being allowed the right of representation in the Imperial parliament. A comparison between the grievances which drove the colonists to the assertion of their complete independence, and the innumerable wrongs under which the people of Ireland groaned during the prevalence of the penal laws, and particularly at the time when the revolutionary movement which exploded in '98 was maturing, would be simply absurd; as scarcely any possible exaggeration of the conduct of the English government towards its trans-Atlantic subjects in the matters of Stamps and tea,[252] could, in point of despotic acts or monstrous injustice, equal one-fiftieth of the provocation given to our unfortunate people by the same ruling authority. The same might be said in reference to the causes which led to the English Revolution that overthrew the dynasty of the Stewarts [*sic*], if it were necessary to seek for further examples to show how readily a nation will adopt the *dernier resort*[253] of peoples, when tyranny becomes unbearable and Freedom may be won by effecting its overthrow. The difference between the action of the English people under Cromwell and Hampden, that of the Colonists under the father of American liberty, and that which was resolved upon by Fitzgerald[254] and Wolfe Tone,[255] is, morally speaking, nil; but an *essential* difference is of course drawn in political morality, because the latter led to failure, while the two former achieved the glorious ends for which they were undertaken. Hence it is that history has consecrated certain English and American

names to be forever invoked in the cause of Freedom and
Mankind, while it—or rather *English* history—condemns the
memory of the Irish patriots of 1798 as "rebels," or speaks of
them, with reluctant charity, as men who loved their country
"not wisely but too well". It is not my purpose, in this short
lecture however to trace the history of the event, which, from
the sacrifices it called forth, from the gallant souls who freely
offered their lives for liberty and fatherland, will ever remain
in endearing memory in the national heart of Ireland; but
rather to bring forth once more from historic record some of
the testimony given by those who carried the Bill of Union,
as to the means by which the infamous transaction was
accomplished. The plan upon which Pitt and his chosen Irish
instruments relied for the carrying out of the Imperial scheme,
was a three-fold one; and as unprincipled and immoral in its
conception as were the gang of scoundrels who undertook to
carry it into execution, unscrupulous and inhuman in the
employment of means to so nefarious an end. To goad the
people into desperation by unheard of cruelties in order that
a pretext might be given, in putting down insurrection, to wipe
out the insult of 1782[256] and wreak vengeance upon the Celtic
race for refusing to efface itself into a willing attitude of abject
slavery; to fool and cajole the leaders of the Catholics with
promises of Emancipation on condition of their remaining
passive spectators of the drama which was to end in the destruction of their country's autonomy;[257] and to bribe all those
who could be corrupted among the Irish Commons, with money
and promises of peerages. Such was the plan which Castlereagh
undertook to carry out in furtherance of Pitt's scheme of
crushing Irish liberty, and such was the state of political morality
in the landlord and ascendancy parliament of Ireland, that the
men who achieved its independence from that of England
eighteen years previously, were now found ready and willing
to barter the very parliament itself as so much profitable mer-
chandise, excepting from this stigma, of course, the incorruptible
minority, who, with Grattan, nobly spurned the bribes which
were being offered and contended to the last true to national

liberty in resolute and unflinching opposition to the proposal of Union.[258] The abortive rebellion of '98 fomented in order to be crushed out by the employment of every species of slaughter known to a ferocious soldiery, there remained, after deluging the country with the blood of tens of thousands of its people and consigning thousands more to the mercies of martial law and the torture which was resorted to after the insurrection was quelled, the civil portion of the Pitt-Castlereagh plan to be carried out in order to secure the success of the Union scheme. If English vengeance was fortunate in selecting Carhampton,[259] Lake[260] and Cornwallis[261] as its chief instruments in the butchery of the insurgents and the outraging of Irish homes and virtue, Pitt was doubly so in being able to entrust the general superintendence of his scheme to the hands of Fitzgibbon[262] and Castlereagh. Never was an English Minister, bent upon the execution of a great but infamous project, more happy in the choice of instruments to effect its execution. Until the time of Pitt the important posts of Lord Chancellor and Secretary of State for Ireland were conferred upon Englishmen; but that far-seeing statesman had the sagacity to discern that in the carrying out of an anti-national scheme, like that which he had planned for Ireland's humiliation, no hands would be so willing or effective in the work as those that would be alike thoroughly familiar with Irish character and the state of Irish parties, while being actuated, in addition, with that deep and quenchless hatred towards an abandoned cause or forfeited principles, which constitute the character of renegades.

The energy and enthusiasm displayed by these traitors to once-professed national and popular principles, in the work of carrying out the English minister's purpose against their country's rights and liberties, would put to shame the most devoted attachment to England's supremacy and interests ever exhibited in Ireland by former English occupants of their respective offices. In politics as in religion the renegade is generally the most implacable of foes; hence it is that the atrocities committed under the rule of Fitzgibbon, Castlereagh and Carhampton surpass in pitiless fiendishness and horror even those which marked the footsteps of that Servant of the Lord's, Oliver, during his pious butcheries of those of the people of Ireland who disputed his right to trample upon them, in the name of the Parliament of England.[263] Every possible scheme of blood, intimidation, bribery or duplicity by which the cause of Union might be advanced was as coolly and unconscionably carried out, as if to sanction wholesale murder and rapine were a religious duty with Fitzgibbon, and the employment of every disreputable means known to political knavery were but a pastime to Castlereagh. No other two men alive could have carried the Union measure. "All that could be accomplished by gold or by iron, by bribes or by threats, or by promises," relates the younger Grattan, "was set in motion; every effort strained to bring round those who were disinclined, to seduce those who were hostile but necessitous, to terrify the timid, and bear down the fearless and those who had at heart the interest and independence of their country. The doors of the Treasury were opened and a deluge of corruption covered the land. The bench of bishops, the bench of judges, the bar, the revenue, the army, the navy, civil offices, military and naval establishments; places, pensions and titles, were defiled and prostituted for the purpose of carrying the great government object—this ill-omened Union."[264] Aye! Truly ill-omened has it proved, indeed. Born of the foulest agencies of political corruption and injustice—treachery and fraud—and written as it were in the blood of thousands of slaughtered Irishmen, how could it possibly become otherwise than an ill-omened measure for Ireland, or ultimately prove otherwise for the country in whose behalf it was carried? "Successful crime alone is justified"—but only when the crime is *completely* successful either in the recognition by the victim of the hopelessness of endeavouring to subvert its decree, or in his political annihilation by the monster criminal. Neither of these events are likely to happen to Ireland while the record of how the union was effected can be read, and its lesson studied by the light of the past eighty-two years' experience. The attitude of the Catholic leaders, pending the passage of the Act, was of vital import to the success or failure of the measure; and the task of cajoling them into the assumption of a neutral if not a friendly part toward the Government scheme with underhand assurances of Emancipation being granted as a reward of such unpatriotic bearing, was undertaken by both Castlereagh and Cornwallis, and formed a trump card in the hands of the former by which he ultimately secured the game.

In reviewing the part which the Catholic leaders took in the Union Scheme, or rather the use which they permitted Castlereagh and Cornwallis to make of their name and cause in the furtherance of that infamous measure, considerable allowance must be made for the action of men who were still living under the atrocious laws which had endeavoured during the preceding century and a half to exterminate the Catholic religion from Ireland. When to be persecuted on account of one's faith becomes, as it were, an inheritance.

. . . [List of Political, Military, Constabulary & Judicial Divisions of Ireland from *Thom's Official Directory;* The roll of Ladies' Precedence in Ireland; draft of a note to MD's sister, Sabina, 22 April 1882, to be enclosed with a letter to another sister, Mary, on hearing of the death of her husband, Neil Padden] . . .

MY 36th BIRTHDAY

There are two circumstances in connection with that single line just written, which afford me very little consolation; or putting it in the "habilements of direct meaning," that are very unpleasant to dwell upon: The one is that I am thirty six years old today, and the other, that I am recording that unpalatable fact—in prison. Were I a Fatalist, I suppose I would endeavour to derive some "philosophic compensation" in the thought that both of these disagreeable events were inevitable, and, as being such, should only be regarded as two among a fixed number of occurrences that make up the sum of my chequered exis-tence. Without, however, endeavouring to point out the exact latitude in which my mind is being tossed about in the metaphysical ocean that stretches between the poles of Fatalism and Free Will, I am no more responsible for being where I am, on this interesting occasion, than, if, supposing I had the privilege of fixing my own age and chose to be twenty one, some meddling earthly power should please to ordain that the detestable number "thirty six" should fix me on the downward journey toward three-score years and ten, and charge the same upon my own desire to be younger than I ought to be. All the consolation that can be derived from personal disinclination in the matters of approaching the "sered and yellow leaf"[265] epoch of life, and being "cribbed, cabined and confined"[266] in the bargain I can lay claim to, and I sup-pose, possess, while being confronted with that ominous line at the head of this prison-stamped sheet of paper: I would not be thirty six if I could help it, no more than would I select the companionship of white-washed walls and the ceaseless censorship of my own reflections had I the power of locating myself where ere I pleased in this wide stretching world. As I might possibly be able to find a satisfactory—though sad-factory—answer to "why I am six and thirty years of age on this day," I should experience considerable difficulty in an effort to explain why I am [residing?] in Portland instead of being abroad among those who are busy prosecuting the duties of life. Well, I have read in grand old Will Shakespere [*sic*] somewhere, "I have done no harm!—but I remember now,

I am in this earthly world, where to do harm

Is often laudable; to do good, sometimes,

Accounted dangerous folly."[267]

Here is a choice, anyhow:

"Laudable Harm or Dangerous Folly—otherwise, Good; *laquelle voulez vous?*[268] I vote for the latter even with its consequences, though I am not going to sanction or remain satisfied with a state of society or law from which such an anomaly in morality emanates.

That ugly "36" is made up of four nines, and one or two of which fractional parts are anything but pleasure-affording reminiscences. With the exception of five years of the first nine, I recollect every year of the remainder, and *almost* every *day* of *one*. At nine years of age I commenced work, thereby bidding adieu to the "happy days of childhood," which extended over four years only, and *they* not of unclouded happiness, either. For nine years more[269] I toiled at daily labour, comparatively happy in adding my very little wages to the scanty "family pool"—excepting three or four years enforced idleness in consequence of having lost my right arm in the battle for daily Bread (during which period I obtained all the schooling it has been my good fortune to get outside of my own exertions in the task of mental improvement[270]). During the next nine years I may say I worked for what I believe to be the good of Ireland and the welfare of its people;[271] while as a consequence of this period of "dangerous folly" I am now completing the remaining nine years of that confounded three dozen—*a convict!*[272] From the 14th of May 1870 date of my arrest in London to the 19th of December 1877 that of my liberation from Dartmoor — . . . . 7 ys 7 months and 5 days.

From 3rd of Feb 1881 date of my re-consignment to Prison
. . . . 1 yr 1 month and 22 days.
In Sligo Jail on untenable charge of "Sedition" in November 1879 . . . . 7 days
    Total. . . . . 8 yrs 9 months 4 days

If, from this reckoning there wants the space of three months and twenty six days to make up the fourth nine of that miserable 36, there is the consolation—that is if consolation comes from *certainty*—that on my *next* birthday, the first three "nines" will be about nine months in the rear of the Convict nine—unless the whole four combine in forming *that* "36" between a "*Hic Jacet*" and R.I.P. down among the worms—somewhere on a coffin lid.

NOTES

ABBREVIATIONS USED IN THE NOTES

HC   House of Commons
HO   Home Office
PRO   Public Record Office, London
TCD   Trinity College, Dublin
UCD   University College Dublin

NOTES TO INTRODUCTION

1   One of these was Detective Officer Sheridan. TCD MS 9641, "Recollections of Portland Prison, 1881–2".

2   Chief Superintendant Adolphus Frederick Williamson was head of the Criminal Investigation Department, Scotland Yard.

3   Brennan, Harris, Patrick Egan (treasurer of the Land League) and Dr Kenny were allowed to go on board to see him before the mailboat left.

4   It was enacted on 2 March 1881.

5   TCD MS 9534, f. 2. Diary 31 December 1881.

6   On 16 December, in a long letter to John Devoy, written from Paris to avoid detection, he suggested that he was considering leaving Ireland to avoid arrest if *Habeas Corpus* were suspended: "I don't like running away from *any* danger; but I would be a fool to allow myself to be caught like a rat and be shut up for a year incapable of doing any good." William O'Brien and Desmond Ryan (eds), *Devoy's Post Bag, 1871–1928*, vol. 2 (Dublin, 1953), p. 24.

7   TCD MS 9320/3/1. Davitt to Brennan, 8 February 1881.

8   *Hansard*, 3rd series, cclvii, para 649–52, 13 January 1881. This was in response to a question by Randolph Churchill, calling on the government to cancel his ticket of leave on the grounds that he had made seditious speeches.

9   Forster only made up his mind to have Davitt arrested on 31 January. See *Florence Arnold Forster's Irish Journal*, ed. T. W. Moody and R. A. J. Hawkins, with Margaret Moody (Oxford, 1988), p. 61.

10 For details on the background to Davitt's arrest, see T. W. Moody, *Davitt and Irish Revolution, 1846–82* (Oxford, 1981), pp. 263–4.

11 *Hansard*, 3rd series, cclvii, 2038 ff.

12 F. S. L. Lyons, *Charles Stewart Parnell* (London, 1977), pp. 146–7.

13 A. Mcintyre, *The Liberator: Daniel O'Connell and the Irish Party, 1830–47* (London, 1965); Oliver MacDonagh, *The Emancipist: Daniel O'Connell, 1830–1847* (London, 1989), pp. 237–43.

14 *Freeman's Journal*, 5 February 1881.

15 Quoted *Newcastle Daily Chronicle*, 4 February 1881.

16 *Freeman's Journal*, 5 February 1881. The meeting, held at the Land League offices at 39 Upper Sackville Street, was described as having "an extremely large attendance". At one stage Dillon addressed the crowd that had gathered outside from a window in the building.

17 *Florence Arnold Forster's Irish Journal*, p. 66.

18 M. Davitt, *Some Particulars of Treatment while a Prisoner in Clerkenwell, Newgate, Millbank, Portsmouth and Dartmoor Prisons*, serialised in *The Nation*, 12, 19, 26 February, 5, 12 March. Written in March 1878, it was initially given as evidence to the Kimberley Commission on Penal Reform; it was included the following year in *Irish Political Prisoners: Speeches of John O'Connor Power*, and published in pamphlet form in 1882. It was reprinted in Carla King (ed.), *Michael Davitt: Collected Writings* (Bristol, 2001), vol. 1. In it Davitt described the appalling conditions he had undergone and witnessed while being held in various prisons between 1870 and 1877.

19 *Annual Register 1881*, 13 February. The third resolution was a reference to government measures to curb obstruction using closure; *Freeman's Journal*, 14 February, p. 6.

20 PRO HO 144/5/17869/46b. Stephen Price, Hon. Sec. Chelsea and Westminster Radical Association to Harcourt, 15 February 1881; PRO HO 144.5.17869/91. James Beckett, Hon. Sec., Combined Political Committee of the Four Radical Clubs of the Borough of Chelsea, 27 April 1881; PRO HO 144/5/17869/92 Telegram from Birmingham Reform League, 29 April 1882; PRO HO 144/5/17869/75. Marcus Collisson and James G. Pollard, Gympie Branch of the Irish National League, Queensland, 7 September 1881.

21 PRO HO 144/5/17869/44.

22 Davitt petition. PRO HO 144/5/17869/51. This is a view with which Davitt's biographer, T.W. Moody, concurred. Moody, *Davitt*, p. 472.

23 Davitt received visits from Mrs Sullivan 15 February 1881; Dr Kenny 3 March 1881; Mrs Sullivan and Mrs Kenny 2 June 1881; Dr Kenny 27 June 1881; Archbishop of Cashel and Archbishop of Ross 8 September 1881; Thomas Brennan requested permission, May 1881 (refused); John J. Louden requested permission, 12 September 1881 (refused); Alfred Webb requested permission, 10 November 1881 (refused); Mrs Sullivan requested permission, 17 November 1881 (refused); Francis W. Soutter and Samuel Bennett requested permission, 18 October 1881 (refused);

Rev Harold Rylett requested permission, 13 December 1881 (refused); John Daly requested permission 15 December 1881 (refused); Mrs Sullivan requested permission, 2 January 1882 (granted); Mrs Kenny asked to accompany Mrs Sullivan, 4 January 1882 (refused); Dr Kenny requested permission 17 February 1882 (refused); Henry George requested permission, 30 March 1882 (refused). PRO HO 144/5/17869/56–91.

24 He was also allowed to send out letters, eight of which have survived, although it appears that there were others.

25 A. G. Gardiner, *The Life of Sir William Harcourt, vol I, 1827–1886* (2 vols, New York, 1923), p. 394. In fact, Queen Victoria was displeased with him on several occasions on account of his leniency. *Ibid.*, pp. 396–402.

26 PRO HO 144/5/17869/64. Dr Gover to Sir E. Du Cane, 26 June 1881.

27 PRO HO 144/5/17869/65. Memo 7 July 1881.

28 Jeremiah O'Donovan Rossa, *O'Donovan Rossa's Prison Life* (1874).

29 See above, note 14.

30 TCD MSS 9640, 9643.

31 This is further explored in an article by me, "Michael Davitt: Irish nationalism and the British Empire", in Peter Gray (ed.), *Victoria's Ireland? Irishness and Britishness, 1837–1901* (Dublin, forthcoming 2003).

32 The Illuminati were established in 1776 in Ingolstadt, Bavaria, by Adam Weishaupt.

33 The Philadelphic Society, founded in Besançon in the 1790s, was led by Lieut. Col. Oudet, and developed from a literary and philosophical society into a political one, aimed against Napoleon Bonaparte.

34 The Tugenbund was a German nationalist federation of societies directed against Napoleon. It was founded by the Prussian minister Heinrich Friedrich Karl von und zum Stein (1757–1831).

35 Davitt had been expelled from the Supreme Council of the IRB on 8 May 1880 (see Moody, *Davitt*, p. 381), although he continued as a rank-and-file member. Several of the more traditional, hard-line Fenians were bitterly opposed to the Land League and to Davitt. In his letter to Devoy of 16 December 1880, he recounted an effort to blow up the platform on which he was to address a meeting in Sligo, which he attributed to P. N. Fitzgerald. Henry George related that when Davitt went to collect his overcoat from Scotland Yard a few days after his release from prison in May 1882, there had been five threatening letters in the pockets. Davitt habitually carried a gun and it is worth noting that on the day of his arrest in Dublin, although he had not bothered to bring his coat on his way to lunch (someone had to be sent back to the office for it on his arrest), he was carrying his gun.

36 Davitt was to repeat this device in his lecture "The Castle Government of Ireland", delivered in the Foresters' Hall, Clerkenwell, on 23 October 1882. It was printed as a pamphlet the same year and free copies distributed.

37 C. Keating, "Sir Horace Plunkett and Rural Reform, 1889–1914", unpublished PhD thesis, NUI, 1984.

38 Philip Bull, *Land, Politics and Nationalism: A Study of the Irish Land Question* (Dublin, 1996), pp. 116–42.

39 Emmet Larkin, *The Roman Catholic Church and the Plan of Campaign, 1886–1888* (Cork, 1978), pp. xiii–xiv.

40 William F. Feingold, "The tenants' movements to capture the Irish poor law boards, 1877–1886", *Albion* (Fall, 1975) pp. 216–31; and William F. Feingold *The Revolt of the Tenantry: The Transformation of Local Government in Ireland* (Boston, 1984).

41 See TCD MS 9664; scrapbook of reviews of *Leaves from a Prison Diary*, presented by Miss A. Murray.

42 Martin J. Wiener, *Reconstructing the Criminal: Culture, Law and Policy in England, 1830–1914* (Cambridge, 1990), pp. 327–8.

43 *Freeman's Journal*, 28 December 1880.

44 Conor Cruise O'Brien, *Parnell and His Party, 1880–90* (Oxford, 1957), p. 57. The seceders were Shaw, Blennerhassett, Brooks, Collins, Colthurst, Errington, Mitchell Henry, Meldon, O'Beirne, O'Brien, O'Conor, and Smyth. Davitt made scathing comments about several of these in his table (see below, pp. XX–XX).

45 Laurence J. Kettle (ed.), *Material for Victory: The Memoirs of Andrew J. Kettle* (Dublin, 1958), p. 63.

46 On 28 February 1882 the House of Commons declared the election void because Davitt was a convict.

47 Davitt thanked the electors of Meath in an open letter to Bishop Nulty, published in *Freeman's Journal*, 24 May 1882, p. 3.

48 Kay had been an economist, barrister and judge, Liberal MP, and was brother of the great educational reformer Sir James Kay-Shuttleworth. His book, *Free Trade in Land* (1878) made a strong case for farmer-ownership, as opposed to landlordism, and he based his case on Continental examples.

49 Henry George, *The Irish Land Question* (New York, 1881).

50 He was to repeat this phrase in his address on land nationalisation, delivered in Liverpool's League Hall, on 6 June 1882.

51 John Stuart Mill, *The Principles of Political Economy* (1848).

52 Alfred Webb, *A Compendium of National Biography, Comprising Sketches of Distinguished Irishmen and of Eminent Persons Connected with Ireland by Office or By Their Writings* (Dublin, 1878). Webb had sent a copy of this to Davitt in prison.

53 The letters were to Mr Hugh King, New York (24 February 1882); to Davitt's aunt, Ellen Davitt (30 Jan 1882); and to his sister Sabina enclosing a letter to another sister, Mary Padden, on the death of her husband, Neil (24 April 1882).

54 *Irish World*, 10 June 1882.

55 Pauric Travers, "Address to Parnell Summer School", 12 August 1997. If this interpretation is correct, Davitt might have intended the motif as an olive branch, since relations between himself and Parnell were cool at the time.

56 T.W.Moody, " Michael Davitt and the British labour movement, 1882–1906" *Transactions of the Royal Historical Society*, 5th ser., III (1953), pp. 53–76.

57 He refers to at least 33 authors in the *Jottings*, a combination of writers, poets, historians, economists and social thinkers.

58 He had committed himself to speak in public on the topic only a week after his release. See *The Radical*, 13 May 1882.

59 Michael Davitt, *The Fall of Feudalism in Ireland* (London and New York, 1904), p. 356. Davitt must be mistaken in his suggestion that Parnell expected land legislation from Forster, as he would have been aware that the Chief Secretary had resigned four days earlier.

60 See Francis William Soutter, *Recollections of a Labour Pioneer* (London, 1923), pp. 99–127 for an account of the origins and running of *The Radical*.

61 This is not dated in Soutter's account but probably refers to some time in the six weeks from the first seizure of the paper on 17 December 1881. See Sally Warwick-Haller, *William O'Brien and the Irish Land War* (Dublin 1990), p. 59.

62 *The Radical*, 10 June 1882.

NOTES TO JOTTINGS IN SOLITARY

1 Martin Davitt was born some time between 1811 (family album, cited by Patrick M. Davitt, "Michael Davitt, 1846–1906, Ancestors and Descendants", prepared for Trinity College Manuscript Department, 2001) and 1814 (T. W. Moody, *Davitt and Irish Revolution, 1846–82* (Oxford, 1981), p. 6) in the parish of Straide, County Mayo. He married Catherine Kielty around 1840 (Moody, *Davitt*, p. 6. The date is estimated from the birth of the first child) and the family emigrated to Haslingden, Lancashire in 1850 and to Scranton, Pennsylvania in 1870, where he died on 16 October 1871.

2 On 22 August 1798 French forces landed at Killala to support the 1798 Rebellion. They won a victory at the "Races of Castlebar" on 27 August but were defeated and surrendered at Ballinamuck, County Longford on 8 September.

3 Patrick Sarsfield (*c.*1655–1693) commanded James II's Irish troops in England in 1688. He returned to Ireland in March 1689; expelled Williamites from Connaught and defended Limerick in 1690. He was appointed Governor of Connaught and created Earl of Lucan in 1691. He attempted to defend Limerick for a second time in 1691 and was one of the principal negotiators of the Treaty of Limerick, signed on 3 October 1691. He sailed for France in December 1691 and died at the battle of Landen, Flanders, July 1693. See Piers Wauchope, *Patrick Sarsfield and the Williamite War* (Dublin, 1992).

4 Colum Cille (St Columba) (*c.*521–597), saint and missionary born at Garten, County Donegal. A large number of poems and prophecies are traditionally

attributed to Colm Cille. An anthology of prophetic poems ascribed to him was published in 1856 and several times subsequently. It has had a great influence on popular lore in Ireland as the "prophecies of Colm Cille" were taken to refer to many of the developments of the twentieth century.

5   Catherine Davitt, *née* Catherine Kielty was born between 1820 and 1824. She married Martin Davitt *c.*1840. They emigrated to Haslingden, Lancashire, 1850 and to Scranton Pennsylvania, 1870. She moved to Manayunk, Philadelphia, 1873, where she died 18 July 1880.

6   MacDaibhid, McDevitt. The eponymous ancestor of the family of MacDaibhid of Inishowen was Daibhid O'Dochertaigh, who according to the annals was killed in battle in 1208. See Fergus Gillespie, "Gaelic Families of Co. Donegal", in William Nolan, Liam Ronayne and Mairead Dunlevy (eds), *Donegal: History and Society* (Dublin, 1995), pp 759–838.

7   In April 1608 Sir Cahir O'Doherty of Inishowen rose in arms against Sir George Paulet, captured Culmore Fort and burned Derry. He was killed in battle at Kilmacrenan and his land allocated to Sir Arthur Chichester. See Gillespie, "Gaelic Families", pp. 800–4. Davitt called his fourth child Cahir Felim Davitt (b. 15 August 1894, d. 3 March 1986). However, there is a possibility that the Davitts were not of Gaelic but of Anglo-Norman stock, descended from a David Burke.

8   Mayo, which already had the lowest per capita income of any county in Ireland in the 1830s, was particularly dependent on potato cultivation and therefore severely hit by the onset of potato blight. During the worst year of the Great Famine, 1847, over 70 per cent of the population of all of Mayo's poor law unions received some assistance. Joel Mokyr has estimated that Mayo, with Famine deaths numbering between 100,000 and 120,000, had the highest mortality rate of any county in Ireland (unpublished estimates, quoted in Donald E. Jordan, *Land and Popular Politics in Ireland: County Mayo from the Plantation to the Land War* (Cambridge, 1994), p. 108 n.

9   On 1 February 1880 a monster meeting was held at Straide at which Davitt was a principal speaker. The platform was erected over the ruins of the house from which his family had been evicted in 1850. His speech at the meeting was later published as "The Crimes of Irish Landlordism", *Irish Bits*, 13 August 1898, pp. 588–90; see also *Michael Davitt Collected Writings* (2001) vol. 2, "Pamphlets, speeches and articles".

10 He was referring to the passage of the *Land Law (Ireland) Act, 1881.* 44 & 45 Vict., c. 49. The act enacted the tenant demand of the 3 Fs (fair rent, fixity of tenure and freedom of sale of tenant right) and intervened in the contract between landlord and tenant by establishing land courts to determine what was a fair rent.

11 Brian O'Lynn had no watch to put on,
    He scooped out a turnip to make him a one;
    Then he planted a cricket in under the skin
    "Whoo, they'll think it's a tickin'," says Brian O'Lynn
    (from *Brian O'Lynn*, popular ballad).

12 This date is incorrect: it should be 1850.

13 Haslingden was 17 miles from Liverpool. In 1851 its population was 9,000, of whom around 430 were Irish. It was built around the industries of cotton and woollen manufacture and some stone quarrying.

14 The words: "a distant relative" are crossed out in the manuscript and replaced by "an acquaintance". It is likely that the family were distant relatives but that Davitt was anxious to spare them embarrassment. It has proved impossible to trace the identity of the family.

15 James Bonner was a tin plate worker from County Armagh.

16 Here Davitt is simplifying a little. Moody traced the family as lodgers in the home of Owen Eagan in Wilkinson Street on 30 March 1851; then in their own house in Rock Hall by 1853, where they took in lodgers in turn. See Moody, *Davitt*, pp. 11–12.

17 Irish Famine emigration to Britain was large-scale and sudden. In 1841 there were some 419,256 Irish-born residents in Britain but by a decade later this figure had shot to 727,326, reaching a peak in 1861 of 806,000 (Ó Tuathaigh, "The Irish in Nineteenth-Century Britain: Problems of Integration" in R. Swift and S. Gilley (eds), *The Irish in the Victorian City* (Kent, 1985), p. 14). As Ó Tuathaigh puts it in explaining British responses: "The huge famine influx of Irish brought native fear and resentment to fever pitch. The flooding of ghetto areas by impoverished and disease-ridden Irish, and the violence and social misery which was a by-product of such a brutalizing environment, together with a ready acceptance of the notion that Irish peasant society was inherently violent, formed for sizeable sections of the British public an explanation for all Irish troubles and misfortunes which rested on 'the fundamental weaknesses of the Irish national character'. A stereotype of the brutalized "Paddy" was formed, in greater detail and enjoying wider currency than ever before; intemperate, improvident, violent, totally innocent of any notions of hygiene, mendacious and undependable – not so much a loveable rogue as a menacing savage." (*Ibid.*, p. 22).

18 Jeffrey Williamson, in "The impact of the Irish on British labour markets during the industrial revolution", has argued that overall British incomes were little affected by the Irish immigration, and that "the British unskilled suffered a bit, while all other classes gained, landlords and capitalists in particular." (R. Swift and S. Gilley, *The Irish in Britain* (London, 1989), pp. 134–62.) However, it was from the unskilled British labourers that much of the physical antagonism came.

19 Anti-Irish feeling aroused by Famine immigration took on a sectarian hue in response to the creation of twelve Catholic bishoprics in 1850. From 1850 "No popery" agitation occurred in various parts of the country and in 1852 Lord Derby's Conservative government forbade Catholics from processing through the streets with symbols of their religion. The anti-Catholic feeling culminated in the Stockport riots of June 1852, in which one man was killed, 51 Irish injured and two Catholic chapels were ransacked.

20 No one strikes me with impunity.

21 This refers to an unsuccessful Fenian raid on Chester Castle on 11 February 1867, in which Davitt took part. John Newsinger, *Fenians in Mid-Victorian Britain* (London, 1994), pp. 53–4.

22 Col Thomas J. Kelly and Timothy Deasy were arrested on 11 September 1867. A week later they were rescued from a police van returning them from a court appearance to prison. The rescue was carried out by about thirty armed Fenians and in the course of the operation an unarmed policeman was shot dead. Three men, William Philip Allen, Michael Larkin and Michael O'Brien were hanged in Salford jail on 23 Sep 1867 and became Fenian martyrs. Paul B. Rose, *The Manchester Martyrs: The Story of a Fenian Tragedy* (London, 1970).

23 The Danish War was actually in 1864.

24 This is a reference to the Franco-Prussian War of 1870–1. France was required to pay five milliard francs. See Michael Howard Eliot, *The Franco-Prussian War: The German Invasion of France, 1870–1872* (London, 1961).

25 In 1875 risings against Turkish power in the Balkans took place in Bosnia and Herzegovina. A year later they were followed by revolts throughout the Bulgarian provinces, which were put down with great violence. In September 1876 Serbia sought the intervention of foreign powers and in April 1877 Russia went to war with Turkey, in which Balkan states and nationalists joined in. The war ended in March 1878, with the Treaty of San Stefano. Misha Glenny, *The Balkans, 1804–1999: Nationalism, War and the Great Powers* (London, 1999), pp. 127–34.

26 The Bashi-Basouks were Turkish irregular troops, who suppressed revolts in the Bulgarian provinces in which between 12,000 and 15,000 men, women and children were massacred. The events caused great indignation in the West. W. E. Gladstone's pamphlet, *The Bulgarian Horrors and the Question of the East* sold 40,000 copies in the first week after its publication in 1876.

27 This is a bay near Constantinople to which the Mediterranean fleet was sent in 1877–8, known in Classical times as Bithynia.

28 This is a reference to a popular music-hall song by G.W. Hunt, which appeared at the time of the Russo-Turkish War (1877–8) when anti-Russian feeling ran high and Disraeli ordered the Mediterranean fleet to Constantinople. The text ran:
We don't want to fight, but by Jingo if we do,
We've got the ships, we've got the men, and got the money too.

29 Herodotus of Halicarnasus (*c.*484–*c.*420 BC), author of the *History of the Persian Wars*, sometimes known as the "Father of History".

30 He was referring to James Anthony Froude (1818–94), historian and man of letters. Froude made his name with the publication of his twelve-volume *History of England* (1856–64). Later he published *The English in Ireland in the Eighteenth Century* (3 vols, 1872–4), which aimed to show the folly of attempts to conciliate Ireland, such as Gladstone's measures of

disestablishment and land reform. W. H. Dunn, *James Anthony Froude: A Biography* (2 vols, Oxford, 1963). Davitt often cited Froude's opinions of Ireland and the British Empire as examples of British Tory attitudes.

31   Exeter Hall was the building in the Strand, London, where missionary societies held May meetings every year.

32   Warren Hastings (1732–1818) began as a clerk in the East India Company and succeeded Robert Clive as Governor-General of Bengal 1774. From 1778 to 1784 he engaged in several wars, returning to England in 1785, where he was impeached before the House of Lords, 1788–95 and finally acquitted. Jeremy Bernstein, *Dawning of the Raj: The Life and Trials of Warren Hastings* (London, 2001).

33   Sir Robert Clive (1725–74) made a fortune as an employee of the East India Company. He eventually bought out the company and became its director.

34   Sir Elijah Impey (1732–1809), first Chief Justice of India. He was born in London, the son of a merchant trading with India. He was appointed Chief Justice of India in 1774 and was the presiding judge in the dispute between Nand Kumar and Warren Hastings, which ended in the execution of Nand Kumar. It was asserted that Impey acted throughout the trial as a tool of the Governor and there were unsuccessful attempts in the House of Commons to impeach him in 1788. He resigned his office in 1789. Bishwa Nath Pandey, *The Introduction of English Law into India: The Career of Elijah Impey in Bengal, 1774–1783* (Asia Publishing House, 1967).

35   What Davitt may have in mind is the quotation: "successful and fortunate crime is called virtue", Lucius Annaeus Seneca, *Hercules Furens*, *c.*50 CE.

36   Thomas Babington Macaulay, Baron Macaulay (1800–59). If Froude was the spokesman for conservative views of history in Victorian Britain, Macaulay was one of the leading Whig historians of his day. He was also a Liberal MP, secretary at war (1839) and served on the Supreme Council of India (1834–8), writing an "Essay on Clive" (1839) and on "Warren Hastings" (1841), based on his knowledge of India, among many other works. John Clive, *Thomas Babington Macaulay: The Shaping of the Historian* (London, 1973).

37   This is a reference to Nawab Siraj-ud-daula, who succeeded his grandfather, Ali Vardi Khan, nawab of Bengal in 1756 and attacked the British fortress at Calcutta the same year. It was in this incident that forty-three English prisoners died in the "Black Hole" of Calcutta. In 1757, Siraj-ud-daula was overthrown by Clive and Mir Jafar and killed.

38   Davitt appears to be referring to Raja Nand Kumar, who had alleged corruption against Hastings but before the case came to court he was arrested on 6 May 1775, found guilty and executed on 5 August. Several commentators had suggested that he was framed. Impey was later threatened with impeachment because of the treatment of Nand Kumar.

39   Rohilla war. This was a war fought by the Nawab Vasir of Oudh, Shuja-ud-daula, against the Rohilla Afghans in 1774.

40 Warren Hastings extorted vast sums from the Raja of Banaras and the *begums* of Oudh, acts for which he was later subject to impeachment proceedings by Parliament.

41 François Guizot (1784–1874), historian and statesman. From 1812–30 Guizot was professor of History at the Sorbonne but was deprived of his post because of his liberalism. He was elected to the Chamber of Deputies in 1830 and appointed Minister of Interior and Minister of Public Instruction. He introduced the French system of primary education. He was Ambassador to London in 1840 and Foreign Minister in 1840–7. Among many works he wrote *Histoire de la révolution d'Angleterre* (1854–56); *Histoire générale de la civilisation en Europe* (1828); *Méditations et études morales* (1851); *Méditations sur l'essence de la religion* (1864); *Méditations biographiques et littéraires* (1868). Ceri Crossley, *The French Historians and Romanticism: Thierry, Guizot, the Saint Simonians, Quinet, Michelet* (London, 1993).

42 Dives is the name popularly given to the rich man in the parable of 'The Rich Man and Lazarus' (*Luke* 16: 19).

43 This was a point made both by Kay, *Free Trade in Land* (see n. 47 below) and by Mill in *Principles of Political Economy*.

44 This was the Bishop of Oxford, William Wilberforce who, when introducing the second reading of the Protection of Females bill in the House of Lords, on 26 Mar 1848, referred to the existence of 80,000 prostitutes in London. *Hansard* 3rd ser. ic, 333, 5 June 1848. My thanks to Dr Maria Luddy for assistance in tracing the reference.

45 *Hamlet*, Act II, scene I, 83.

46 The *Royal Commission of Inquiry into Primary Education (Ireland)*1868–70 H.C. 1870 (c. 6) xxviii (Powis Commission) had recommended that attendance in rural areas should not be made compulsory. Thomas Joseph Durcan, *History of Irish Education from 1800* (Wales, 1972).

47 Joseph Kay (1821–1878) economist, influenced by his travels in Europe in 1846–9. He was also a barrister and later a judge of the Salford Hundred Court of Record. He was brother of Sir J. P. Kay-Shuttleworth (see note 123 below) and twice unsuccessfully contested the borough of Salford in the Liberal interest. He is best known for his influential book, *Free Trade in Land*, published posthumously in 1878.

48 *Ibid.*, p. 286.

49 "Dieu et mon droit" was the parole of Richard I at the Battle of Gisors (1198), meaning that he was no vassal of France, but owed his loyalty to God alone. It was the royal motto of England from the time of Henry VI.

50 This quotation is from Cicero and translates: "I approve the higher course of action but I follow the lesser one." My thanks to John McColgan for assistance with the quotation (ed.).

51 The original is: "I see the right and I approve it too. Condemn the Wrong and yet the wrong pursue." Ovid, *Metamorphoses*, vii, 20. Translated by Tate and Stonestreet, edited by Sir Samuel Garth (1661–1719).

52 French revolutionary name for Louis XVI.

53　Perhaps a subconscious reference to Charles Stewart Parnell?

54　Louis-Napoleon Bonaparte, who in December 1848 won the Presidential elections in France and on 2 December 1851 staged a coup, following which he declared himself Emperor Napoleon III of France. J. M. Thompson, *Louis Napoleon and the Second Empire* (Oxford, 1954).

55　This is a reference to British support for Napoleon III's effort to install the Austrian archduke Maximilian as Emperor of Mexico, 1864–7 in order to act as a barrier to the expansion of the United States republic and republican ideas. See Alfred Jackson Hanna and Kathryn Abbey Hanna, *Napoleon III and Mexico: American Triumph over Monarchy* (North Carolina, 1971).

56　In 1878 Lord Lytton launched the Second Afghan War. The Amir of Afghanistan, Sher Ali, fled Kabul and died in exile the following year.

57　Cetshwayo or Cetewayo (1826–84) last great king of the Zulus, ruled 1873–9. Leader of an army of 40,000 men, he was considered a threat to British colonial interests and his power was destroyed in the Zulu War (1879).

58　Gavan Duffy, *Young Ireland: A Fragment of Irish History, 1840–1850* (London, 1880), ch. IV, "A bird's eye view of Irish history", pp. 81–150.

59　Davitt probably means 1170 here, the date of the landing of the Normans in Ireland, led by Richard FitzGilbert, "Strongbow".

60　Hugh O'Neill (1550–1616), third Baron Dungannon and second Earl of Tyrone. With Red Hugh O'Donnell he defeated an English army at the Battle of Yellow Ford in 1598. On 24 December 1601 the two leaders were defeated at the Battle of Kinsale. In September 1607 O'Neill left Ireland in the "Flight of the Earls". He died in exile in Rome. The Flight of the Earls left the way clear for the Plantation of Ulster. Nicholas P. Canny, 'Hugh O'Neill, Earl of Tyrone and the changing face of Gaelic Ulster', *Studia Hibernica* (1970), vol. 10, pp. 7–35; John McCavitt, *The Flight of the Earls* (Dublin, 2002).

61　Red Hugh O'Donnell (1571–1602), chief of the O'Donnell clan. He joined forces with Hugh O'Neill at the Battle of the Yellow Ford and at the Battle of Kinsale (see above) and sailed to Spain on 6 January 1602 to seek aid but was poisoned and died at Simancas on 10 September 1602. McCavitt, *Flight of the Earls.*

62　Theobald Wolfe Tone (1763–98), often seen as the "father of Irish republicanism". In 1791 Tone participated in the foundation of the United Irishmen in Belfast. In 1792 he became Secretary of the Catholic Committee and in December of the same year he organised the Catholic Convention in Dublin. He sought French assistance for rebellion in Ireland from 1796 and was captured at Lough Swilly when he attempted to land in Ireland in 1798. He committed suicide in prison on 19 November 1798. Davitt had requested a biography of Tone in Portland Prison, for which permission was granted. (PRO HO144/5/17869/62)

63　Lord Edward Fitzgerald (1763–98), son of the Duke of Leinster and leader of the United Irishmen Rebellion in 1798.

64 Robert Emmet (1776–1803). Having participated in the United Irishmen Rebellion, he led a second unsuccessful rising in Dublin on 23 July 1803, for which he was hanged on 20 September 1803. Patrick Geoghegan, *Robert Emmet: A Life* (Dublin 2002).

65 The Penal Laws were a series of acts passed in Parliament in the late seventeenth and early eighteenth centuries, devised to disenfranchise and otherwise disadvantage the Catholic population of Ireland.

66 Catholic Emancipation was the progressive removal of restrictions on Roman Catholics, a process largely completed in 1829 as a result of Daniel O'Connell's efforts, with legislation to permit Catholics to become MPs and other government officers. At the same time, the franchise qualification in Ireland was raised from 40s to £10.

67 The tithe, or tenth, was an annual tax levied by the established church in Ireland on the produce of the land; paid either in kind or cash. The Tithe Rent-Charge Act of 15 August 1838 converted the tithe into a rent charge and made landlords responsible for paying it.

68 St Patrick's College, Maynooth, was established in June 1795 with an annual grant of £8000. This was raised in 1845 to £26,000.

69 Disestablishment of the Church of Ireland, passed 26 July 1869 by the Liberal government of W. E. Gladstone, provided that from 1871 the Church of Ireland was to be a voluntary body.

70 Time will reveal all.

71 Latifundias ruined Italy.

72 Pliny the Elder (23–79 CE), a Roman scholar and writer; completed his encyclopaedia of science, *Natural History* about 77 CE.

73 John Stuart Mill (1806–1873) philosopher and social thinker. He was also proprietor of *Westminster Review*, to which he sometimes contributed articles. His *Political Economy* (2 vols, 8vo, 1848, 1849, 1852, 1857, 1862, 1865) was influential in shaping thought on the Irish land question.

74 Léonard Simonde de Sismondi (1773–1842) historian and political economist, who wrote *Nouveaux principes de l'économie politique* (1819), which is said to have influenced the Saint-Simonians.

75 See note 47 above.

76 Émile de Laveleye. Henry George, in *Progress and Poverty*, refers several times to de Laveleye's "Systems of land tenure in various countries", a paper published by the Cobden Club and to his book, *Primitive Property*.

77 Léonce de Lavergne (1809–80), author of *Économie rurale de la France depuis 1789* (1866), quoted Kay, *Free Trade in Land*, pp. 115–16.

78 For what benefit?

79 Lord Derby (1826–1893), Foreign Secretary, 1876–8, son of former Prime Minister. Quoted Kay, *Free Trade in Land*, pp. 18–19.

80 On Macaulay's social and political ideas, see Joseph Hamburger, *Macaulay and the Whig Tradition* (Chicago, 1976).

81 James Thorold Rogers (1823–1890), liberal economist at Oxford. His most important work was *The Economic Interpretation of History* (London, 1888).

82   Herbert Spencer, *Social Statics* (1851), p. 142; quoted in Henry George, *Progress and Poverty*, p. 258 (see also note 85 below).

83   Henry George (1839–1897), land reformer and economist. In 1881–2 he was Irish correspondent for the *Irish World* and got to know Davitt on his release from prison (the two men had already met in 1880). He published a pamphlet, *The Irish Land Question: What it Involves and How Alone It Can Be Settled: An Appeal to the Land Leagues* (New York 1879) and London, 1881), proposing a solution to the Irish land question on the basis of nationalisation of the land. Henry George, Jr, *Henry George* (New York, 1900).

84   *Progress and Poverty* was Henry George's most important work. In it he proposed the single tax, that is, that the state should nationalise all the land and charge a tax for use of it. All other taxes and rents would then be abolished.

85   Herbert Spencer (1820–1903), philosopher and early sociologist, he insisted on a synthesis of knowledge from close scientific investigation of biological and social phenomena. He believed in the continuing development of species from simple to complex forms. His works include: *The Proper Sphere of Government* (1843); *Social Statics* (1851), which Davitt expressed an interest in reading in a note in "Jottings"; *The Man Versus the State* (1884); and *The Synthetic Philosophy* (1896). Jonathan H. Turner, *Herbert Spencer: A Renewed Appreciation* (Beverly Hills, Calif., 1985).

86   Henry George, *Progress and Poverty. An Inquiry into the cause of Industrial Depressions and of Increase of Want with Increase of Wealth—The Remedy* (London, 1883), pp. 258–9.

87   Sir George Otto Trevelyan (1838–1928) introduced a resolution for extending the county franchise to the agricultural labourer to the House on 4 March 1879. It was unsuccessful.

88   Augustin Thierry (1795–1856), historian. He wrote *Considérations sur l'histoire de France* (1840) and *Dix ans d'études historiques* (1834).

89   William Wallace (?1272–1305) was a Scottish general and patriot who led a struggle against Edward I of England. He was captured and executed in London in 1305.

90   This word is illegible in the manuscript but since the rest of the text is identical to that in Davitt's speech on Castle Government [see below], I substituted it—ed.

91   Sir Edmund Henderson, Commissioner of the London Metropolitan Police.

92   He is probably referring here to the Dublin *Daily Express* and the Dublin *Evening Mail*.

93   R. B. McDowell, *The Irish Administration, 1801–1914* (1964).

94   Sir Bernard Burke was editor of *A Genealogical and Heraldic History of the Landed Gentry of Ireland*. Davitt transcribed in his "Jottings" the roll of ladies' precedence from *Thom's Directory*, 1881, p. 768.

95   Joseph Cowen (1831–1900) Liberal politician and journalist. MP for Newcastle-upon-Tyne, 1873–86, he inherited a lucrative fire-brick business from his father and was an active supporter of revolutionary movements

on the continent and the Chartists in England. He also supported the Irish Home Rule movement, to the disapproval of his constituency supporters. He was proprietor and editor of the *Newcastle Chronicle*.

96 Sir Charles Wentworth Dilke, 2nd baronet (1843–1911), Radical liberal politician with republican sympathies, and author. Under Secretary at the Foreign Office 1880, he was offered the post of Chief Secretary for Ireland to succeed W. E. Forster in April 1882 but declined on the ground that it did not carry a seat in cabinet. In 1882 he was made president of local government board. In 1885 Dilke and Chamberlain recommended a local government board for Ireland as a measure of devolved government alternative to Home Rule. He was named in a divorce case in 1885 and owing to the scandal he was not included in Gladstone's third cabinet.

97 Henry du Pré Labouchère (1831–1912) politician, journalist, served in British diplomatic corps, 1854–64, then sat in the House of Commons as a Liberal MP (1867–8) and as a Radical (1880–1906). He urged abolition of the House of Lords. He opposed the imperialist expansionism of Joseph Chamberlain and others. His periodical, *Truth* (founded 1877) was devoted to the uncovering of organised frauds. He helped in the exposure of the Pigott forgeries in *The Times*'s allegations against Parnell in 1889.

98 Joseph Chamberlain (1830–1914), industrialist, social reformer and politician; leader of radical element in the Liberal party. He was liberal MP for Birmingham, 1876–85, and opposed a coercion policy in Ireland. He became involved in negotiations resulting in the "Kilmainham Treaty" with Parnell in April 1882. He broke with Gladstone over the Home Rule Bill 1886, following which he became a liberal unionist. Secretary of State for the Colonies in Salisbury's third administration, 1895–1903, when Davitt opposed his colonial policies.

99 Sir Wilfred Lawson, 2nd baronet (1829–1906), politician and temperance advocate, born at Brayton near Carlisle. Radical liberal and champion of Gladstone's policy of disestablishment. He was an advocate of women's rights and defended Charles Bradlaugh's right to sit in the House of Commons as an atheist. He opposed coercion in Ireland and supported Home Rule, although by 1886 he had lost his seat in parliament and could not vote for it. He supported the Boer side during the Second Anglo-Boer War.

100 James Howard was a Liberal land reformer. Early in 1880 he established the Farmers' Alliance to coordinate the efforts of land reformers in Britain and Ireland.

101 John Bright (1811–1889), Radical Liberal, best known for his campaign, with Richard Cobden, for repeal of the British Corn Laws. For over thirty years, following his election to parliament in 1847, Bright urged that attention to be given to Irish reforms. He was also interested in reform of conditions in India and other imperial issues, resigning his chancellorship of the duchy of Lancaster and seat in cabinet on 15 July 1882 in protest against the bombardment of Alexandria by British forces.

However, he broke with Gladstone over Home Rule and spoke out in public against its introduction.

102 The point Davitt is making here is that these men were all Radical Liberals and relatively sympathetic to Irish demands and grievances.

103 Davitt was referring to the grazing of cows in Phoenix Park but I have not been able to establish which Lord Lieutenant this was. —ed.

104 Davitt may have in mind the Chief Secretary at the time he was writing, W. E. Forster, who had come to the office of Chief Secretary as a man of Liberal sympathies, and had helped his father in distributing relief in Ireland during the Great Famine but ended up advocating coercion as the only means of pacifying the country. See T. Wemyss Reid, *Life of the Right Honourable William Edward Forster* (2 vols, London, 1888); and *Florence Arnold-Forster's Irish Journals*, ed. T.W. Moody and Richard Hawkins (Oxford, 1988).

105 John Howard (?1726–90), known for his efforts to reform the wretched conditions of English prisons. The Howard League for Penal Reform, established in 1921, was named after him.

106 St Vincent de Paul (1581–1660) spiritual leader of the Counter-Reformation, founder of the Vincentian Order.

107 *Thom's Official Directory of the United Kingdom of Great Britain and Ireland.*

108 Davitt discusses the state trial of Parnell and others *vs* the Queen in *The Fall of Feudalism in Ireland* (London and New York, 1904), ch. xxii, "The State Trials", pp. 286–95.

109 See also TCD MS 9634, Papers relating to the prosecution of Parnell and other Land Leaguers, 1880–1.

110 Francis McDonogh QC, the leading counsel for the defendants. Davitt described him as "a veteran lawyer who had seen nearly eighty summers", *The Fall of Feudalism in Ireland*, p. 293.

111 George Augustus Chichester May (1815–92), Lord Chief Justice of Ireland. May's remarks on 4 December against an application from the traversers for a postponement of the trial had been so partisan that the storm of controversy they raised caused him to withdraw from the bench on 28 December and leave the conduct of the trial to his two colleagues, John D. Fitzgerald and Charles R. Barry.

112 Justice Peter O'Brien (1842–1914), Attorney General 1888, largely responsible for administering A. J. Balfour's Crimes Act (1887). He was appointed Lord Chief Justice in 1889 and raised to the peerage in 1900. He was known among his nationalist critics as "Peter the Packer", owing to his tendency to pack juries to secure the verdict required.

113 John David Fitzgerald (1816–89), Judge of the Queen's Bench. MP for Ennis, 1852; he was appointed Attorney General, 1855–6. During his career he tried Fenians and nationalists, including A. M. Sullivan, Richard Pigott and Parnell. He was made a life peer in 1882.

114 George, first baron Jeffries of Wem (1648–89), Jeffries took an active part in the trials of those charged in connection with the "Popish Plot". He amassed

a considerable sum during the "bloody assizes", chiefly by means of extortion. He became notorious for the misconduct of trials, abuse of prisoners and drunkenness. He was appointed Lord Chancellor, 28 September 1685 but eventually lost the confidence of James II. During the revolution of 1689, he was captured while attempting to flee to France and died in prison.

115 Judge Scroggs (*c.*1623–1683) Lord Chief Justice of England, active in prosecuting those connected with the alleged "Popish Plot" in 1678.

116 See Donal J. O'Sullivan, *The Irish Constabularies, 1822–1922* (Kerry, 1999).

117 This is a reference to The Closure, which had been introduced to limit the effects of parliamentary obstruction on 2 February, the day before Davitt's arrest.

118 I have not been able to establish who this was [ed.].

119 Davitt later wrote more on Canada in his article "Impressions of the Canadian North-West", *The Nineteenth Century*, vol. 31 (April 1892), pp. 631–47.

120 Disestablishment of the Church of Ireland.

121 The lack of a Catholic university was one of the political issues of the late nineteenth century. The Roman Catholic hierarchy had refused to accept non-denominational, state-funded colleges as represented by the Queen's Colleges established in 1845. The situation was resolved in 1908, by the Irish Universities Act.

122 The Intermediate Education Act, 1878, permitted the state to give indirect funding to denominational secondary schools by establishing an examination board which disbursed funds to school managers on the basis of the success rates of their students at the public examinations.

123 Sir James Phillips Kay-Shuttleworth (1804–77) founder of the English system of popular education, was a physician who became concerned with improving the conditions of the poor. In 1835 he was appointed Assistant Poor Law Commissioner and in 1839 nominated to administer a grant voted by the House of Commons for public education in Britain. He founded the first training college for teachers at Battersea, 1839–40. He also was a Liberal party activist in Lancashire. R. J. W. Selleck, *James Kay-Shuttleworth: Journey of an Outsider* (London, 1993).

124 No one has ever done all that he could have.

125 The argument here, one frequently made by land reformers of the time, was that if tenants showed signs of improving their holdings, landlords immediately and arbitrarily raised the rent.

126 The Irish were frequently portrayed in the pages of the magazine *Punch* and similar papers with simian features. See L. Perry Curtis, *Apes and Angels: The Irishman in Victorian Caricature* (Washington, 2nd ed., 1997).

127 This is quoted from *Thom's Directory 1881*, p. 631.

128 Davitt included the establishment of Mechanics' Institutes in Ireland in the proposal for a National Land Reform and Industrial Union of Ireland, to replace the Land League "submitted to and strongly disapproved of by Parnell, August '82", as he later wrote above his draft of the proposal. Article 8: "To improve the scientific and practical Education of the

Artizan & Laboring classes by the establishment of Mechanics Institutes throughout the country." (TCD MS 9398/1500b).

129 Such measures were eventually introduced by the Congested Districts Board, in 1898, under its Parish Committee Scheme, which offered prizes and grants through parish committees for improvements to homes and gardens. See *Eighth Annual Report of the Congested Districts Board*, 1899, pp. 27–8.

130 9 May–20 November 1880.

131 Westminster Hall was the chief law court of England.

132 John Philpot Curran (1750–1817), lawyer and politician. In Parliament he was a strong advocate of Catholic Emancipation and a severe critic of patronage and corruption. He defended the United Irishmen, Hamilton, Rowan, Napper Tandy and Wolfe Tone in their trials following the 1798 Rebellion.

133 Isaac Butt (1813–79) born County Donegal; co-founder of *Dublin University Magazine*, 1833. He was professor of Political Economy at Trinity College Dublin, 1836–40 and was called to the Irish Bar in 1838, where he made a name as a brilliant orator. He served as Conservative MP for Youghal 1852–65. He became President of the Amnesty Association in 1869 and founder of the Home Government Association in 1870. He sat as Home Rule MP for Limerick, 1871–9.

134 Brahmins or Brahmans are the highest *varna* or social class in Hindu India. The ritual purity of the Brahmins is maintained through the observance of taboos, many of which relate to diet and contact with lower castes. Most Brahmins are strictly vegetarian.

135 John Hampden (1594–1643). Hampden led the opposition to the payment of ship-money in 1635.

136 In the National Covenant (1638) and the Solemn League and Covenant (1643) Scottish Presbyterians pledged to maintain their chosen forms of church government and worship.

137 The correction was inserted by Professor Moody.

138 See note 41.

139 St Paul (*c.*3–*c.*64 CE) was a Hellenised Jew from Tarsus who shaped early Christianity and moved it away from Judaism.

140 Alexander III of Macedon (Alexander the Great) (336–323 BCE) conqueror of Egypt and large parts of Asia, leading an expedition as far as northern India.

141 This is a rather mysterious reference. I have not been able to identify any people known as the Guanacas. Nor is the Sago Palm (*Metroxylon*) native to the Orinoco region. However, it is the staple carbohydrate for many people in Southeast Asia, Oceania and the Pacific Islands. The Asmat of Borneo subsist on a combination of the highly productive sago palm and from hunting and gathering.

142 Benjamin Franklin (1706–90), printer and publisher, author, inventor and scientist, and diplomat. Franklin was the leading Enlightenment figure in America. He helped to frame both the Declaration of Independence and the US Constitution.

143 Davitt's call for an international tribunal was ahead of his time, although he did live to see the establishment of the international permanent court of arbitration at the Hague, under the Hague Convention, May 1899. Unfortunately it was unable to prevent the outbreak of wars.

144 Adam Smith (1723–90) social philosopher and political economist, best known for *An Inquiry into the Nature and Causes of the Wealth of Nations* (1776). He studied at the University of Glasgow and Balliol College, Oxford. He was appointed professor of logic (1751) and later of moral philosophy (1754) at Glasgow.

145 Davitt was a supporter of equal rights for women and women's suffrage. See, for example, his arguments in favour of the vote and women's candidacy for parliament in his *Life and Progress in Australasia* (London, 1898), pp. 366–7.

146 Jeremy Bentham (1748–1790) Utilitarian philosopher, economist and theoretical jurist whose scientific approach to social problems greatly influenced nineteenth-century reforming thought.

147 Isidore August Marie François Xavier Comte (1798–1857) philosopher, founder of sociology and Positivism – a system of thought and knowledge proposed as capable of providing a basis for political organisation in a modern industrial society. His works include *Course of Positive Philosophy* (1830–42) and *System of Positive Polity*.

148 John Stuart Mill (1806–73) philosopher, political economist and exponent of Utilitarianism. His major works include *A System of Logic* (1843), *Principles of Political Economy* (1848), *The Subjection of Women* (1869), *On Liberty* (1859) and *Considerations on Representative Government* (1871). His *England and Ireland* (1868) is believed to have influenced W. E. Gladstone in shaping his first land act of 1870; Kay, *Free Trade in Land*, pp. 244–8, quotes his *Principles of Political Economy*, vol. I, in favour of peasant proprietorship.

149 John Frederick William Herschel (1792–1871), astronomer, son of the astronomer Sir William Hershel, and lifelong friend of William Whewell (see note 150) since their Sunday morning "philosophical breakfasts" at St John's College Cambridge. He studied for the law at Lincoln's Inn but his main contributions were in astronomy. He specialised in the study of astronomical observations from the southern hemisphere.

150 William Whewell (1794–1866), Master of Trinity College, Cambridge. He was the son of a master carpenter who won an exhibition to Trinity College, Cambridge in 1811, where he later became lecturer and moderator in mathematics. He was ordained an Anglican clergyman in 1825 and was appointed Master of Trinity College Cambridge in 1841. His interests extended to philosophy, theology and geology and he engaged in debates and disputes with J. S. Mill.

151 François Marie Arouet Voltaire (1694–1778), French philosopher of the Enlightenment. He was imprisoned in the Bastille, 1717–18 and 1726. He lived briefly in Potsdam under the patronage of Frederick II and corresponded with Catherine the Great. He criticised dogmatic religions,

especially Catholicism. A consistent theme in his writings is a lack of respect for authority and institutions, therefore it has been argued that he helped to prepare the intellectual climate for the French Revolution. He campaigned on behalf of victims of religious and political persecution.

152   Samuel Johnson (1709–1784), poet, essayist, critic, journalist, lexicographer and conversationalist, is regarded as one of the outstanding figures of English eighteenth-century life and letters.

153   Joseph Addison (1672–1719), essayist, dramatist, poet and statesman. Son of a distinguished clergyman, he studied at Oxford. He was appointed secretary of state for southern affairs 1705, MP in 1708 and was Chief Secretary in Ireland (1708–10). He was appointed secretary of state in 1717.

154   Davitt had already served a seven-and-a-half-year term of imprisonment between 18 July 1870 and 18 December 1877.

155   The Cynics were a sect that flourished from the fourth century BCE into the Christian era. Founded by Diogenes of Sinope, they challenged social conventions and sought to return to a "natural life". The Stoics were a school of philosophy in Greco-Roman antiquity that stressed duty and held that, through reason, man can come to regard the universe (both physical and moral) as governed by fate and, despite appearances, as fundamentally rational.

156   Antoine-Laurent Lavoisier (1743–94) was a scientist and is regarded as the father of modern chemistry.

157   Joseph Priestley (1733–1804) was a clergyman, political theorist, educator and scientist, one of the discoverers of the element oxygen.

158   Davitt is thinking here of the three more years until the completion of his original sentence. In the event, this was to be his last Christmas spent in prison, although not the last time he was jailed.

159   Yet I argue not Against Heavn's hand
                 or will, nor bate a jot
          Of heart or hope; but still bear
                 Up and steer Right onward.
                        John Milton (1608–74) Sonnet XXIV, *To Cyriac Skinner*

160   Thomas Brennan (1854–1915), born at Slane, County Meath, he entered employment as a clerk in Castlebar, working for the North Dublin Milling Company and later in the company's Dublin office, where Patrick Egan was manager. He became a Fenian as a young man. He was a founder and secretary of the Land League and was Davitt's closest confidant in the movement. Brennan emigrated to America in 1882 but the men remained friends until Davitt's death in 1906.

161   Matthew Harris (1825–90) was born in County Galway. He became a successful building contractor and supported Repeal, Young Ireland, the Tenant League, and Fenianism. He founded the Ballinasloe Tenants' Association in 1876 and enlisted Davitt's support for the Mayo land reformers in 1879. He served as MP for East Galway.

162   Detective Officer Sheridan of the Dublin Metropolitan Police.

163 Dublin Castle. Davitt was under arrest.

164 Mr Williamson and Inspector Swansea.

165 The arrest warrant was signed by Sir William Harcourt, the Home Secretary.

166 Davitt had already been in London on 2 February for meetings.

167 This refers to Davitt's armed guard from Willesden station to Bow Street Magistrates' Court.

168 Bow Street Magistrates' Court

169 Millbank Prison. Davitt had been incarcerated here before, in 1870.

170 Portland Prison

171 Davitt's prison number.

172 Mr George Clifton was the Governor. This may have referred to a private joke between them.

173 Joseph Edward Kenny was allowed to see Davitt as his doctor. The administration was suspicious of him and the likelihood that he might try to make political capital from the situation and denied him subsequent visits. (HO 144/5/17869/60, 64). He was later one of those held in Kilmainham Jail.

174 Margaret Frances Sullivan was the American-Irish wife of A .M. Sullivan and lived in London, where she was active in forming a branch of the Ladies' Land League.

175 Elizabeth Kenny was the wife of Dr J. E. Kenny. She visited Davitt with Mrs Sullivan on 27 June 1881.

176 Thomas William Croke, Archbishop of Cashel (1824–1902). Bishop of Auckland, New Zealand (1870–5); Archbishop of Cashel and Emly (1875–1902). He was a staunch supporter of the Land League and the leadership of Parnell. See Mark Tierney, *Croke of Cashel: The Life of Archbishop Thomas William Croke, 1832–1902* (Dublin, 1976).

177 Dr William Fitzgerald, Bishop of Ross.

178 By the time of their visit, the 1881 land bill had passed into law as the Land Law (Ireland) Act, 44 & 45 Vict. c.49 (22 August 1881).

179 Under the original terms of the 1881 Act tenants in arrears were unable to claim relief. This was amended by the Arrears of Rent (Ireland) Act 45 & 46 Vict. c. 47 (18 August 1882), as agreed in the "Kilmainham Treaty".

180 John George McCarthy (1829–92), MP for Mallow, 1874–8; MRIA; author of *Irish Land Questions, Plainly Stated and answered by John George MacCarthy* (1870); *A Plea for Home Government of Ireland* (1872); *A letter on waste land reclamation* (Cork, 1879); land commissioner 1885.

181 "Fearless and beyond reproach", from Bayard, a French soldier known as "le chevalier sans peur et sans reproche". It is difficult to tell whether this is pure admiration or expresses a hint of irony.

182 A. M. Sullivan was also returned for Meath and decided to sit for that county. In a new election on 28 May 1880 Bellingham was elected.

183 Croke was so much in favour of the bill that he had publicly disagreed with Parnell over it. See Tierney, *Croke of Cashel*, pp. 120–8.

184 This is a reference to the Elizabethan, Jacobite and Cromwellian Plantations.

185 W. E. Vaughan, *Landlords and Tenants in Mid-Victorian Ireland, 1848–1904* (Oxford, 1994) appendix 9, p. 249, gives annual rentals for Ireland, 1850–86, which vary between £10.2 and £12.2 million.

186 Because the good old rule
Sufficeth them, —the simple plan
That they should take who have the power
And they should keep who can

William Wordsworth (1770–1850), *Rob Roy's Grave*

187 This was a common argument among nationalist economists. R. D. Collison Black, in *Economic Thought and the Irish Question, 1817–1870* (Cambridge, 1960), questioned this assessment, commenting: "Since the nationalists of the time were never called to take on the task, they could paint Utopian pictures of an Ireland in which a population of ten or fifteen millions would be comfortably supported from a combination of small-scale agriculture with manufactures of a rather nebulous form and organisation. On an appraisal of the facts it appears that to make this situation a reality would have been a virtual impossibility" (p. 248).

188 Davitt's figure seems about accurate. Cormac Ó Gráda, *Ireland: A New Economic History, 1780–1939* (Oxford 1994), pp 178–87, suggested that the country lost some 985,000 people during the famine (out of *c.*8.4 million). During the decade 1846–55 about 2½ million more people emigrated, while between 1850 and 1914, some 4 million more were to leave.

189 This was an argument favoured by the proponents of "high farming" in Britain in the mid-nineteenth century, who advocated a form of high input – high output mixed farming that was already being questioned by the time Davitt was writing, owing to the onset of an agricultural depression in the 1870s and 1880s.

190 Concern with the post-Famine decline in tillage levels was a frequent theme in the 1880s and 1890s.

191 John Joseph Mechi (1802–80), author of various works on agriculture published in the 1840s-1870s, based on experience of his own farm, Tiptree Hall. He brought his knowledge of soil chemistry to bear in advocating and advising on the use of fertilisers.

192 Jean Antoine Chaptal, comte de Chanteloup (1756–1832), author of *De l'industrie française* (1818) and *Chimie appliquée à l'agriculture*. 2 tom. (1823).

193 Quoted Kay, *Free Trade in Land*, p. 318.

194 Chaptal, *De l'industrie française* (1818).

195 Arthur Young (1741–1820), agriculturalist and traveller, and an early publicist of the Norfolk husbandry. He went to Ireland in 1776, where he became agent to Lord Kingsborough in County Cork, 1777–9; he published his *Tour in Ireland* (1780) and his *Travels in France during the Years 1787, 1788, 1789* (1792–4); quoted in Kay, *Free Trade in Land*, p. 318

196 Heinrich Friedrich Karl von und zum Stein (1757–1831) and Karl August von Hardenberg implemented a social transformation of Prussia, the most important provision of which was the liberation of the Prussian serfs in 1810. The "Edict for better cultivation of the land" formed part of the Stein and Hardenberg reforms. The provisions Kay had before him when he wrote about the reforms are listed in a note by his widow. See *Free Trade in Land*, p. 102 [the book was published posthumously].

197 This argument is made in Kay, *Free Trade in Land*, pp. 18–20 and 60–1.

198 Aimable Guillaume Prosper Brugière, baron de Barante (1782–1866), litterateur, historian and diplomat. See J-P. de Beaumarchais, Daniel Conty and Alain Rey, *Dictionnaire des Littératures de Langue Française* (Paris, 1984), vol. I, p. 148.

199 De Barante, *Des Communes et de l'Aristocratie* (1820); quoted in Kay, *Free Trade in Land*, pp. 318–19. Kay is quoting from Peter Franz Reichensperger, *Die Agrarfrage aus dem Gesichtspunkte der Nationalökonomie* (Trier, 1847), p. 388.

200 Kay, *Free Trade in Land*, p. 303.

201 *Ibid.*, p. 200.

202 *Ibid.*, pp. 306–7

203 This might be Albert Chester Ives, who was the *New York Herald*'s Irish correspondent in 1880–1.

204 Davitt was deeply opposed to agrarian outrages, describing them as "these damn petty little outrages" in his letter to Devoy of 16 December 1880. They undermined the discipline of what he aimed to create—a mass peaceful organisation—and invited retaliation in the form of government coercion.

205 Thomas Drummond (1797–1840) Under Secretary of State for Ireland, 1835–40. He is quoted in Kay, *Free Trade in Land*, p. 63.

206 In April 1838 a letter was addressed to the Irish Government from Lords Glengall and Lismore and thirty other Tipperary magistrates, relating to the murder of a Mr Cooper. It gave a dreadful account of the state of the country and called on the Government to introduce more stringent measures to suppress crime. Drummond replied in a long letter of 22 May 1838, pointing out exaggerations in the letter and condemning the manner in which Irish landlords generally neglected their duties towards their tenants. It contained the phrase: "Property has its duties as well as its rights; to the neglect of those duties in times past is mainly to be ascribed that diseased state of society in which such crimes take their rise." This set off a storm of indignation on the part of the landlords and in both houses of Parliament Drummond's policies were attacked. This account is from Alfred Webb, *A Compendium of Irish Biography, Comprising Sketches of Distinguished Irishmen and of Eminent Persons Connected with Ireland by Office or By Their Writings* (Dublin, 1878), p. 159. Davitt had a copy of the book with him in Portland.

207 An Act of 1711–12 instituted and regulated the payment of compensation to owners whose stock had been houghed. 9 Anne, chap 9. See also

S. J. Connolly, "The Houghers: Agrarian protest in early eighteenth-century Connacht," in C. H. E. Philpin (ed.), *Nationalism and Popular Protest* (Cambridge, 1987), pp. 139–62.

208 Frances Sullivan referred in a letter to the press written shortly after her visit to Davitt to his denunciation of the mutilation of animals. *The Nation*, 14 January 1882. This was clearly an issue that Davitt felt strongly about. He returned to it in his letter to the *London Standard* in May 1882, where he criticised Forster for imprisoning him and thereby removing the restraining hand he could have exerted: "had I been permitted to continue my crusade against outrages, to have levelled all the influence of the Land League against the commission of murder and the mutilation of cattle, I could have prevented numbers of crimes that now stain the name of Ireland, and have averted the horrible deed of Saturday last [the Phoenix Park murders]. This is no vain boast." *London Standard*, 11 May 1882.

209 This was written shortly after Frances Sullivan's visit on 10 January 1882.

210 War and peace are the same.

211 Davitt's Aunt Ellen, *née* Ellen (or Eleanora) Gorman, was married to his uncle Henry Davitt, his father's brother. I should like to thank Patrick M. Davitt for this information. From the tone of this letter Davitt may have expected that it would be published.

212 Alexander Martin Sullivan (1830–84). Editor of *The Nation* (1858–77), he favoured constitutional agitation and opposed Fenianism. He was a barrister, practising in London, and Home Rule MP for County Louth (1874–80) and for Meath (1880–1). He was author of *The Story of Ireland* (1870).

213 The Knight of the Sorrowful (or Rueful) Countenance was Sancho Panza's name for Don Quixote.

214 Davitt had visited Washington on 5 August 1880.

215 Davitt's mother had died on 18 July 1880.

216 Epicurianism was a Hellenistic philosophy based on the teachings of Epicurus (341–270 BCE) who regarded pleasure (which they defined as freedom from pain and anxiety) as the greatest good.

217 Aphrodite was the goddess of love, identified in Rome with the ancient Italic goddess Venus. She was also identified with a fertility cult on the island of Cyprus. Doves and sparrows were considered sacred to her.

218 In the manuscript Davitt had written Mary Ann and then changed the last name to Ellen. He is almost certainly referring to his niece, Mary Anne Agnes Padden (b.15 March 1870), daughter of his sister, Mary Padden. I should like to thank Patrick M. Davitt for this information.

219 This was Davitt's sister, Sabina Davitt (1850–1922), who had planned to come to Ireland. She came in August 1882.

220 Aunt Ellen Davitt had a son called Joseph Davitt, to whom Davitt may be referring here. Alternatively, he may be joking, as in his earlier term of imprisonment, he had referred to the writer of his letters smuggled out of prison as "Joe" or "Poor old Joe", in a sort of code with his family.

221 This was the Poor Rate, used for the upkeep of workhouses and dispensaries and payment of poor relief.

222 Davitt got this figure from *Thom's Directory*, 1881, p. 673, which gives the revenue collected within Ireland for the year ended 31 March 1870 as £7,287,127. The Treasury estimated Ireland's true revenue in 1893–4 at £7.5 million, whereas the Childers Committee's estimate for the same year was £6.6 million. See Pauric Travers, "The financial relations question, 1800–1914" in F. B. Smith (ed.), *Ireland, England and Australia: Essays in Honour of Oliver MacDonagh* (Canberra and Cork, 1990), pp. 41–69.

223 It is unclear how Davitt came to an estimate for the annual agricultural product of the country of £70 million. *Thom's Directory, 1881*, p. 694 shows the value of the principal crops in 1879 as £22,743,006, but it only gives the number of livestock exported that year, which was 1,744,464, and not their value.

224 In February 1882 the Fifth Ward branch of the American Land League in New York held an entertainment and lodged the proceeds, $633, to a bank account opened for Davitt in a New York savings bank. Davitt obtained special permission to reply in a letter dated 24 February, a draft of which is included in "Jottings", thanking the committee for their efforts but refusing to accept it, claiming that "As I am wholly unconscious of any pecuniary loss sustained by me that should call for such action as that of the fifth Ward Branch of the Land league on my account, neither can I imagine any contingency in my personal affairs as likely to arise pending my release from prison that will need any monetary assistance outside of my own resources", and suggesting that the money should be put to "whatever purpose might possibly advance the interests and wellbeing of the people of Ireland". The letter was published in America and Ireland, which is the reason it is not included here.

225 Robert Stewart, Viscount Castlereagh, second Marquess of Londonderry (1769–1822). Chief Secretary 1797–8. The 1798 Rebellion convinced him that Union with Britain was essential to preserve the Empire and he expended large sums to secure the passage of the Act of Union in the Irish Parliament.

226 Charles Cornwallis, 1st Marquess and 2nd Earl (1738–1805). Cornwallis was an English general who had served in the American War of Independence, where he was forced to surrender at Yorktown in 1781, and governor general of India, 1786–92. In June 1798 he was appointed joint viceroy and commander in chief to suppress the rebellion of that year. In the aftermath of the Rebellion he worked to secure legislative union between Great Britain and Ireland. He resigned in 1801 when George III refused to allow Catholic emancipation to accompany union.

227 *Correspondence of Charles, first Marquis Cornwallis* ed. Charles Ross (3 vols, London, 1859) and *Memoirs and Correspondence of Viscount Castlereagh*, ed. Charles Vane, Marquess of Londonderry (12 vols, London, 1848–53) are quoted by W. E. H. Lecky in *Leaders of Public Opinion in Ireland* (London, 1871).

228 William Pitt the Younger (1759–1806), British Prime Minister who legislated for the Act of Union.

229 Henry Grattan (1746–1820), political leader. He was the son of James Grattan, recorder of, and MP for the city of Dublin; he entered the Irish parliament in 1775; carried the address in favour of Irish free trade 1779; successfully moved addresses in favour of Irish legislative independence 1782; declined office but championed the cause of Catholic relief; seceded from the Irish Commons 1797 but he returned to oppose the Union, 1800; sat in the Imperial Parliament 1805–20.

   The Volunteers arose as an attempt to establish a militia to strengthen the Irish army against apparent threats of a French invasion. It was a formally Protestant movement, although some Catholics were admitted to Volunteer ranks in several places. R. F. Foster, *Modern Ireland, 1600–1970* (London, 1988), p. 246, puts their number in 1782 at between 30,000 and 40,000 which is considerably lower than Davitt's figure of 60,000. However, contemporary estimates by Dublin Castle were higher. See James Kelly, "Select documents viii: The secret return of the Volunteers of Ireland in 1784", *Irish Historical Studies* XXVI, 103 (1989): 268–92.

230 W. E. H. Lecky (1838–1903), historian. His major works on Irish history were *Leaders of Public Opinion in Ireland* (1862) and *History of England in the Eighteenth Century* (1878–90), which includes five volumes on Ireland refuting the anti-Irish claims of J. A. Froude. He was a Liberal Unionist.

231 W. E. H. Lecky, *Leaders of Public Opinion in Ireland* (London, 1871), pp. 79–80.

232 Introduced by Sir Edward Poynings in December 1494, "Poynings' Law" prevented the Irish parliament from meeting without royal licence and provided that all parliamentary business must first be approved by the King's Deputy and his Council in Ireland and by the King and his Council in England.

233 The French invasion scare of 1778–9 was a major stimulus to Volunteer recruitment.

234 This was Poynings' Law—see note 232 above.

235 James Caulfeild (1728–99) born Dublin; created Earl of Charlemont, 1763. Commander-in-Chief of the Volunteers, 1780; he supported Grattan on the Regency question; he opposed Catholic emancipation and the Union.

236 J. A. Froude, *The English in Ireland in the Eighteenth Century* (1874), pp. 425–98.

237 Lecky, *Leaders of Public Opinion in Ireland*, p. 182.

238 Cost what it may.

239 Charles Lucas (1713–71) born in County Clare; elected to the Common Council of the City of Dublin, 1741 where he advocated municipal reform. Riotous behaviour during his candidature as parliamentary representative for Dublin 1748 led to his imprisonment; he escaped to London, studied medicine at Paris, Rheims and Leyden and returned to Ireland, where he served as MP for Dublin, 1761–71.

240 1785 [not 1784] Pitt attempted to form a commercial union between Ireland and Britain. See James Kelly, *Prelude to the Union: Anglo-Irish Politics in the 1780s* (Cork, 1992).

241 The Regency Crisis, 1788–9, arose when the Irish government, during King George III's illness, favoured proceeding by a bill to create a regency. The Irish opposition, in a bid to assert its independence, supported Charles Fox's tactic of asking the Prince of Wales to assume power on his own account. The situation was resolved when the King recovered.

242 Sectarian strife emerged in the 1780s, initially in Armagh, where the improving relative status of Catholics aroused Protestant fears. Groups of Protestants, known as Peep-of-day-boys, later followed by Orange lodges, were organised and Catholic counter-groups, calling themselves Defenders, also secret and oath-bound, were formed. Tension spread and escalated with armed skirmishes and arson attacks in the 1790s.

243 "Tithe mongers" or "tithe proctors" were men who undertook for a fee to collect the tithe (payment by landholders for the upkeep of the Church of Ireland). Payment of tithe was much resented and tithe mongers were unpopular.

244 Quoted in Webb, *Compendium of Irish Biography*, p. 227.

245 This was a proposal by Grattan, made in the Dublin parliament on 14 February 1788, that tithes should be commuted in favour of a uniform tax per acre on tillage land. See Webb, *A Compendium of Irish Biography*, p. 227; James Kelly, *Henry Grattan* (Dublin, 1993).

246 The quotation refers to tithe proctors. It is probably from one of Henry Grattan's speeches on the tithe question, 1787–9, see *The Speeches of the Right Honorable Henry Grattan in the Irish and Imperial Parliament*, edited by his son (4 vols, Dublin 1822) but I have been unable to locate it [Ed.].

247 Davitt is referring here to a re-emergence of anti-tithe agitation in Munster in 1785–7, spearheaded by the Rightboy movement. There had been earlier anti-tithe agitation in Tipperary and Kilkenny in the 1760s, led by the Whiteboys. James S. Donnelly 'The Whiteboy movement 1761–65,' *Irish Historical Studies* 21 (1981), pp. 20–54; 'The Whiteboys of 1769–76' *Proceedings of the Royal Irish Academy*, 83C (1983).

248 In the 1790s Whiteboy/Rightboy organisations spread as a southern counterpart to the Defender societies in the north. These secret agrarian societies attempted to enforce tenants' demands on landlords, by means of intimidation and occasional violence. Agrarian secret societies were to remain a feature of Irish rural society through much of the nineteenth century.

249 In 1155, Pope Adrian IV (1154–9) issued a bull called "Laudabilitur" ("It is praiseworthy") which granted King Henry II (1154–89) permission to go to Ireland "to reform its Church". This was one of the reasons used to justify the Norman invasion.

250 The Ten Commandments

251 William [Wentworth-] Fitzwilliam (1748–1833) succeeded as Earl Fitzwilliam in 1756; he was Lord Lieutenant of Ireland from December 1794 to March 1795. Keen to introduce reforms, he alienated the London government and Dublin authorities and was dismissed after only seven weeks in government.

252 One of the contributory factors in the deterioration of relations between the British government and the American colonies was a dispute over Stamp Tax that arose in 1765.

253 Last resort.

254 See note 63 above.

255 See note 62 above.

256 The winning of legislative independence by the repeal of the Declaratory Act (Sixth of George I) on 21 June 1782.

257 Catholic leaders were promised that emancipation measures would be included with the Act of Union but in the end these were vetoed by the King, George III.

258 Henry Grattan opposed the Union bill in the Irish parliament.

259 Henry Lawes Luttrell, second Earl Carhampton (1743–1821), commander of armed forces in Ireland in 1796, and general in the army 8 January 1798.

260 Gerard Lake, first Viscount Lake of Delhi and Liswaree (1744–1808), army general appointed commander of armed forces in Ulster, December 1796 and commander-in-chief 25 April 1798. He led his forces against the 1798 Rebellion, including the Battle of Vinegar Hill, Wexford, 21 June 1798 and defeated the French invasion forces at Ballinamuck on 8 September 1798.

261 Charles Cornwallis, see above note 226.

262 John FitzGibbon (1749–1802), Earl of Clare, Lord Chancellor of Ireland 1789. Opposed to Catholic Emancipation; supported and promoted the Act of Union.

263 Oliver Cromwell (1599–1658) spent nine months in Ireland—15 August 1649–26 May 1650—and carried out a military campaign aimed at visiting "Godly retribution" on those who had carried out the 1641 rebellion. He stormed and massacred Drogheda and Wexford, causing a succession of towns to surrender. He introduced a new Protestant land settlement aimed at destroying the economic base of the Catholic elite.

264 Henry Grattan, *Memoirs of the life and times of the Right Honourable Henry Grattan by his son* (5 vols, London, 1839), I, p. 49; quoted in Webb, *Compendium of Irish Biography*, p. 229.

265 *Macbeth*, Act 5, Scene 3, l. 25: "I haue liu'd long enough, my way of life Is falne into the Seare, the yellow Leafe".

266 *Macbeth*, Act 3, Scene 4.

267 *Macbeth*, Act 4, Scene 3.

268 Whichever you wish.

269 Davitt's division of his life into nine-year sections is very approximate, see below. From 1855 until 1865 he was employed, first at Parkinson's cotton

mill at Ewood Bridge, followed a month later by work at Holden Mill; then at Stellfoxe's Victoria Mill, where his arm was crushed in an accident in 1857. After four years in school he worked in the Haslingden post office and its associated printing business, from 1861 until his resignation to become a full-time Fenian activist in 1869. For a detailed account of Davitt's youth, see Moody, *Davitt*, ch. 1, pp. 1–23.

270 When Davitt recovered after the accident in which his arm was amputated in 1857, he was sent to John Poskett's school in Haslingden, where he remained until 1861.

271 Davitt joined the Irish Republican Brotherhood in 1865, becoming a full-time activist in 1869, where he remained until his arrest in May 1870.

272 Davitt was serving out the remainder of his fifteen-year term of imprisonment, handed down in 1870. He had served seven-and-a-half years in 1870–7. From 1877–81 he had been at liberty. In theory he had over three more years left when he wrote, to bring him to 1885 (the original end of his sentence). In fact, he was to be released just over a month after this entry (on 6 May 1882).

INDEX

Index